D1082855

WORK AND FAMILY

Policies for a
Changing Work Force

Edited by
Marianne A. Ferber and Brigid O'Farrell
with La Rue Allen

Panel on Employer Policies and Working Families

Committee on Women's Employment and
Related Social Issues
Commission on Behavioral and Social Sciences and Education
National Research Council

NATIONAL ACADEMY PRESS
Washington, D.C. 1991

NATIONAL ACADEMY PRESS • 2101 Constitution Avenue, N.W. • Washington, D.C. 20418

NOTICE: The project that is the subject of this report was approved by the Governing Board of the National Research Council, whose members are drawn from the councils of the National Academy of Sciences, the National Academy of Engineering, and the Institute of Medicine. The members of the committee responsible for the report were chosen for their special competences and with regard for appropriate balance.

This report has been reviewed by a group other than the authors according to procedures approved by a Report Review Committee consisting of members of the National Academy of Sciences, the National Academy of Engineering, and the Institute of Medicine.

Library of Congress Cataloging-in-Publication Data

Work and family : policies for a changing work force / edited by
  Marianne A. Ferber and Brigid O'Farrell with La Rue Allen ; Panel on
  Employer Policies and Working Families, Committee on Women's
  Employment and Related Social Issues, Commission on Behavioral and
  Social Sciences and Education, National Research Council.
      p.   cm.
  Includes bibliographical references and index.
  ISBN 0-309-04277-1
  1. Dual-career families—United States. 2. Work and family—
  United States. I. Ferber, Marianne A., 1923–   . II. O'Farrell,
  Brigid. III. Allen, La Rue, 1950–   . IV. National Research Council
  (U.S.). Committee on Women's Employment and Related Social Issues.
  Panel on Employer Policies and Working Families.
  HQ536.W62 1991   91-25484
  306.3'6—dc20   CIP

Printed in the United States of America

Preface

The increase in dual-earner and female-headed families has led to significant research and policy interest in the relationship between employer policies and families. In February 1987 the National Research Council's Committee on Women's Employment and Related Social Issues convened a planning meeting, which included experts in the area of work and family, as well as representatives of private industry, federal agencies, and foundations, to explore the feasibility of conducting a study that would explore these issues further. Following that meeting, the committee established the Panel on Employer Policies and Working Families to synthesize and assess the research on employer policies and working families, to evaluate policy alternatives, and to assess the need for further research. Although the research on many of the relevant topics is limited, analysis of the available data and discussions with experts enabled the panel to assess the major areas of conflict between work and family responsibilities.

A panel of 12 experts conducted the study. Members included scholars with expertise in the disciplines of economics, demography, sociology, developmental psychology, social psychology, organizational behavior, and employment and family law, as well as experts in employment policy (public and private) and public policy related to social welfare. Within these categories, the panel included both researchers and practitioners from management and labor. To enhance its understanding of these issues, the panel commissioned background materials and heard presentations by and held discussions with a wide range of experts from management, labor, and government, as well as scholars specializing in related areas of research. A list of the background materials, their authors, and the experts who were consulted appears in Appendix A.

In the course of conducting this study, each of the panel members took an active role in reading drafts, writing individual sections, providing data, working with paper authors, leading discussions, and participating in the meetings. La Rue Allen bore primary responsibility for Chapter 3. Marianne Ferber not only chaired the panel and guided the writing throughout the report, but also took primary responsibility for the analysis of work and family issues in Europe. The panel's study director, Brigid O'Farrell, also played an important role in the project: her expertise in family and work interaction was a valuable resource, and her part in the drafting and editing of the report reflects a thorough understanding of complex issues. The commission deeply appreciates all of these contributions.

Lucile DiGirolamo, the panel's staff associate, was indispensable in organizing the various activities of the panel as well as providing critical research support, especially for Chapter 7. Excellent administrative support was provided by several very patient support staff during this lengthy process. We would like to thank Michelle Daniels, Carey Gellman, Lisa Sementelli-Dann, Kasey VanNett, and Sheryle Decareau from Wheaton College.

This report has benefited from extensive review by a large number of people. Members of the Commission on Behavioral and Social Sciences and Education (CBASSE) and of the National Academy of Sciences' Report Review Committee carefully reviewed several drafts. Joan Huber, chair, and Gene Smolensky and Dianne Pinderhughes, members of the panel's parent committee, provided detailed comments on successive drafts of the report. Emily Andrews and Martha Zaslow made presentations at the panel's meetings and reviewed specific chapters of the report. Eugenia Grohman, assistant director for reports, and Christine McShane, commission editor, greatly improved the clarity of this report. Susanne Stoiber, director of the Division of Social and Economic Studies, provided extensive comments and support. Sincere thanks to all of these readers and reviewers for their time and effort on so important a topic.

The project would not have been possible without the generous financial support received from the Women's Bureau of the U.S. Department of Labor, the Ford Foundation, the Russell Sage Foundation, the German Marshall Fund, Aetna Life and Casualty, IBM Corporation, and the National Research Council Fund, and we gratefully acknowledge them. Special acknowledgment and thanks for their support and patience go to June Zeitlin at Ford and Collis Phillips and Harriet Harper at the Department of Labor.

This study has required a great deal of hard work, mutual commitment to the task, and respect for differing points of view. The commission is grateful to the panel members for their prodigious efforts, especially those of Chair Marianne Ferber, and trust that it has been both personally and professionally gratifying to work together on a topic that is so vitally important. Our hope is that the findings, conclusions, and supporting data found in this volume will make an important contribution to helping families and employers adjust to the ongoing changes in our society.

SUZANNE H. WOOLSEY, *Executive Director*
Commission on Behavioral and Social
Sciences and Education

Contents

Summary   1

1   Introduction   7

2   The Family and the Workplace   18

3   Linkages Between Work and Family   42

4   How Adults Cope: Dependent Care   64

5   Standard Employee Benefits   87

6   New Family-Related Benefits   114

7   Family-Oriented Programs in Other Countries   155

8   Findings and Conclusions   179

References   202

APPENDIXES

A   Background Materials   233

B   Data Needs and Research Agenda   237

C   Biographical Sketches   243

Index   247

WORK AND FAMILY

Summary

The last quarter century has produced a fundamental change in the composition of American families and the participation of women in the work force. Women now constitute 45 percent of the labor force, and the dominant pattern is for both parents to be employed, even when children are very young. The proportion of households headed by a single adult, usually the mother, has also increased sharply—almost a quarter of all workers who maintain families. Although social institutions are gradually adapting to the new work force configuration, the process is slow and there is little consensus about how the burden of adaptation should be shared. The Panel on Employer Policies and Working Families was asked to synthesize and assess what we know about these changes, to evaluate policy alternatives, and to assess the need for further research. Although the research on many of the relevant topics is limited, analysis of the available data and discussions with experts in the field enabled the panel to assess the major areas of conflict between work and family responsibilities and possible ways of easing them.

Our examination focuses on existing policies and programs, recognizing both the possibilities and the limitations of employer actions within the broader context of current economic conditions and public policies. Thus our findings and conclusions are embedded in a perspective that recognizes not only the needs of workers, but also the constraints faced by employers in attempting to improve their operations and maintain the financial health of their organizations. Some consideration is thus given to a range of related government policies addressing issues of economic security, equal opportunity, dependent care, and health care.

CONSEQUENCES FOR FAMILIES AND FOR WORKPLACES

An estimated one-half of U.S. employees have responsibility for at least one dependent, 37 percent have children under the age of 18, and fewer than one-third have a spouse at home full time. In 1988, 57 percent of married women with children under the age of 6 were in the labor force compared with 19 percent in 1960. Approximately 10 percent of full-time employees are actual or potential caregivers for elderly relatives. This group is expected to increase substantially over the next several years, as both the number of elderly people requiring care and the number of employed women continue to grow. An estimated 2 to 3 percent of employed people are caring for working-age adults.

Employers now provide an extensive base of benefits, accounting on average for about 28 percent of total compensation. Benefits arrived at voluntarily or as the result of collective bargaining account for about 19 percent of compensation. Commonly provided benefits include vacations, health insurance, sick leave, and pensions. Recently, some employers have added new types of benefits, such as child and other forms of dependent care. The availability of these types of benefits, however, is very uneven across organizations, industries, and occupations. Paralleling the emergence of new family-oriented benefits, many employers have begun to reduce health insurance coverage—particularly dependent care. The loss of health insurance protection increases the likelihood that family members will not receive necessary health services and exposes families to the threat of financial ruin. Over 30 million people in this country have no health insurance, including 12 million children, most of whom live in families with an employed adult.

While the number of firms offering family-related benefits has been growing, many employers have not yet adapted to the legitimate needs of workers with family care responsibilities. In some firms, workers lack benefits that are now considered essential in mainstream employment. It appears that the majority of employed women have no paid leave for pregnancy and childbirth, and a small number of employees have no leave for their own illness. Small, less profitable, and more labor-intensive firms, often in the retail trade and service sectors, tend to provide few benefits. Only 46 percent of employees in small firms have paid sick leave, compared with 67 percent in large firms. While small firms are somewhat more likely to offer part-time work and flexible schedules, part-time jobs usually pay less and have fewer benefits than comparable full-time jobs. Small firms employ 38 percent of all workers and a large proportion of women and minorities, so the absence of benefits places already vulnerable groups at increased risk.

While research shows that many results of combining work and family are positive, there are negative results as well, particularly for women, who continue to be the primary caretakers. Especially for families with single parents, there is evidence that economic and psychological stress has negative developmental effects, particularly on children from low-income families, which includes many minority children. For employers, there is tentative evidence that family responsibilities exacerbate such workplace problems as retention, absenteeism, tardiness, and work interruptions. Factors found to be associated with these concerns include: terms of employment, such as the number of hours and weeks worked and the degree of flexibility in work schedules and locations; the availability of services for family members, such as child care; and the extent to which family concerns are recognized as legitimate in the workplace. The scarcity of affordable, good-quality dependent care for children and elderly people, as well as parents' lack of time to handle family matters, underlie most factors noted.

We believe that families need additional supports. To be successful, these must involve men as well as women and take into account variations in family preferences, income and occupation, and different points in the life cycle. Our reading is that the current system of employee benefits, although substantial, is inadequate for the new, diverse labor force.

Employers facing tight labor markets, particularly for skilled workers, will continue to innovate in providing benefits as an aid to recruitment and retention. These innovations are important for testing new concepts and establishing their costs and benefits. However, the constellation of tax policies and rising real incomes that sustained the growth of benefits from the 1950s through the 1970s has altered. Stagnant real incomes, low income tax rates, and increased domestic and international competition no longer support widespread growth in benefits. The panel sees little prospect that benefits will improve for the majority of workers absent government action.

The panel assessed a range of public policies for family-related benefits, including tax incentives, regulations, and other legal requirements. Our conclusions suggest general directions and broad outlines for policies and programs, but, in the absence of clear evidence pointing toward preferred options, the panel does not make recommendations on specific public policies or implementation mechanisms.

CONCLUSIONS

The panel's conclusions are based on the assumptions that family issues are a legitimate employer responsibility, but that the burden of adaptation should not rest exclusively with employers. A substantial base of family-related employee benefits and government supports already exists. We believe improvements will bring about a better match between institutional practices and social and economic conditions.

Terms of Employment

Because flexible policies and choices among a variety of programs are likely to reduce work and family tensions, the panel concludes that openness to experimentation on the part of both managers and workers is important in solving existing problems and meeting constantly changing conditions. The panel concludes that:

For the economic, physical, and psychological well-being of employees and their dependents, some form of paid sick leave, including paid leave for medical-related disabilities for pregnancy and childbirth, and some form of family leave, to care for infants and ill family members, are essential. The panel urges policy makers to explore various approaches to financing and phasing in such benefits so as to minimize economic disruption, spread costs equitably among the community at large, and prevent discrimination against those who use leave.

On the basis of experiences in this country and Western Europe, employers and unions should consider increasing a variety of options, including part-time work, flexible schedules, and alternative work locations. Ensuring that unintended negative effects, such as the loss of benefits, do not occur is also essential.

Direct Provision of Services

The panel found that employers can in some circumstances efficiently gather and disseminate information about the availability and quality of family services, provide services or supports when they are not available elsewhere, and offer indirect support for services through flexible benefit systems, thus increasing employee choices. The panel draws the following conclusions:

As far as economic conditions permit, employers and unions are encouraged to support the development and expansion of resource and referral programs, employee assistance programs, and various types of direct and indirect assistance for the care of children and elderly and disabled family members.

Employers should review the structure of their current benefit systems, on the basis of needs assessments of current employees and an examination of utilization data on existing benefits. Employers are encouraged to consider adopting flexible benefit packages, balancing the need for core benefits against the advantages of more choice.

While recognizing the need for health care cost containment, we strongly encourage employers who provide health insurance to maintain coverage for workers and their dependents. Employers offering very minimal health coverage are encouraged to improve it when possible. Access to health insurance and health care services is an urgent national problem that deserves a place high on the national agenda.

Program Implementation and Dissemination

Because changes in organizations are likely to meet with resistance, special efforts must be made to encourage the adoption of programs and to facilitate their implementation. The panel encourages:

Managers and union representatives to reassess the needs and preferences of employees, taking into account occupational, income, and cultural differences and to give high priority to identified programs and needs.

The development of training programs for manager, workers, and union representatives to help them recognize the importance of family issues and to encourage the participation of both men and women in family-oriented programs.

Governments (federal, state, and local) to support employers in the development and implementation of useful programs and demonstration projects, including education and dissemination.

Data Collection and Research

We have noted throughout the report where the research evidence is weak or contradictory and where there is simply a need for more data. Collecting and analyzing information is costly, however, and a good many decisions can be made without waiting for further research. We therefore urge collection and analysis of additional data only when they are necessary for formulating policies and when they are most likely to be cost-effective. The panel concludes that priority should be given to two areas:

Augment data collection efforts at both the individual and the firm level, including institutionalizing the national longitudinal data collection efforts that have made possible a great deal of useful research on important issues, as well as developing better measures of time use, benefits, and working conditions and expanding the collection of establishment-level data.

Expand the research agenda to include more research on the long-term effects of various ways of caring for children on their development, on the work performance of caregivers in general, and on the changing roles of men and women at home and at work. Additional research is also needed on program evaluation and on differences in work and family issues by occupation, income, and race and ethnicity.

In summary, this study offers an ambitious agenda for employers and suggests the need for additional public policies. We note, however, that some employers, particularly large firms, are already doing more than what is suggested in this report. New programs would nonetheless increase the costs for others, especially small and labor-intensive firms, as well as for taxpayers and consumers. In return, however, the large and growing proportion of working people with responsibilities to job and family would be helped to do justice to both.

In terms of national interest, it is difficult to overstate the importance of finding a new equilibrium for work and family. Greater awareness on the part of all interested parties of the extent to which their interests coincide is crucial in meeting workplace challenges. Conflicts are inevitable, but much can be achieved by relying not only on altruism, but also on the far-sighted self-interest of all the parties involved.

1

Introduction

Because of the dramatic increase of dual-earner and single-adult families and the related decline of households with full-time homemakers over the last 25 years, an increasingly greater proportion of workers in the United States have responsibilities for family care as well as for their jobs. Yet little systematic attention has been paid to the effects of these workers' dual responsibilities. The Panel on Employer Policies and Working Families was asked to synthesize and assess the research on employer policies and working families, to evaluate policy alternatives, and to assess the needs for further research.

The rapid changes in the labor force participation rate of women, which underlie the recent changes in the work force, have meant increased income for many families, wider employment choices for women, and an expanded supply of labor for employers. At the same time, women working outside the home have less time, energy, and opportunity to attend to family and community needs. The implications of this shift are gradually becoming clearer—but how to compensate for the loss remains a very divisive issue.

The sea change in composition of the employed population in the United States raises questions of balance among competing social needs. Difficulties have increased for employees who must balance their responsibilities to work and family, especially single heads of families; for dependents who need care and can no longer count on the services of a full-time homemaker; and for employers who can no longer count on workers who give their jobs undivided attention. The potential conflicts between work and family obligations have implications for work performance, for the cumulative stress on workers and their families, and for the health and well-being of children—the nation's future.

Finding appropriate ways to strike the balance must take into account the diversity of the labor force, which includes larger proportions not only of women but also of workers of different ethnic and cultural identities. Many household needs vary with income and by family composition, as well as with the terms of the job.

The current search for means to do justice to both families and jobs occurs within a framework of employment-related laws and regulations developed over the last 75 years. They include a wide range of programs designed to ameliorate social ills through the mechanism of employment status: Social Security, Workers' Compensation and Unemployment Insurance, equal employment statutes, occupational safety and health rules, and regulations governing health insurance and pension plans.

The engine that keeps the system functioning is the economic reality of individual enterprises in the private sector, whose dynamics vary dramatically by such factors as sector, size, region, regulatory burden, quality of management, and degree of unionization—at least as many variables as characterize family and worker differences.

FOCUS OF THE STUDY

Tensions related to work and families are receiving a great deal of attention. Members of the administration and of Congress, employers, unions, and academicians all agree that families need to be supported and have joined the debate about the mix of policies and programs that will best advance this goal. Underlying the debate is the recognition that new approaches to benefits must more flexibly meet the requirements of a diverse work force. So far, however, there is no consensus on what new approaches should be taken.

Recognizing the complexity of these issues, it was believed that an objective, analytic review would shed much-needed light. The panel was therefore established to synthesize and evaluate what is known in three major areas related to work and family: (1) the effects of different employer policies (such as work scheduling, benefit and leave policies) on families; (2) the effects of employees' family composition (such as dual earner, single earner, female headed) and responsibilities (such as child care, elder care) on their work availability, commitment, and performance; and (3) the factors that influence employers to adopt new, family-related policies (such as size, industry, economic conditions, public policies).

The panel's focus is the effect of two of the most central aspects of American life—paid employment and family—on one another. So it should not be surprising that both strongly held beliefs and differing definitions of crucial terms could be found within the panel as well as across our society. As the panel pursued its review, the immense size, complexity, and rich variation of our national life made the critical task of developing inclusive definitions very difficult.

The definition of a family that we adopted from U.S. government data is two or more people living together, who are related by blood, marriage, or adoption. It comprises both a social and an economic unit. Employment is defined here as paid employment or self-employment found primarily in the private for-profit sector of the economy. We also recognize that much work in the United States is performed by those employed by government and nonprofit organizations; important variations among enterprises are noted as they relate to the issues at hand. The majority of the workplace policies and programs that are the focus of this report are nonwage benefits, including leave policies, health insurance, employee subsidies, and resource and referral programs as well as terms of employment such as scheduling and location of work. Wages and salaries, the core of total compensation, while crucial to family well-being, are not the focus of this review.

In the course of our deliberations we recognized that the functioning of employers and the well-being of families are influenced by a broad set of social issues and policies, and the role of employer policies must be placed within this larger context. We reviewed briefly the range of employee benefits that have been built up over the last 75 years and are already in place—such as pensions and health insurance—and examined information that sheds light on employers' reasons for implementing benefit changes. Finally, we examined the extensive role of public policy in shaping the economic and social environment for both businesses and workers.

Constraints

Because of the complexity of these issues, the limitations of available research, and the diverse perspectives of the panel members, it is important to clarify both the considerable constraints encountered and the shared assumptions underlying this report. Essentially the panel's assignment was to examine the facts underlying a current policy debate and to report on what is known about the interactive effects of work and family. The nature both of the question and of the focus of study makes this a difficult assignment.

The research literature in this area turns out to be quite sparse; this is especially true of data on the effect of family status on various measures of employee performance and especially on the important question of productivity. Herein lie at least two constraints that increase the difficulty of attaining statistically useful data: productivity research in general has had very little success beyond a few studies of production workers in the manufacturing industry. Nor are any great advances expected in measuring the wide range of service, administrative, and professional and managerial tasks that increasingly constitute the employment situation in the late twentieth century. Similarly, research has been very sparse on what causes employers to change benefit structures. Employers have come to make management decisions on the basis of information they have on tardiness, absenteeism, turnover, etc., that is thought to be related to productivity. They may also use more informal assessments and an understanding of general practice. What works to inform management practice does not in this case aggregate to form a solid scientific base. We present the data that exist, but there is very little solid research evidence on productivity and benefit structures.

A very different constraint on available data is the sensitivity of questions about how family affects work. Employees, particularly women, may be anxious to maintain their often precarious position in the work force. Employers, for their part, may be anxious to avoid charges of unfairness. Our review of available research therefore draws on a wide range of related sources, from data on macro trends to small-sample opinion surveys, in an effort to display as comprehensively as possible what is known.

A final constraint is the lack of research and experience on the costs and benefits of existing or proposed public policies. There is also disagreement in interpreting the effects of particular programs; value judgments are frequently involved. In light of this we have tried to make our assumptions and value judgments explicit, and we have used caution in carefully evaluating the probable gains and losses.

Framework

In the course of our review, the panel met five times and also held a 2-day workshop. The panel consulted a large number of experts from management, labor, government, public policy, and research. Our work benefited from the work of scholars who prepared background materials crucial to our deliberations on a wide range of topics; a list of the background materials, their authors, and the experts we consulted is found in Appendix A.

Throughout the report, to the extent that they are described by the data, we clarify the variations among businesses in size, type, extent of unionization, and location, as well as the differences among workers in family status, income level, gender, and ethnic characteristics. In assessing the policy alternatives, we paid careful attention to three questions: who decides on programs and policies, who provides them, and who pays for them?

Who Decides?

Employers inevitably play a large role in finding solutions to the problems of workers with dual responsibilities to jobs and families, although the extent to which they play a proactive role, rather than simply making adjustments to stay competitive in local labor markets, varies considerably.

Some employers have adopted innovative policies on their own initiative, taking into account different market conditions. But such actions have frequently been taken in isolation, without regard to the broad implications of the changes they introduce. At other times, employers have introduced new programs as a result of collective bargaining. On occasion, federal and state governments have imposed requirements.

Voluntary Benefits

During periods of labor shortages—whether general, regional, or for particular skills—there is considerable incentive for employers to voluntarily provide benefits that will attract and hold workers. For example, day care centers to provide care for workers' children were established during World War II (with a good deal of government support); in recent years, hospitals are among the institutions that have most frequently provided them (Auerbach, 1988). In both these instances, there was not only a labor shortage, but also a specific need to attract women.

When there is an ample labor supply, incentives for business to provide "extra" benefits are very limited. Tax policies encourage employers to provide new benefits voluntarily, but they reduce public-sector revenues and are very uneven in their reach. Also, today's diverse labor force, coupled with national economic and organizational shifts, presents an enormous challenge in designing fair and appropriate benefits. Future labor shortages, now predicted by a number of experts, may provide the impetus for better-designed benefits for the new work force. However, to the extent that U.S. industry must compete in world markets with firms having lower labor costs, incentives to decrease total compensation costs will work against benefit improvements unless greater productivity can be achieved.

Collective Bargaining

Organized labor is one source of pressure for employers to provide new benefits. Freeman and Medoff (1984) found that unions have had a greater effect on the provision of benefits than on wages. For a long time, however, unions, representing mainly male workers who were the family breadwinners, were concerned almost exclusively with standard benefits such as pensions, vacations, and health insurance. Recently, unions have become more interested in family-oriented benefits in response to large numbers of women members. This trend is particularly pronounced among public-sector unions (Cook, 1989). Overall change has nonetheless been slow, in part because of the general weakening of the labor movement in organized industries and the declining percentage of organized workers in the labor force as a whole. Also, the fear that new programs would be offered only at the expense of wages, which have in many instances barely kept up with inflation, has been a constraint.

Government Actions

The benefit packages available today have, in significant part, been shaped by government actions: tax policies (such as unemployment insurance and Social Security), tax incentives (such as the dependent care tax credit), and various regulatory policies. Those who seek to ensure that specific benefits are available to all working people favor government action, because establishing benefits under law is the only way to ensure universal coverage. Moreover, to the extent that productivity increases as a result of such programs—because firms can hire more qualified people, receive greater loyalty from present employees, have a more stable labor force, or benefit from better public relations—net costs to employers will be reduced. It is also true that, when all firms offer comparable benefits, businesses are in a better position to shift the cost burden to consumers without being at a competitive disadvantage to domestic competitors.

The difficulty with this course of action—apart from serious philosophical differences about the appropriateness of government interventions in labor markets—is that adding benefits normally results in higher total wage costs for employers, and the ability to provide them differs greatly among employers. Increased labor costs may result in fewer jobs, as employers attempt to offset increased benefit costs. Exemptions for small or low-wage firms are the most frequently proposed means of minimizing job losses. However, creating exemptions from benefit coverage often results in low-wage workers' not being covered.

Small enterprises pose a particular challenge in crafting benefits legislation. Many benefits are more costly to small firms because they do not profit from economies of scale. For example, health insurance is considerably less expensive when it is purchased for large groups. Developing less expensive alternatives for small firms has proved a difficult and elusive goal. In addition, there is skepticism about governments' making the appropriate decisions about what benefits are needed, in part because they lack knowledge about the particular needs and problems of specific groups of workers and employers.

Who Provides the Programs?

The policies and programs discussed in this report can be grouped into two categories: terms of employment and direct services. Terms of employment—such as leaves, work schedules, and work locations—directly affect the work process. Although they may be influenced by unions and by governments, they are available only to employees and can be implemented only by employers. Services—such as insurance, counseling, care for children, and care for the elderly—can be provided and paid for by employers, but they can also be provided by governments or communities, and they can be sold in the marketplace. Services are beneficial not only to employees, but also to people who do not work. The responsibility for paying for such services is often shared in many different ways. Flexible spending accounts, for example, enable employees to spend part of their earnings, in pretax dollars, on programs they choose from among a specified assortment. They are offered only by employers to employees; however, government must establish enabling tax policies and bear the burden of reduced revenues.

With respect to programs that are increasingly accepted as necessary, or at least very desirable, the debate focuses on who should provide them. Summers (1989) suggests that some people favor government programs because they need not be restricted to workers and their dependents and because the taxes needed to pay for them can be related to income. In addition, they emphasize that governments are generally the only available providers of benefits for nonemployed people and their dependents. Other people prefer employer-provided benefits because they expect employers to avoid government inefficiencies, and this approach offers more choices for both employers and employees.

Governments—local, state, and federal—are the representatives of the community and act on its behalf. People with common interests, however, can also form voluntary associations in order to pursue their goals. This country has a long tradition of many worthy ends being achieved through voluntary efforts. The social utility of voluntary programs is recognized in the tax-exempt status accorded many voluntary organizations. Some of the services needed by employees—such as the provision of information about the availability and quality of child and elder care programs—are probably best provided in this manner. We note, however, that, as more women have been entering the labor force, the supply of volunteers has diminished. Over time this is likely to affect the ability of these organizations to function in their traditional capacity.

Who Pays?

The costs of nonwage benefit programs can be borne by the workers themselves, sometimes in the form of lower incomes; by consumers, who purchase the goods and services produced by the workers who need the benefits; by investors, who receive profits from the sale of the firm's product; or by taxpayers, as members of a society that benefits in a variety of ways when everyone is adequately cared for. All too frequently it is simply taken for granted that making the initial outlay is tantamount to carrying the total burden. This is by no means necessarily the case: how the burden is shared is largely determined by underlying economic forces.

To cover the cost of a new benefit, a firm may raise prices, but that is an option only if sales will not fall so much as to do more harm than good. Perhaps the most important factors influencing this situation are whether competing firms also increase their prices, which is far more likely when they provide the same benefits to their workers, and how responsive consumers are to a change in the price of the particular product. Under favorable conditions, most of the additional cost can be passed on to consumers, although even then output and employment of the firm would be expected to decline somewhat, because it is unlikely that a business would be able to find an equally favorable combination of price and quantity to sell under the new conditions.

Alternatively, a business can pay lower wages or provide fewer of the other benefits than would otherwise have been the case. If workers value the new benefits at least as much as what they are giving up, there will be no negative effect on the amount and quality of labor available. Should they value them more, the supply of available workers might increase. If particular programs are worth more to some people than to others, however, it will be easier to attract those workers who value the benefit and harder to attract those who do not. There is some evidence that employers pay somewhat lower wages when benefits are increased (Ehrenberg and Smith, 1982).

A third alternative is for the federal (or other) government to help businesses that are confronted with providing increased benefits. This can be done by offering direct subsidies, by permitting the employer to make payments in pretax dollars (as is the case for ordinary and necessary business expenses), and by not taxing employees for the value of the benefits received (which may induce employees to accept decreases in wage compensation). Governments can also directly administer a benefits program but require that it be funded to a greater or lesser extent through taxes. In any case, either government expenses are increased or revenues are decreased, and the costs are borne by the public, in the form of higher taxes, reductions in other government programs, or an increase in the public debt. In sum, the costs of employee benefits are likely to be shared by consumers, workers, and the public. How the costs are shared, however, is likely to vary considerably.

THE BROADER CONTEXT

While employer policies are inevitably part of any solution for work and family conflicts, they are necessarily limited in scope and must be considered in a broader perspective. Individuals, employers, community groups, and governments all have a stake in productive workers and families that raise healthy and capable children. Government policies beyond those directly related to the terms and conditions of employment are beyond the panel's charge. Employers do undertake policies and programs in each of the following areas, and in that context they are discussed throughout this report. Government policies that go beyond the role of employers are broader than the panel's charge; however, because they are so intimately related to the issues we are concerned with, we briefly consider the issues of economic security, equal opportunity, dependent care, and health care.

Economic Security

In order to enjoy an adequate standard of living, all families need a minimum income. Workers should also have the opportunity to obtain jobs commensurate with their individual abilities, have access to health care for themselves and their families, and be able to obtain satisfactory dependent care. These goals are interrelated. Sufficient income will enable most households to purchase their own health insurance and provide their own dependent care, although this may be a very expensive way to achieve these goals. But even getting the best job warranted by a worker's qualifications may not provide a family with an adequate income.

Currently, there are three main approaches to economic security for working people: require a sufficiently high minimum wage; offer supplements to incomes, such as earned income tax credits for low-wage workers; and improve workers' skills so they can compete for higher-wage jobs. Each is a way of increasing the wage earnings of workers and preserving the dignity of being self-supporting.

Equal Opportunity

The goal of equal opportunity for similarly qualified people is a very broad one. The absence of equal opportunity inhibits both efficiency and equity; failing to employ workers according to their individual abilities robs both the worker and society. Workers lose the income and benefits that would have been paid absent discrimination, and society loses the contribution that those workers could have made. Most people agree that government should intervene in a case of overt discrimination. It is beneficial to individuals and efficient for business when employers are prevented from discriminating against qualified people solely on the basis of their race or gender. What it takes to prove discrimination and in what form restitution should come, however, are matters of continuing dispute.

More generally, as long as there is inequality in areas other than the labor market, such as access to good schooling or unequal burdens of household responsibilities, the group that is disadvantaged in these respects will not have equal opportunity to acquire valuable work-related experience.

Dependent Care

The basic problem with respect to child care, so crucial to the well-being of the family, the economy, and society, is that without assistance many families cannot afford to pay the price of good-quality care. In addition, however, there are chronic problems in arranging child and elder care, in part because consumers, and even some providers, lack adequate knowledge of how to evaluate quality. Research on dependent care is only beginning and is very inadequate. Making information about existing facilities and their quality more readily available would be useful, but arguments are also made for a variety of other policies. Possibilities range from government-operated centers to subsidizing private centers, making payments to families, and providing tax deductions for dependent care expenses. All these approaches exist already in some form and are currently being considered further by policy makers.

No single approach will be best for both children and dependent adults or for all families. Needs and preferences differ widely. Public and private policies making possible a variety of approaches could ensure the availability of care while preserving a range of choices. The availability of good, affordable dependent care would benefit a large proportion of the population directly—and everyone indirectly—by giving a better start to the next generation. Therefore, the substantial costs that would be incurred, especially if caregivers were paid a high enough wage to attract and keep capable, responsible people, might well be justified.

Health Care

Most Americans believe that the country's health care system is seriously flawed. Health care costs are increasing much faster than other costs, yet more than 30 million Americans have no health care coverage and millions more have very inadequate coverage. In addition, the costs of some types of health care, notably long-term care, are not covered under existing insurance arrangements. Critics suggest that these shortcomings help explain why the United States lags behind other advanced industrialized countries in terms of important health indicators, particularly infant mortality.

One proposed solution with a large government role is a system of universal health care not tied to employment. An alternative that would reduce the need for an expanded government role is to require that employers provide health insurance for all full-time workers and their families, with prorated contributions for part-time workers. Because of high and rising costs for health care, there is great resistance in the business community to any required expansion of health care coverage. Although public and expert opinion favors broad reforms, no consensus exists on how to proceed or on the appropriate roles for the public and private sectors. Addressing problems in health care financing and delivery is both critical to the future health of the society and the economy and part of the larger context in which this report must be read.

ORGANIZATION OF THE REPORT

The panel's assigned tasks and the broader context establish the framework for this report. We begin in Chapter 2 by tracing the history of family structure and composition in the United States, the changing nature of employment, and the central role of the employment relationship to the social welfare system. In Chapter 3 we review available research on the advantages and disadvantages for adults, children, and the elderly of being members of families in which all the adults are employed. Given extensive changes in the family and the workplace and identified problems, we examine how dependents are currently cared for, as well as the outcomes and costs of various types of programs in Chapter 4.

Chapters 5 and 6 provide a detailed review and evaluation of existing programs offered by employers and ideas for innovative programs, including what can be learned about their costs and benefits. Among these are such standard benefits as sick leave and health insurance, as well as such new family benefits as leave and flexible schedules. Chapter 7 examines the practices of other advanced industrialized countries and what we can learn from their experiences. Finally, Chapter 8 presents the panel's findings and conclusions for policies, programs, and future research.

2

The Family and the Workplace

Only by recognizing the ongoing evolution of the family, changing opportunity structures in the economy, and evolving government policies in the United States can we consider what potential policies are appropriate to the situations of today and tomorrow. This chapter first examines the historic development of the family, then that of the workplace; it then considers changes that have occurred in the labor force by sex, level of education, and family status. As far as possible, we also examine the factors of race and ethnicity, but, for the most part, data are available only for blacks, whites, and, in recent years, Hispanics. (These are the terms currently used in official sources for racial and ethnic groups.) We review changes in the labor market in terms of the extent to which jobs are available, where and in what occupations and industries, earnings in various occupations, incomes of different types of families, and future trends.

CHANGING FAMILIES

In all societies, those who work, in or out of the home, collectively produce the output that is then available to maintain them as well as those who do not work. Throughout history, at any given time, there has always been a range of family types, varying by personal circumstance as well as by race, ethnicity, and social class. In addition to this diversity at any given time, there have been changes in what people consider the "typical" family unit.

Preindustrial Economies

If we go back far enough, the basic economic unit was an extended family or a tribe (Friedl, 1975; O'Kelly, 1980). Subsequently, some of what later came to be viewed as functions of the family was assumed by various other institutions, including the manor system, the church, and slavery. Slave families and their owners together comprised an economic unit. Similarly, in the feudal manor, lords had a claim on part of the output of serfs and in turn had responsibilities to them (Heilbroner, 1972). By colonial times in New England, extended families living separately but supporting one another both economically and socially were the rule. In this century as well, immigrant groups to the United States have often bonded together in extended family constellations (Hareven, 1982).

Perhaps the most self-sufficient family existed in peasant societies, in which family farms were the basic unit of ownership, production, consumption, and social life (Shamin, 1987). Extended families consisting of three generations or siblings and their families were frequent. In such households, although husbands and wives often did different work, specialization was not sharply defined: men did much of the labor on the farm, in workshops, and, occasionally, in a store; women also worked in the fields and shops, cared for gardens and small animals, and did the bulk of the housework and instructed their daughters in these tasks. Husbands were seen as heads of households, and wives were partners rather than dependents. Women generally had the skills necessary to carry on in case of their husbands' illness or death, and history records many instances of widows operating farms and workshops (Handlin and Handlin, 1982). They were also major participants in household industries (Brownlee and Brownlee, 1976). Overall, adults did the physically demanding chores, and the less exacting tasks were relegated to the elderly and to children. Everyone, except the very young and the disabled, participated in the necessary maintenance of the household to the extent they were able. Parents took care of dependent offspring and expected that their children, in turn, would take care of them when they became dependent (Degler, 1980; O'Kelly, 1980).

The system worked, albeit imperfectly. There were great differences in the standard of living among families. The poor might be hungry, and they generally did not have sufficient resources to provide their children with adequate nutrition and health care, let alone education or an inheritance. In that way, poverty was often perpetuated for generations. Households unfortunate enough to have handicapped members were at a great disadvantage. The high degree of interdependence, however, tended to make families stable, and there were social pressures on all members to fulfill their responsibilities. Marriages were seldom dissolved; the implicit contract between generations was rarely broken (Degler, 1980).

Industrial Economies

The situation began to change substantially with industrialization and the rapid expansion of the market economy. Growing businesses were more and more dependent on hired labor, and workers became more and more dependent on wages. Industrial employment away from home became more prevalent than work in family enterprises, and purchased commodities increasingly replaced those that had been produced in the household. During this period of industrialization and urbanization the family arrangement of father as the provider and mother as the caretaker came into being—as a reality among the well-to-do and as an ideal to which the poor aspired.

In what we now refer to as the traditional family, husbands were the sole wage earners, and they worked at a site distinct from their homes. Employers could expect men's undivided allegiance to their jobs, because their full-time "housewives" took care of home and hearth. Although women produced goods and services in the household, combining their own time and purchased products, they came to be seen not as producers but as facilitators of consumption. The basic standard of living was determined by husbands' incomes. Children's responsibilities to help to provide for the household dwindled; they came to specialize more and more and, for increasingly longer years, in acquiring education for their own adult lives, while their parents continued to support them (Blau and Ferber, 1986; Welter, 1978).

Under these conditions the concept of a "living wage," adequate to enable a male worker to maintain not only himself but also his wife and children, became a common goal of unions in collective bargaining in many industries, especially among the emerging large corporations. All too often men did not receive a wage large enough to support their families; hence, in many less affluent families, in particular nonwhite and immigrant families, women worked for pay to supplement family income. Eventually, pensions and social security systems were instituted to help take care of retired people. Public education was greatly expanded to help young men acquire the skills needed in the labor force and to teach young women those needed for homemaking (Degler, 1980). Although these programs reduced the financial burdens on families, other problems remained.

In the course of the twentieth century, growing numbers of married women entered the labor force. The time needed for housework declined as labor-saving devices became available and as more of the goods and services previously produced in households became available for purchase in the marketplace. The time needed for child care declined as fertility declined, and longer life expectancy gave women more years when there were no children in the family to care for. In addition, the invention of new products, from automobiles and radios to telephones, air conditioners, and television sets, raised aspirations for a higher standard of living. Finally, the increasing possibility of divorce made women more cautious about being entirely dependent on their husbands' earnings.

These developments, together with the higher wages made possible by improved technology, larger amounts of capital used in production, and higher levels of education, made it more costly than previously—in terms of "lost income"—for women to be full-time homemakers. This, in turn, caused an increase in the number of women opting for employment. Growth in the clerical and service occupations also increased demand for women's labor. But these new occupations often paid lower wages than what was needed to support a family, and the growing number of families with two wage earners weakened the case for a family wage. Thus, two-earner families became more and more necessary to achieve the standard of living to which families aspired. Wives nonetheless have continued to look after households and care for children and, as needed, for infirm family members (O'Kelly, 1980). Exploration of the resulting tensions and how they affect both work and family is the subject of this study.

THE CHANGING WORKPLACE

The historic development of the workplace provides an important perspective for understanding the strengths and weaknesses of today's mix of policies and programs for families. Employer concern with family issues is by no means unprecedented. Wage and benefit packages linked to assumptions about the family status of employees began early in the industrial revolution. Since the 1930s, federal and state governments have also been playing a major role in regulating wage and benefit decisions. They too largely still assumed the prevalence of traditional families.

The Modern Era Through World War II

As long ago as the beginning of the textile industry in New England, young single women were carefully supervised in company housing. In mining towns, company housing and company stores were common. Such programs, often labeled *paternalism* or what Brandes (1976) refers to as *welfare capitalism*, reached their height during the period of rapid industrialization from 1880 to 1920.

Workers, mainly from farms and small villages either in the United States or abroad, came from a background of small family enterprises. They had to be acculturated to a life that revolved around industrial employment and to newly emerging technology. Under these circumstances, it was common for large companies to provide not only housing and stores, but also social services and, for immigrants, English-language classes. These programs were intended both to improve productivity and to make workers more dependent on and loyal to their employer.

An extreme example of a company committed to welfare capitalism was the Ford Motor Company. It instituted a Sociological Department in 1914, which lasted until 1921 (Meyer, 1984). Under the personal supervision of Henry Ford, department employees visited the homes of all assembly line workers. These visits were intended to ensure conformity of workers' home life to company standards of order, cleanliness, and temperance. Children's attendance at school was strongly encouraged. Penalties for nonconformity included withholding part of one's wages until the shortcomings were corrected.

Welfare capitalism declined after World War I. Little research has been done to ascertain the reasons for the decline. It may have been related to the rise of the labor movement, which relied on bargaining to make sure the interests of workers were protected. The growing availability of a disciplined urban labor force and sharp restrictions on immigration may have convinced employers that there was less need for such programs. In the 1930s, the Great Depression seriously weakened the ability of employers to provide such support. By 1936, the base of a federal social insurance system—most particularly Social Security—was established.

During World War II, employers again provided some family services, with government help; the major reason was to attract women into the war industries. Over 2,000 employer-based child care centers were established to help deal with the conflicting demands of work and family (Auerbach, 1988); these programs were generally discontinued at the end of the war when there was no longer a shortage of male workers.

Post World War II

In the period immediately following World War II, the great majority of workers were still either heads of families that included full-time homemakers or single people. Both these categories of workers were relied on to give full allegiance to their jobs, not being distracted by responsibilities for the care of dependents. Many were willing and eager to work overtime as needed, to take on greater responsibilities requiring longer hours as opportunities arose, and to maintain or establish residences as dictated by the location of jobs. These workers were first and foremost breadwinners, concerned with earnings and security. Far from permitting family to interfere with work, the expectation was that they would permit their jobs to make demands on other family members. This was most common in high-status occupations, especially among managers and executives (Kanter, 1977a; Whyte, 1951). In some cases wives were assumed to provide essential but unpaid work as part of their husbands' careers (Papanek, 1973).

Under these circumstances, what most employees wanted, what unions bargained for, and what employers offered when they sought to attract more and better qualified workers was mainly a wage adequate to support a family. Beyond that, the emphasis was on provision for such contingencies as unemployment, illness, disability, and retirement—in part because employers were able to secure better terms than individuals. Thus, insurance and pensions increasingly came to be included in fringe benefit packages.

Government also played a role in furthering this trend by providing tax preferences for employers to provide benefits and by mandating certain programs. Employer contributions to legally required benefit programs now stand at an estimated 9 percent of total compensation. These are primarily for old age, survivors, disability, and health insurance; unemployment compensation; and workers' compensation (Bureau of Labor Statistics, 1990a). Programs that are not required but that are often provided voluntarily or because of union negotiations include pensions, life and health insurance, death benefits, paid time off for vacations, and sick leave (Woodbury, 1989). Together these nonwage benefit programs account for almost 28 percent of total compensation. Although many of these programs benefit dependents as well as workers, most are still built on the assumption that the employee is the sole breadwinner of the family.

In recent years, as a result of the increase in two-earner families, pressure from employees and unions for different, family-oriented benefits for workers has increased, and it is likely to continue to do so. Similarly, employers' concerns over family commitments that tend to interfere with the ability of workers to perform their job as traditionally defined has also grown, and it too is likely to continue to do so.

Related Developments

Other historic changes that also helped to shape the present are only beginning to receive attention. People who came of age in the 1940s and 1950s were unusually fortunate. There were no major recessions in those years; they were members of relatively small birth cohorts; most of them achieved job security before the long-term rise in unemployment began in the 1970s; and labor market opportunities for women were improving. They were also the first generation that was largely relieved of the financial burden of taking care of their parents, most of whom received at least partial support through Social Security.

The situation for subsequent labor force entrants has been far less favorable. As baby boomers came of age, beginning in the middle 1960s, the supply of workers grew rapidly. It was augmented by immigration, both legal and illegal, which grew from about 3.3 million a year in the 1960s to about 6.4 million in the 1980s. The influx of women into the labor force has also continued. As noted above, women were entering the labor force not only in response to inflation and a slowdown in the growth of real wages, but also partly in response to the growing social acceptance of family life that included two wage earners. As a result of all these changes, in recent generations one-earner families have found it increasingly difficult to even maintain the living standards of their parents—let alone to exceed them, as had long been the accepted norm.

EMPLOYMENT AND EARNINGS

It is very difficult to determine to what extent the change in available jobs has influenced the entry of new workers and to what extent the availability of workers has influenced the number and kinds of jobs in the economy. In any case, the overall image that emerges is one of rapid changes in both the work force and the job market. Among labor force entrants, women now substantially outnumber men. The proportion of blacks, other non-whites, and Hispanics in the work force has been increasing rapidly. At the same time, a major shift in available jobs has taken place from manufacturing to service industries. Large numbers of jobs are being created, but they tend to be of two kinds: either well-paying white-collar positions for well-educated workers or jobs that do not pay enough for workers to maintain themselves above the poverty level. The employment and earnings data described below reflect these changes.

Sex, Race, and Education

One of the most dramatic developments in the U.S. labor force over the last century has been the rapid increase in women's participation in response to industrialization, rural-to-urban migration, rising levels of education, increases in real wages (until relatively recently), declines in fertility, and increases in life expectancy. Another reason for the increase is that, as goods and services once produced at home (as well as new products) have become available for purchase, the need to spend time at home has been reduced and paid employment has become more attractive.

Women's earnings have raised overall spending and hence the demand for labor, particularly in the service sector. Women with better job opportunities are likely to postpone marriage and have fewer children and to get more education and training, which in turn further increases their labor market opportunities. In the 1970s, the situation changed when inflation and recession reduced the rate at which women's wages increased; men's wages even declined at times in that period. Some women entered the labor force in response to husbands' falling wages while others entered although their husbands' wages were rising. The desire to achieve and maintain the expected standard of living provided an important additional impetus for women to seek employment. The rapidly rising divorce rate, itself perhaps related to women's greater ability to support themselves, further added to women's need for paid jobs (discussed in Chapter 3).

In sum, it appears that, in times of rising wages, women have entered the labor market in response to greater incentives and, in times of falling wages, they have entered in order to avoid a decline in family income. The result has been a long-term upward shift in women's employment, which has taken on a life of its own (England, 1989). Along with all these developments, attitudes toward women's roles have gradually changed. Social pressures to stay at home have diminished—some people say they may even have been reversed—and in recent years there is evidence that men's participation in household work is slowly increasing (Pleck, 1989).

Between 1950 and 1989, the percentage of all women in the labor force (working for pay or looking for such work) increased from about 34 percent to 57 percent, while the percentage of all men in the labor force declined from almost 87 percent to 76 percent. The latter change has resulted from the fact that young men have tended to stay in school longer and older men have been retiring earlier. There may also be more men who despair of finding a job and drop out of the labor force because of structural changes in the economy or because they live in depressed areas; this is especially likely to be true for minority men.

Since women have also been acquiring more years of schooling and retiring at younger ages than earlier, the rise in women's labor force participation rate in their middle years has been even greater than is suggested by the data for the total adult population: more than 70 percent of all women between the ages of 18 and 50 are now in the labor force (Bureau of Labor Statistics, 1990b). As a result of the increasing percentage of all women in the labor force and the decrease in the percentage of all men in the labor force, the proportion of the labor force that is female has changed from about 20 percent at the turn of the century to more than 45 percent today. Projections suggest that this ratio is likely to reach about 48 percent by 2000 (Johnston and Packer, 1987).

Interestingly, the proportion of women who work for pay does not currently vary a great deal by race and ethnicity. As shown in Table 2-1, the participation rate of nonwhite women in 1955 was considerably higher than that of white women. Now, black women are only marginally more likely to be working for pay than white women, although a larger proportion of white women work part time by choice. At the same time, the labor force participation of black men, which was virtually the same as for white men as late as 1955, is now about 6 percentage points lower. Thus, overall, the labor force participation of blacks increased less than that of whites. It is also worth noting that among ethnic groups the labor force participation rate of Hispanic women is the lowest and that of Hispanic men the highest.

There is a strong positive relation between education and labor force participation for women. This is true even though better educated women tend to be married to better educated men with higher incomes. In 1987,

TABLE 2-1 Labor Force Participation Rates, 1955-1989

Year	Men			Women		
	White	Nonwhite	Hispanic[a]	White	Nonwhite	Hispanic[a]
1955	85.4	85.0	n.a.	34.5	46.1	n.a.
1965	80.8	79.6	n.a.	38.1	48.6	n.a.
1973	79.5	73.8	81.5	44.1	49.1	40.9
1981	77.9	70.6	80.6	51.9	53.6	47.5
1984	77.1	71.4	80.5	53.3	55.3	49.9
1989	77.1	71.0[b]	82.0	57.2	58.7[b]	53.5

NOTE: Data are for civilian labor force age 16 and older.
[a]Hispanics are also included under the relevant racial category.
[b]Data are for blacks rather than nonwhites.
n.a. = not available.
SOURCE: Data for 1955-1984 from Blau and Ferber (1986:Table 4.2); data for 1989 from Bureau of Labor Statistics (1990b:Table 39).

the labor force participation rate for women ages 25-64 ranged from about 60 percent for those with less than 4 years of high school to almost 90 percent for those with 4 or more years of college (Bureau of Labor Statistics, 1990b). The availability of good job opportunities, of course, itself plays a role in attracting women into the labor market.

Family Status

Throughout this report, we refer to families and households. As noted in Chapter 1, in U.S. government data a family is defined as two or more persons living together who are related by blood, marriage, or adoption. Increasingly, bonds equivalent to marriage are also recognized, and we do so in this report. A household is defined as one or more persons living in the same dwelling unit and sharing living expenses. Thus, all families are households, but all households are not families.

Family circumstances continue to influence the labor force status of women. For instance, there is a difference in the labor force participation rate between women who maintain families (62.3 percent) and those who are married with their husband present (55.8 percent), although the difference was not as great in the 1980s as it was in the 1960s. The labor force participation of married women with their spouse present also differs by age of youngest child. In 1988, 72.5 percent of these women with children ages 6 to 17 and 57.1 percent of those with children under age 6 were in the labor force. The rates for both groups have increased dramatically since 1960, when the figures were only 39 percent and 18.6 percent, respectively (Bureau of Census, 1990b).

With this influx of married women and mothers into the labor market, there has also been a substantial increase in part-time workers, who often make such an arrangement by preference. As shown in Table 2-2, a far larger proportion of women than men—both black and white—work part time, and a substantially larger percentage of unemployed women than men are looking for part-time work.

Part-time employment is no doubt viewed as a useful compromise by many women who have families to care for, but it also tends to be costly for them. In general, part-time employees not only earn a lower wage rate, but also rarely receive the benefits that full-time workers usually get. This need not be a serious problem if a worker's spouse has substantial earnings and receives benefits for family members, but it may be for others, especially a single head of household.

Single Earners

People who are the sole adult in their family clearly have relatively more difficulty in balancing their responsibilities as wage earners and homemakers. This is especially so for low-income men or women who cannot afford to purchase the services and conveniences that make caring for a household less onerous. The proportion of families with only one adult is now quite

TABLE 2-2 Labor Force Status of Men and Women by Race, Average Annual Percentage, 1989

Labor Force Status	White		Black	
	Men	Women	Men	Women
Working full time	84.7	68.8	76.7	70.5
Working part time				
For economic reasons[a]	3.1	4.5	5.4	6.7
Voluntarily	7.7	22.2	6.4	12.0
Unemployed				
Looking for full-time work	3.8	3.2	10.0	9.2
Looking for part-time work	0.7	1.3	1.7	2.3
Total number (in thousands)	58,988	47,367	6,702	6,796

NOTE: Data are for civilian labor force age 16 and older. Total percentages do not add up to 100.0 due to rounding.
[a]Includes reasons such as slack work or could only find part-time work.
SOURCE: Bureau of Labor Statistics (1990b:Table 7).

large (Table 2-3). Approximately 23 percent of all working men and women who maintain families do not have a spouse present in the household; four-fifths of them are women who most often are divorced or never-married parents. Such families comprised 8.7 percent of all families in 1970 and 11.6 percent in 1988 (Bureau of the Census, 1989d).

These households fare much worse than those with two adults. Poor people do not have the unpaid family care of a full-time homemaker, which is an often overlooked addition to family well-being (Morgan, 1984). They also suffer in terms of money income; the situation is particularly serious for black and Hispanic families. For example, in 1987 among female heads of household who were married but whose spouse was absent, the mean household income for whites was $15,680; for blacks, $12,651; and for Hispanics, $10,812. For the same year, the mean household income for white households with the spouse present was $41,129; for blacks, $31,494; and for Hispanics, $30,253. Table 2-4 shows that over 56 percent of families headed by black women fall below the poverty level (measured in 1988 as $12,091 for a family of four, counting money income only); more than 59 percent of those headed by Hispanic women do.

Because divorce rates are higher among poor people and because they have higher fertility rates, single-adult families maintained by mothers have, on average, 0.7 more children than do married couples with children (Bureau of the Census, 1989a). Overall, the poverty rate among children in the United States is almost double that of adults (Bureau of the Census, 1989b).

The proportion of Americans living in poverty was somewhat higher in the 1980s than in the 1970s using a constant standard of poverty adjusted

TABLE 2-3 Employment Status of Adults Who Maintain Families by Work Status of Spouse, 1989 (in thousands)

Spouse's Work Status	Men		Women	
	Employed	Percent	Employed	Percent
Employed spouse	25,618	62.4	25,618	73.4
Unemployed spouse	877	2.1	685	2.0
Spouse not in labor force	12,478	30.4	2,261	6.5
Spouse not present	2,113	5.1	6,338	18.2
Total	41,086	100.0	34,902	100.0[a]

NOTE: Excludes persons living alone or with nonrelatives, persons in married-couple families where the husband or wife is in the Armed Forces, other relatives 16 years and over, and persons in unrelated subfamilies.

[a]Does not equal 100.00 due to rounding.

SOURCE: Bureau of Labor Statistics (1990b:Table 8).

TABLE 2-4 Percentage of Families in Poverty, 1988

Total	All Races	With Children Under 18			
		All Races	White	Black	Hispanic[a]
All families	10.4	15.7	11.9	36.0	29.7
Married couple	5.6	7.2	6.4	12.5	19.0
Male householder (no wife present)	11.8	18.0	14.5	31.4	26.1
Female householder (no husband present)	33.5	44.7	38.2	56.3	59.2

NOTE: Poverty status in 1988 meant an income of $12,091 for a family of four, counting money income only.

[a]Persons of Hispanic origin may be of any race.

SOURCE: Bureau of the Census (1989b:Table 20).

only for changes in the consumer price index (CPI) (Bureau of the Census, 1989c). In relative terms, however, the situation has worsened in recent years because of a growing trend of greater income inequality. As can be seen in Table 2-5, this is a reversal from the trend of somewhat more equality up to about 1970. Particularly significant is the continuation of this trend between 1984 and 1987, a period of recovery from the recession of the early 1980s, in which the opposite would be expected. It has been suggested that changes in family size would tend to mitigate these changes, but Danziger et al. (1989) found that adjusting for differences in the number of family members leaves the outcome essentially the same.

Employment does not always solve the problem. In 1989, approximately 10 percent of all families with children under 18 and an employed householder were below the poverty level. The labor force participation rate of divorced women is 70 percent. Among families headed by women, how-

TABLE 2-5 Distribution of Family Income, 1950-1987

Year	Total Income, by Quintiles (percentage)				
	Lowest	Second	Third	Fourth	Highest
1950	4.5	12.0	17.4	23.4	42.7
1969	5.6	12.4	17.7	23.7	40.6
1984	4.7	11.0	17.0	24.4	42.9
1987	4.6	10.8	16.9	24.1	43.7

SOURCE: Bureau of the Census (1989c:Table 12).

ever, as many as 21 percent of those who worked were still below the poverty level: 17 percent of whites, 29 percent of blacks, and 31 percent of Hispanic women (Bureau of the Census, 1990a).

Dual Earners

Unlike families with one adult, two-adult families have the option of having (1) two wage earners and more money or (2) a wage earner and a full-time homemaker, reducing the likelihood that either partner experiences stressful conflicts between job and family demands. The pressure to opt for the first solution may have been especially great in recent decades when real wages, contrary to historical trends, have been declining. Mean hourly earnings (in 1977 constant dollars) rose from $3.36 in 1950 to $5.04 in 1970, then declined to $4.89 in 1980, and to $4.80 in 1989 (Bureau of Labor Statistics, 1985b, 1990c). Even the growing proportion of two-earner families (although somewhat offset by the growth of families maintained by women) has not resulted in long-term growth in real family income. In 1988 dollars, family income was $32,109 in 1973 and $32,191 in 1986, having gone down to $28,727 during the 1982 recession (Bureau of the Census, 1989b). Adjusting these data for the decline in average family size from about 3.5 to 3.2 during this period (Bureau of the Census, 1989d), there is only a modest rise in family income of 10 percent over 13 years. Moreover, young families with children fared substantially worse than the average.

Wives' participation in the labor force is not significantly influenced by their husbands' occupations. For example, almost 33 percent of managers and executives and 36 percent of machine operators have wives who are not employed. In fact, the only two instances of wives who are substantially less likely to be employed are those married to farmers or to men in the military; they undoubtedly have less opportunity to find and hold a job (Bureau of Labor Statistics, 1988c). The reason for the lack of association between husband's occupation and wife's employment may be that families of men in low-income occupations are in greater need of more income, offsetting the tendency for women married to men in high-income occupations to be highly educated and thus have better opportunities in the labor market.

Whatever the occupation of wives, for whites and Hispanics husbands are generally in the labor force, and for blacks they are only slightly less so. Even among men who are not employed, it appears that few are likely to be homemakers: only 2 percent of men compared with 57 percent of women cite homemaking as a reason for not working for pay (Bureau of Labor Statistics, 1990b). Hence, the vast majority of employed women, as well as a growing minority of employed men, now tend to have some family responsibilities.

The number of children per family has declined in recent decades and is, on average, less than two per family today. While the proportion of households with three or four members remained steady between 1970 and 1988, the proportion with five or more members declined from 20.9 to 10.5 percent (Bureau of the Census, 1989d). Nonetheless, children make the most demands on parents' time and energy during the stage of the life cycle when earnings are still low and the demands of getting established in a career are high. It is estimated that the elderly (defined as those over age 65), who constituted 4 percent of the population in 1900 and 12 percent in 1988, will constitute more than 20 percent by 2030. Moreover, the greatest relative growth in life expectancy has occurred at age 85 and above (McGill, 1988). Because women in their forties and fifties are increasingly more likely to be in the labor force and people have fewer siblings to share in caring for parents, the challenge of caring for frail elderly parents is likely to grow in the foreseeable future.

The effects of family pressures, discussed in more detail in Chapters 4 and 5, continue to be greatest for women. Despite substantial increases in women's labor force participation, changes in men's participation in housework have been very slow. Estimates of the number of hours per day devoted to housework in 1960 ranged from 4.0 to 5.3 for employed wives and from 1.1 to 1.6 for their husbands. By 1970 the number of hours for employed wives declined to between 2.3 and 4.0, but for their husbands the number remained essentially unchanged at 0.6 to 1.9. As recently as 1981-1982, it was estimated that wives spent 4.2 hours daily on housework but husbands only 2.1 hours. These recent figures are not quite comparable, because they include couples with full-time homemakers; still, they are the only ones available. The one sign that greater changes may be imminent is that in 1981-1982, among people ages 25-44, women spent 0.14 hours per day less on housework and men 0.42 hours more than did their counterparts in 1975-1976 (Blau and Ferber, 1986).

As men are slowly taking on more household responsibilities, they are also increasingly experiencing the pressures of dual allegiance that women have lived with for a long time (Pleck, 1989). Thus, it is not surprising that a recent study at the DuPont Company showed "that the attitudes of men concerning work and family issues are rapidly approaching those of women, a significant change over . . . just four years ago" (Wohl, 1989:183).

The heavy commitments of dual-earner couples are suggested by estimates that, in 1970, husbands and wives who were both in the labor market together spent only about 2.5 hours less per day on housework but about 4.5 hours more at their jobs than couples with a full-time homemaker (Blau and Ferber, 1986). The increase in total time worked would be even greater if there were data for couples with both spouses working full time. Families are "time poor" when all the adults are employed and there are dependents who need care (Vickery, 1977).

Occupation

The degree of hardship encountered by men and women because of the dual responsibilities of jobs and families depends in part on earnings, because money can be used to purchase substitutes for household work. It also depends on occupation, for there are great differences in the demands made by and the flexibility of different kinds of work. Analysis of a national sample showed that, as hours of work increase, so does work-family conflict (Staines and Pleck, 1983). One survey of young professional men found that 59 percent claimed that their long hours tended to disrupt family life (Mortimer, 1980). Both earnings and type of work vary considerably for various population groups.

Women and men, and whites and nonwhites, remain concentrated in different occupations, although sex segregation appears to have declined somewhat in recent years. For example, 29 percent of white women and 27 percent of black women are employed in administrative support (formerly clerical) positions, compared with 5 percent of white men and 9 percent of black men. Similarly, almost 15 percent of white men and 11 percent of white women are in the executive and managerial category, compared with only 6 percent of black men and 7 percent of black women (Bureau of Labor Statistics, 1990b).

Table 2-6 provides information on median incomes of men and women by occupation. In 6 of 12 categories, women on average earn less than

TABLE 2-6   Median Income of Year-Round Full-Time Workers, 1988

Occupation	Median Income	
	Men	Women
Executive, administrative, managerial	$36,759	$23,356
Professional specialty	37,490	25,789
Technical and related support	30,369	21,039
Sales	27,022	15,474
Administrative support, including clerical	24,399	16,676
Precision production, craft, repair	25,746	16,869
Machine operators, assemblers, and inspectors	21,382	13,289
Transportation and material moving	23,453	13,021
Handlers, equipment cleaners, helpers, and laborers	17,042	13,397
Service workers, private household	[a]	7,299
Service workers, others	18,648	11,232
Farming, forestry, and fishing	14,300	9,926

[a]Base less than $75,000.

SOURCE: Bureau of the Census (1989b:Table 11).

TABLE 2-7 Median Household Income, 1988

Family Composition and Location	Race or Ethnic Origin		
	White	Black	Hispanic[a]
All Households	$28,781	$16,407	$20,359
Number of earners			
No earners	11,269	5,577	6,063
1 earner	24,263	14,920	16,139
2 earners	38,998	31,334	28,044
3 earners	50,050	41,435	36,563
4 or more	65,192	54,151	46,620
Residence			
Farm	24,415	[b]	[b]
Nonfarm	28,884	16,431	20,454
Metropolitan	31,088	17,418	20,825
Nonmetropolitan	22,405	12,003	15,978
Region			
Northeast	31,578	19,108	18,574
Midwest	28,875	15,012	24,142
South	26,949	15,029	17,986
West	29,160	23,175	21,790

NOTE: Restricted to households with civilian householders.
[a]Persons of Hispanic origin may be of any race.
[b]Base less than $75,000.
SOURCE: Bureau of the Census (1989b:Table 1).

$15,000. In 1988 the poverty level for a family of four was $12,091; clearly, many of these workers, although they are employed full time, find it extremely difficult to provide adequate support for a family, especially if it includes young children or elderly members who need care.

Male workers fare better: 80.9 percent of white men and 67.5 percent of black men are in occupations with median earnings above $15,000 (although this is not a very high standard of affluence). Only 26.2 percent of white men and 12.7 percent of black men are executives and professionals who earn, on average, more than $30,000. Of course the majority of husband-wife families today have two wage earners, but persons in low-income occupations tend to have spouses who also earn little. According to the Bureau of the Census (1989b), almost 10 percent of couples with both spouses employed have earnings below $20,000, and almost 30 percent have earnings below $30,000.

Table 2-7 shows median incomes for families with different numbers of earners by race, ethnicity, residence, and region. The differences by race and ethnicity are much greater than those by region, although, as might be expected, there are substantial differences in earnings between urban and rural areas.

Industry and Unionization

Conditions of work and earnings are determined not only by occupation, but also by the industry in which a worker is employed. For instance, some industries are more cyclically or seasonally stable than others. Recent research has also convincingly demonstrated that workers performing very similar or identical tasks earn considerably more in some industries than in others (Katz and Summers, 1988). Similarly, the number of hours worked and the extent to which workers are employed full time or part time vary considerably, as seen in Table 2-8. As we detail in Chapters 5 and 6, the extent and nature of fringe benefits also varies dramatically by industry.

It is these disparities in rewards by occupation, industry, and work status that in large part account for the variations in the standard of living of different population groups. As we noted above, women are more likely than men to work part time and in low-paying industries, such as the service sector. Women also tend to work fewer hours per week (Bureau of Labor Statistics, 1990b).

TABLE 2-8 Wage and Salary Workers in Nonagricultural Industries, 1989

| Industry | Total at Work (thousands) | Part-Time Workers (percent) | | Average Hours, Total at Work | Average Hours, Full-Time Workers |
		Economic[a] (percent)	Volun-tary		
Total	99,754	4.1	13.5	39.3	43.3
Mining	642	2.5	2.3	45.8	47.0
Construction	5,930	6.1	4.4	40.5	42.8
Manufacturing	20,258	2.3	3.3	42.2	43.4
Durable goods	11,978	1.6	2.3	42.7	43.6
Nondurable goods	8,280	3.4	4.7	41.5	43.2
Transportation and public utilities	7,297	2.7	6.0	42.3	44.3
Wholesale and retail trade	21,322	6.3	23.4	37.1	44.1
Finance, insurance, and real estate	7,038	1.8	9.6	40.1	42.6
Service industries	31,985	4.7	19.3	37.4	43.0
Private household	1,057	18.0	44.1	26.4	45.6
All other service industries	30,928	4.3	18.4	37.8	43.0
Public administration	5,282	0.9	4.9	40.8	42.2

[a]Includes reasons such as slack work or could only find part-time work.
SOURCE: Adapted from Bureau of Labor Statistics (1990b:Table 32).

TABLE 2-9 Employment by Sector, 1948 and 1986

Sector	Shares of Total Employment (percent)		Net New Jobs, 1948-1986 (thousands)
	1948	1986	
Agriculture	4.3	1.6	–587
Mining	2.1	0.8	–234
Construction	4.8	4.9	2,352
Manufacturing	32.3	19.4	2,959
Services	56.5	73.4	42,678
Total	100.0	100.0	47,168

NOTE: Employment is measured in full-time equivalents.
SOURCE: Adapted from Waldstein (1989:Table 2).

Related to growth in the service sector is growth in small firms. According to the Small Business Administration, between 1980 and 1986, 64 percent of the 10.5 million new jobs were created by businesses with fewer than 500 employees, and half of the new jobs in the service sector were in such firms (U.S. Small Business Administration, 1987). Approximately 39 percent of the new jobs came from firms with fewer than 20 employees. There was even some growth in small firms in the manufacturing sector, which showed an overall net loss of 1.7 million jobs during that period. Whereas 64 percent of new jobs are found in small firms, they also represent a lower but still large percentage of ongoing jobs.

Small firms are clearly an important part of the growing economy, but there is also evidence that, because of a relatively high failure rate of new small businesses, some of the new jobs created are short-lived. This fact may explain the discrepancy between jobs created and employment status. A recent analysis of the May 1988 Current Population Survey found that 38 percent of nonfarm wage and salary workers in the private sector were in firms with fewer than 100 employees, a decrease from 43 percent in 1983 (Piacentini, 1990). (Both numbers are slight underestimations because firm size was undetermined for 9 percent of the sample in 1988 and 6 percent in 1983.)

It is significant that growth in new jobs has been in the lower-paying service sector of the economy (Table 2-9). Average hourly earnings are almost $2 an hour less in the expanding industries: $7.70 compared with $9.93 in shrinking industries (Waldstein, 1989). Furthermore, growth in involuntary part-time work has been greatest in the service industries. For example, between 1979 and 1986, involuntary part-time jobs increased 88 percent in miscellaneous services, compared with 61 percent in trade and 21 percent in durable manufacturing (Waldstein, 1989). It is also important to note that considerable job growth has occurred in the public sector. In 1985, governments employed 16.6 percent of the labor force: the federal government accounted for 2.9 percent, and state and local governments accounted for 13.7 percent.

Union representation also varies by industry (Table 2-10). Hamermesh and Rees (1988) estimate that wages of workers who are in unions are about 10 to 15 percent higher than for those not in unions. Union membership as a percentage of the total labor force, however, peaked in 1945 at 34.5 percent. By 1989, union members represented only 16.4 percent of nonagricultural workers. More recently, there has also been a decline in absolute numbers, from 20 million in 1980 to 17 million in 1989. Union membership differs by race and ethnicity and especially by sex. Among men, approximately 19 percent of whites, 25 percent of blacks, and 17 percent of Hispanics are union members; among women, 11.5 percent of whites, 20 percent of blacks, and 13 percent of Hispanics belong to unions (Bureau of Labor Statistics, 1990b). Differences in membership range by region, from a low of 14 percent in the South to almost 27 percent in the North Central part of the country (Hamermesh and Rees, 1988). To some extent, these differences reflect differences in distribution by occupation and industry.

The ethnic and gender composition of unions is changing. Today the proportion of Hispanic workers in unions is about the same as that of whites, and that of blacks is a good deal higher. Women continue to be underrepresented in unions relative to their representation in the labor force, but not to the same extent as previously. In fact, women have accounted for half of all new union members in the last 20 years. Thus, while the proportion of men in unions has declined precipitously since World War II, that of women has grown slightly. It is therefore not surprising that since the 1960s more unions have become advocates for a number of policies furthering women's equality in the labor market, and others are oriented toward helping two-earner couples (Cook, 1989).

Explanations for Race and Sex Differences

Throughout this section on employment and earnings, the data have shown substantial differences by sex and by race. There is evidence that this is true by ethnicity as well, although detailed data are not readily available. Although the difference in the labor force participation of men and women has declined considerably and occupational segregation has declined somewhat, the gender earnings gap has been closing only very slowly. In 1970 women working full time year round earned 62 percent as much as men and, in 1987, 70 percent as much.

TABLE 2-10   Union Affiliation by Industry, 1989 (percentage of employed)

Industry	Members of Unions[a]	Represented by Unions[b]
Agricultural wage and salary workers	1.2	2.1
Private nonagricultural wage and salary workers	12.4	13.7
Mining	17.5	19.7
Construction	21.5	22.6
Manufacturing	21.6	23.1
Durable goods	23.1	24.7
Nondurable goods	19.4	20.8
Transportation and public utilities	31.6	34.1
Transportation	29.6	31.3
Communications and public utilities	34.2	38.0
Wholesale and retail trade	6.3	7.0
Wholesale trade	6.8	7.8
Retail trade	6.1	6.8
Finance, insurance, and real estate	2.3	3.1
Services	5.8	7.0
Government workers	36.7	43.6

[a]Data refer to members of a labor union or an employee association similar to a union.

[b]Data refer to members of a labor union or an employee association similar to a union as well as workers who report no union affiliation but whose jobs are covered by a union or an employee association contract.

SOURCE: Bureau of Labor Statistics (1990b:Table 58).

Even less change has occurred in recent years in earnings differences for racial and ethnic groups. In comparison with the earnings of white men, those of black men rose sharply from 61 percent in the mid-1950s to 77 percent in the mid-1970s, but they have since declined slightly. The earnings of black women in comparison with white women rose even more during the same period, from 51 percent in the mid-1950s to 98 percent in the mid-1970s, but they have since declined to 91 percent. Data for Hispanics are not available for the earlier period, but the ratio of their earnings to the rest of the population has declined modestly since 1975, from 72 percent to 70 percent for men and from 85 percent to 82 percent for women.

A great deal of research has been done in the hope of determining the causes of these differences, but much disagreement remains. Economists who believe in the efficient operation of the competitive labor market explain occupational segregation by sex largely in terms of women's lesser labor market attachment, presumably due in large part to family responsibilities, which cause them to seek out jobs that involve less investment in human capital (such as specialized education, training, and on-the-job experience) and impose lower penalties for work interruptions (Mincer and Polachek, 1974; Polachek, 1981, 1987; Filer, 1989). Segregation by race is mainly attributed to fewer years and lower quality of education of blacks and to some extent to the fact that they tend to work shorter hours. The occupational distribution in turn helps to explain the earnings gap, together with the direct effects of the lesser accumulation of human capital by women and minorities.

Alternative explanations emphasize habit, discrimination, and the rigidity of internal work structures as intentional and unintentional factors that contribute to both occupational segregation and the earnings gap. While not denying that differences in education, training, and experience play a role, proponents of these views point out, first, that none of the numerous studies using a wide variety of human capital variables is able to account for more than 50 percent of the total difference in earnings (Treiman and Hartmann, 1981; Michael et al., 1989). Second, they suggest that some of the shortfall of human capital among women and minorities is itself likely to be caused by societal or labor market discrimination (Arrow, 1973; Bergmann, 1976). Such feedback effects make it difficult to determine the relative importance of individual factors.

The main unresolved points between the two schools of thought are to what extent variables that cannot be measured, but that would presumably favor white males, account for the unexplained earnings gap and how much credence should be put in the claim that, in the absence of discrimination, the differences in qualifications would diminish (Blau and Ferber, 1987; England and Farkas, 1986). Also, the large unattributed differences may indicate that labor markets are simply inefficient in practice.

Unemployment

Even more serious than the plight of workers holding jobs with low pay is the situation of those who are unable to find work. The extent to which unemployment is a problem has varied over time. The overall unemployment rate in this country since World War II has fluctuated from a low of 2.9 percent in 1953 to a high of 9.7 in 1982 (Bureau of Labor Statistics, 1983); it was between 5 and 6 percent in the late 1980s. These figures do not include discouraged workers (people who would like to work but are not actively looking for a job) or part-time workers who would prefer to work full time. There also are variations in unemployment rates among different groups. In general, rates for women have been somewhat higher than for men, particularly so during periods when the labor market is relatively tight (i.e., unemployment is low). This is the case, in part, because women tend to be employed in industries that are cyclically stable, so that their unemployment rate rises less during downswings and declines less during upswings. Women are also especially likely to enter the labor force during prosperous times, so that their unemployment rate does not decline as much (Ferber and Lowry, 1976).

Differences in unemployment rates are substantially greater by age, level of education, and race and ethnicity than by sex. In recent years, the rate for teenagers has been about three times higher than that of adults (age 20 and over). Unemployment rises sharply as the level of education declines; it is more than four times greater for high school dropouts than for college graduates. And Hispanics are almost twice as likely as whites to be unemployed; blacks are somewhat more than twice as likely.

FUTURE EMPLOYMENT TRENDS

We now turn to a brief examination of projections for the future of both women's labor market participation and changes in the total labor force. These developments will have a great impact on the environment in which businesses seek to hire and keep workers and in which workers seek to find and keep jobs that offer satisfactory rewards.

Forecasts are inherently hazardous, yet this is less true of near-term projections of the labor force, because the people who will be working a few years hence have already been born. Furthermore, the near-term age distribution of the population is known, and the labor force participation of the young and the old is not likely to change dramatically. Illegal immigration, however, introduces some uncertainty into projections; because the relevant laws were recently changed, the annual number of undocumented aliens is projected to decline from 200,000 in 1988 to 100,000 in 1998 (Fullerton, 1989). Even so, the assumption that the recent rate of entry of all immigrants, estimated to be 450,000 a year, is likely to continue appears to be realistic, assuming no new legislation affecting entry rates. New immigrants are expected to represent 22 percent of the projected net total of new workers between 1985 and 2000 (Fullerton, 1989; Johnston and Packer, 1987) and to locate in the cities and states that today have large concentrations of recent immigrants. While there may be some effect in regions where immigration is particularly heavy, Johnston and Packer (1987) tentatively conclude that immigrants do not have a negative effect overall on native minority workers, as some fear.

Somewhat more conjectural is the question of to what extent women's labor force participation will continue to rise. For some time there was a tendency to underestimate future increases, but predictions are probably now more accurate. Carefully documented work by Johnston and Packer (1987) and Fullerton (1989) projects that women's labor force participation rate, which was 56.1 percent in 1987, will be approximately 62 percent in 2000. In view of the recent very modest increases in labor force participation among young women, many of whom continue their schooling, as well as a slight decline among elderly women, who retire somewhat earlier than men, these projections seem reasonable.

The total labor force is expected to increase from 115 million in 1985 to 139 or 140 million in 2000. Of the net change of 25 million workers, only 36 percent are likely to be men, and among the men somewhat more than half will be minorities or immigrants. Thus, the change in the composition of the labor force witnessed in recent decades is expected to continue.

Similarly, a changing economy will continue to affect the jobs that need to be filled. The most recent occupational projections expect the long-term employment shift to service industries, particularly in business and health services, to continue (Kutscher, 1989). These are also industries composed of relatively small firms (Johnston and Packer, 1987). The fastest-growing occupations are in managerial, professional, and technical specialties that require high levels of education. However, four of the six occupations that have recently grown most rapidly in absolute numbers pay low wages: retail salesworkers, janitors and cleaners, waitresses and waiters, and general office clerks. The other two occupations with the largest job growth are registered nurses and general managers and top executives (Silvestri and Lukasiewicz, 1989).

Labor shortages are projected for entry-level jobs, primarily because of the decline in the number of young people ages 16 to 24 entering the work force. This shortage will be most noticeable in areas that already have low unemployment rates. The Bureau of Labor Statistics also projects shortages of workers for technical and skilled craft jobs that require some postsecondary education or training but less than a 4-year college degree. This expected shortage in large part reflects continuing low completion rates for high school, especially among black and Hispanic youths. Hispanics are the fastest-growing component of the labor force, but they also have the lowest high school completion rates: 54.7 percent compared with 64.9 percent for blacks and 76.6 for whites (Kutscher, 1989).

CONCLUSIONS

Today's diverse family forms are not unprecedented, nor are the concerns with family issues on the part of employers and governments. What has become known as the traditional family is a relatively new phenomenon, and it was never universal. Some women have always been employed outside the household, initially single women and widows in addition to poor, immigrant, and black women. The evolution of wage and benefit packages, since the beginning of the industrial revolution, has been linked to assumptions about the family status of workers, as have the government programs that began in the 1930s, such as family assistance programs, social insurance, and tax incentives.

The labor force in much of the United States is continuing to become more diverse, not only because of the influx of women, especially those with young children, but also by race and ethnicity because of both rural-urban migration within the country and immigration from abroad. At the same time, projections for the year 2000 anticipate continued growth of employment in the service sector, in small firms, and in entry-level jobs, all of which have traditionally employed a relatively large number of women and minority workers. Although union membership has declined, unions continue to play a role in determining the wages and benefits of this new work force.

Family status is no longer as important a determinant of labor force participation as it was previously, yet married women with husbands present and mothers of young children are still less likely to be employed, as well as more likely to be employed part time, than other women. The number of two-earner families is rapidly rising; they have more money but less discretionary time than families with two adults and one wage earner. Female-headed families have also become increasingly numerous, and they tend to be very short of both money and time. Minority families are disproportionately represented in this group.

Differences in labor force participation of men and women have declined considerably, and occupational segregation has declined somewhat. Women working full time, year round in 1987 earned 70 percent as much as men, compared with 62 percent in 1970. This is still, however, a substantial gap, and even less change has occurred in recent years in the earnings gap by race and ethnicity. Although the reason for these continuing differences remains the subject of debate, there is no question that the low wages of female- and minority-headed families result in fewer resources to deal with family responsibilities.

We conclude that the economic well-being of most families is increasingly dependent on having two wage earners; at the same time, employers, particularly those in the growth areas, increasingly depend on women and minority workers. The combined labor force and labor market trends over the past several decades and projections for the future raise important questions. How are dependents being cared for when all adults in the family who are able to work are employed? What are the effects at work and at home? How and why have families and employers responded to these changes and the new opportunities and problems to which they have given rise? The answers to these questions are the subject of the remaining chapters of this report.

3

Linkages Between Work and Family

One of the questions motivating this study is to what extent changing family structures and employment patterns (discussed in Chapter 2) have interacted to create problems in the workplace and in the family. A particular concern is the effects on children. Historically, researchers as well as employers tended to treat work and family as separate worlds (Kanter, 1977b). In the past decade, however, there has been increasing recognition of the multiple levels of interdependence between work and family (Voydanoff, 1987; Baca-Zinn and Eitzen, 1990). The relationship, although it has changed over time, has always had both positive and negative aspects.

Employment is a major component of family well-being. It is the primary source not only of income and various types of social insurance (including health insurance, Social Security, private pensions, disability and unemployment insurance) but also of other benefits, such as self-esteem. Thus it is one of the most essential sources of both economic and psychological security. The need for financial security increases when one has a family. Married men, in particular, have substantially higher labor force participation rates than do unmarried men.

Long hours, rigid schedules, and an excessively high level of involvement in work, however, can also have negative consequences both for the individuals involved and for their families. Among other things, they may reduce the quality of care available from working family members for their dependents. Similarly, the responsibilities of caring for family members can affect work performance in a number of ways.

In this chapter we review what is known about the linkages between work and family: how they fit together and how they conflict. To the extent possible we summarize the workplace issues for women and men with different racial and ethnic backgrounds, in different kinds of work-places, and for different family structures. For example, the pressures generated by time spent at work and scheduling conflicts precipitate different stresses and coping responses in female-headed households, dual-earner households, and male-earner, two-parent households (Piotrkowski, 1979).

Although men and women are both vulnerable to stress when they are employed and have household responsibilities, women are at greater risk because they perform the bulk of household tasks. Men have been increasing the time they spend in housework and child care (Pleck, 1989), particularly husbands who care for children during mothers' working hours (Presser, 1989). Data show, however, that women continue to bear most of the responsibility for children and elders, whether or not they work for pay, and employed women, especially mothers, have less leisure time than men (Staines and Pleck, 1983; unpublished data, Institute for Social Research, University of Michigan, 1989). For example, in a study of 1,500 employees in two companies, the combined time spent on work, home chores, and child care in a week was, on average, 84 hours for married mothers, 79 hours for unmarried mothers, and 72 hours for fathers, married or unmarried (Burden and Googins, 1987). It has been suggested that employed women with a family tend to have two jobs, one in the workplace and one at home, while it is still assumed that men's primary responsibility is their paid work.

Multiple levels of interdependence make it impossible to consider the sphere of family and the sphere of employment as separate worlds (Baca-Zinn and Eitzen, 1990). The precise nature of the linkages varies considerably, depending on the structural features of both household and work settings (Voydanoff, 1987). Therefore, we assess the effect of labor force participation on the family, of family characteristics on performance in the workplace, and the combined effects of multiple roles and quality of life. We first examine studies concerned with various aspects of workplace conditions, especially those over which employers have some control, such as schedules and leaves, and their impact on employees and their dependents. We then review research on the effect of domestic circumstances, such as a breakdown in child care arrangements, on job performance. We also consider the interaction and feedback, stressful or satisfying, between family and work.

Existing investigations range from descriptive case studies, based on small nonrandom samples or employees of one firm, to research using national samples. Each approach has its strengths and limitations. Case studies provide in-depth information about particular groups, members of a single occupation, or employees of one firm, but they are primarily descriptive and do not provide a sound basis for generalizations or for conclusions about causal relationships (for reviews see, for example, Friedman, 1989b;

Galinsky, 1989b). National survey data based on representative samples allow generalizations and some inferences about causality, especially if longitudinal data are available, but individuals are usually the unit of analysis, with little or no link to a particular enterprise; such data are therefore often not suitable for investigations of employer policies and their impact on the workplace (for reviews see, for example, Pleck, 1983; Repetti et al., 1989; Hayes et al., 1990). Drawing conclusions from such diverse research, based on vastly different data and methodology, is often difficult.

EFFECTS OF WORK ON FAMILY

Employees sometimes report that family responsibilities interfere with their work, but even more so that work interferes with their family. In a survey of two-earner families with children age 12 or under (done for *Fortune* magazine), 16 percent of men and 18 percent of women reported family interference, while 32 percent of men and 41 percent of women reported that paid work interfered with their family life (Galinsky and Hughes, 1987). There is also evidence that people believe they perform better at work than at home: Burden and Googins (1987) found that 86 percent of people questioned in their two-company study rated their job performance as "good or unusually good"; only 59 percent rated their family performance that way. Their interpretation is that jobs take priority. It may also be the case, however, that people set higher standards for themselves at home than on the job.

Research in this field has focused on the effects of employment on families, specifically the impact of women's labor force participation, presumably because men were expected to work for pay, while women were still expected to be responsible for homemaking. Initially, research attention centered almost entirely on potential negative effects on marriage and children of women's employment (see, for example, Hoffman and Nye, 1974; Spitze, 1988). Recently, however, scholars have broadened their studies to encompass the complex interactions between work and family, as well as the multidimensional characteristics of jobs, families, and individuals.

Income and Identity

Men's employment has been taken for granted because it has been the major source of income for the vast majority of families. Income is crucial to family well-being for several reasons. Not only does it determine the basic standard of living, but also a minimum amount of steady income is required to maintain family stability and cohesion (Cherlin, 1979; Furstenberg, 1974; Rodman, 1971). In addition, employment is a central part of the personal identity of most men. Therefore, when a man is not employed, he and his family are likely to have problems. (For a discussion of the negative effects of men's unemployment, especially on children, see Voydanoff, 1987).

Only recently have researchers clearly recognized the importance of women's employment in increasing family income; employed wives often help keep their families out of poverty (Blau and Ferber, 1986). When both spouses work full time all year, wives' earnings, on average, constitute 39 percent of family income (Bureau of the Census, 1986). Women's employment also tends to raise their status in the eyes of other family members, as well as their own. For instance, husbands are more likely to respect working wives' decision-making ability and to listen to their opinions (Blumstein and Schwartz, 1983). About half of all employed women are not married, and they usually depend on their job to support themselves as well as a source of social support (Repetti et al., 1989).

Health

Both longitudinal and cross-sectional studies suggest that in general employment does not have negative effects on women's physical or mental health, despite frequent problems of role conflict and overload (see Repetti et al., 1989, for a review). It appears to have beneficial effects on physical health particularly for unmarried women, black women, and Mexican American women. Some, though not all, studies have also found employed women to be less depressed than nonemployed women.

Positive findings from cross-sectional studies, however, must be discounted because there is substantial evidence that healthier women are more likely to enter the labor force. The causal relationships between employment and health are not clear. Preliminary findings from a national longitudinal survey suggest that health is an important determinant of labor force participation (Maret, 1982). Women who are not employed frequently report poor health as a reason for not working (e.g., Kessler and McRae, 1982); however, when homemakers reporting poor health as a reason for not working were excluded from the analysis, Jennings et al. (1984) found that homemakers reported better health than employed women. Repetti et al. (1989) conclude that more longitudinal data and more appropriate methods of analysis are needed to distinguish between the effects of health on employment and the effects of employment on health.

More sophisticated studies indicate that it may not be employment status per se but the sense of independence and control brought about by work that contributes to the positive outlook of employed women. Rosenfield (1989) suggests that perceived control influences the relationship between employment and role strain. That is, employment is not always a mental health benefit for women when it trades one source of low control (housewife status) for another (a job with little power). A key factor appears to be the woman's preference: two reviews conclude that there are positive effects on women's health when there is congruence between what she is doing and what she would like to be doing (Repetti et al., 1989; Spitze, 1988).

There is also a modest amount of evidence on the relationship between family responsibilities and health. Women who care for dependents—most of all those with a dependent spouse—have been found to be more prone to depression than other women, especially if they have to give up their job (Holmes and Rahe, 1976; Kanner et al., 1981). Men also suffer depression when caring for elders, particularly spouses (McLanahan and Monson, 1989).

Marital Satisfaction

The interaction effects between women's employment and marital status are mixed. Women's employment is associated with higher divorce rates: this might be interpreted to mean that such marriages are worse or, alternatively, that divorce is more affordable. Entering employment could introduce strain, or wives may enter the labor force when the marriage is shaky. Some studies have shown that husbands of employed women are more likely to be depressed and experience greater job pressures (Kessler and McRae, 1982). Others found that both spouses experience greater marital satisfaction (e.g., Simpson and England, 1982). Recent research has also found that, as the proportion of dual-earner couples rose, there was increased emphasis in families on conversation, shared leisure time activities, empathy, and companionship (England and Farkas, 1986), and the proportion of respondents who said that their marriage was either very happy or above average rose from 68 percent in 1957 to 80 percent in 1976 (Thornton and Freedman, 1983).

Clearly, the effect of wife's employment on marital satisfaction depends on a variety of factors. For example, according to one small survey, greater financial security, older age of children, and higher levels of community involvement are all associated with more satisfaction (Thomas et al., 1984). In general, favorable outcomes are most likely to prevail when wives' employment is consistent with both partners' preferences (Ross et al., 1983). When husbands' preferences are inconsistent with wives' employment status, women show lower self-esteem and increased depression (Kessler and McRae, 1982). Research results regarding the effects of employment on marriage continue to be mixed depending on how the questions are approached. In a comprehensive review of the literature, Spitze (1988) reports that recent studies using large national samples find no overall effects of wives' employment on the marital satisfaction of either husbands or wives. She also concludes that causal ordering with respect to employment and marital satisfaction or dissolution is not clear.

Children's Well-Being

There is general consensus that a mother's work status per se has no predictable effects on her children's development (Kamerman and Hayes, 1982; Hayes et al., 1990). Rather, a variety of specific factors interact with mother's employment in determining the outcomes. In general, when mothers work by choice and child care is satisfactory, family stress is not too great and their children are as well adjusted as those with mothers at home. For infants, a small number of stable caretakers to whom the child can become attached is also important (Zigler and Frank, 1988). Although less research has been done on the effects for older children, there is evidence that much depends on what mothers do and how they feel about it (Bloom-Feshbach et al., 1982).

Children of employed mothers are less likely to subscribe to traditional gender stereotypes and in general have more positive views of themselves and their families (Hoffman, 1987). When mothers work by personal choice, daughters are likely to view both parents with admiration; however, sons of working mothers in low-income families tend to be more critical of their fathers. When mothers work in nontraditional occupations, their daughters in college are more inclined to aspire to such occupations (Heyns, 1982). Sons of employed middle-class mothers tend to do less well in school than their counterparts with nonemployed mothers, but this does not hold for lower-class sons (Bronfenbrenner and Crouter, 1982). In her review of the literature, Hoffman (1987) finds that dissatisfied mothers, whether employed or not, appear to have more poorly adjusted children, suggesting that mothers' satisfaction, rather than employment status, may influence children's adjustment.

Research on employed minority mothers, although sparse, shows consistently favorable effects on children's achievement except when arrangements for their care are inadequate (Heyns, 1982). One study focusing largely on minority children suggested that, when mothers' work is highly regulated and demanding, children are more likely to conform to school requirements and to study more diligently (Piotrkowski and Katz, 1982).

A mediating factor for the effects of parental employment on children's well-being is the quality of child care. Despite earlier fears, there is no evidence that high-quality out-of-home care is harmful to children over age 1, and in some cases positive effects have been documented. For infants, the evidence is mixed. Group sizes, staff/child ratios, caregivers' training, stability of care, daily routine, and organization of classroom space are factors in quality care (for extensive reviews of the developmental literature, see Hayes et al., 1990; Phillips, 1987). For instance, children's cognitive and social development has been found to be positively related to group size, teacher qualifications, and the goals of the program, such as focus on cognitive development (Ruopp et al., 1979). Particularly for children from low-income families, high-quality programs appear to have a positive effect on intellectual development, perhaps because they compensate for poor family environment (Slaughter, 1983; Ramey et al., 1985).

With respect to infants, research so far has been inconclusive. Stress in the form of role overload and role conflict appears to be most strongly felt by employed women with infants. A Swedish study shows that employed mothers report more daily fatigue and psychological distress after the birth of a first child (Moen, 1989). Limited evidence suggests that the stress felt by some employed mothers may have negative effects on the relationship with and the development of their infants (Zigler and Frank, 1988; Moen, 1989; Brazelton, 1986; Clarke-Stewart and Fein, 1983).

It is clear that infants need high-quality care from a small number of caretakers, with adequate opportunity to establish close bonds in order to enhance healthy emotional development (Zigler and Frank, 1988). Full-time purchased child care in the first year appears to be associated in some children with insecure attachment to their mothers, often considered an important component in healthy development. Reliance on only one measure, however, as well as other methodological constraints, makes interpretation of the finding difficult (Hayes et al., 1990). Studies also find that group day care at this early age seems to lead to greater orientation toward peers and more competence in interacting with them (Clarke-Stewart and Fein, 1983) but to decreased responsiveness toward adults (Belsky, 1988).

The physical health and safety of children in child care centers are also important issues. A comprehensive review (Jarman and Kohlenberg, 1988) of over 200 existing studies is generally reassuring, but there is agreement that more research is needed on health and safety. Preschool-age children in centers were found to be more likely to contract common infectious diseases than children at home, although there tend to be no unfavorable long-term effects. Group child care also increases the risk of several serious but very rare infectious diseases. Based on more limited research, no evidence has been found of increased risk of neglect, injury, or any kind of abuse in child care centers. The National Research Council's Panel on Child Care Policy (Hayes et al., 1990) concluded that organized care does not involve major risks to children's health.

Other Dependents

With rising life expectancy, the number of elderly parents and spouses in need of care has been increasing. The continued influx of women into the labor market has raised questions about possible declines in the availability of services needed by these people, as well as by a smaller group of disabled working-age adults.

Existing evidence on the effects of women's labor force participation on disabled and elderly dependents is inconclusive. Some studies show that women's employment limits caregiving for elderly parents (Lang and Brody, 1983; Brody and Schoonover, 1986). Other studies have found no effect on the helping behavior of daughters (Cicirelli, 1981; Stoller, 1983). There is little evidence on caring for a disabled spouse, who may or may not be elderly. An early study, however, shows that wives of disabled men are likely to enter the labor force in response to the illness and related economic loss (Franklin, 1977). Thus, employment may offer economic relief and make possible the purchase of care. It may also provide some psychological relief from the demands of caring, which causes depression, as discussed earlier. At the same time, the additional demands of employment add to the mental and physical stress of caregivers and potentially reduce the quality of care for the disabled and the elderly.

Minority Families

Although research specifically on the linkages between work and minority families is sparse, there is evidence of differences between minority and majority families, as well as among various minority groups (Harrison, 1989; Gerstel and Gross, 1987). Primarily, studies have shown that the generally poorer jobs and lower incomes of minorities have a negative effect on their families.

Recent investigations suggest that deteriorating economic conditions have had a major impact on family structure. Wilson (1987) documents relationships between male joblessness and high divorce rates, low remarriage rates, and high ratios of births to unmarried mothers. He concludes that the explosive growth of black families headed by women has been mainly an outgrowth of changes in the U.S. economy, which resulted in declining employment opportunities for inner-city blacks, particularly men.

Among Hispanic communities, important variations exist in economic conditions. While economic conditions for Puerto Ricans have deteriorated in the past decade, the well-being of Cuban Americans has improved considerably, and there has been little change for Mexican Americans (Bean and Tienda, 1988). Understandably, then, there is little evidence of consistent changes in family structure for the Hispanic community as a whole (Baca-Zinn, 1989; Moore, 1989). Structural changes have been greatest for the groups that experienced the most serious economic dislocations. In some cities, Puerto Rican unemployment, poverty rates, and the proportion of families with female heads is reaching or exceeding those of blacks.

Variations in childrearing strategies, value socialization, extended kinship ties, and sex roles may also contribute to different perspectives on work and family (Harrison, 1989). Hence, family care supports and problems tend to vary, and it cannot be taken for granted that findings from studies not specifically focusing on these groups are applicable to them.

Using three national data sets on blacks, whites, and Americans of Mexican descent, Jackson and Antonucci (1989) found that the relationship between roles and well-being or happiness is complicated for each of the populations. While most people reported being satisfied with their lives, the level of satisfaction was influenced by many factors, including gender, race, and employment status. In general, blacks experienced the highest levels of stress, job related and otherwise, and also had the most chronic health problems.

Other smaller studies did not find some of the same differences. Among a sample of black inner-city mothers, approximately 29 percent indicated experiencing moderate to severe family-work conflict (Katz and Piotrkowski, 1983), a figure comparable to that found in a representative national sample by Pleck et al. (1980). Job autonomy and job demands, not income, were the key correlates of strain among the inner-city sample. Similarly, Fernandez (1986) reported no differences in levels of stress among men in various racial and ethnic groups. More surprisingly, he also reported that black women felt less family-work stress than did either white women or other women of color.

An examination of the effects of employment and parental and marital status on the health of a sample of 712 Americans of Mexican descent showed that employment was associated with less illness for both men and women and parenthood with less chronic illness for women (Krause and Markides, 1985). For women there were also interesting interactions between employment and marital status, suggesting that earnings and the greater self-esteem associated with employment are particularly important for single women.

Work Characteristics

Schedules

The 8-hour day and the 40-hour week have been the typical work pattern in the United States for the last several decades. As we saw in Chapter 2, however, a substantial and growing minority of workers are employed part time. Married women constitute the largest group of part-time workers. Married men, in contrast, are most likely to work extended hours and to hold more than one job, slightly more so when their wives are not employed (Moony, 1981; Moen and Moorehouse, 1983). In addition, 13 percent of women and almost 16 percent of men work fixed nonday shifts, while 4 percent of women and 9 percent of men work rotating shifts (Presser, 1989).

Almost one-fifth of workers in the 1977 Quality of Employment Survey complained about excessive work hours (Staines and Pleck, 1983). Several studies, using different data sets, have concluded that long hours are associated with higher levels of family-work conflict and strain for both male and female workers (Burke et al., 1980; Mortimer, 1980; Staines and Pleck, 1983; Voydanoff, 1984; Voydanoff and Kelly, 1984) and at times for the worker's spouse (Keith and Schafer, 1980). One study concluded that the number of hours that wives work increases the divorce rate when the husband disapproves of her working (Spitze and South, 1985). No evidence of negative effects of long hours on marital satisfaction, however, has been found by several other researchers who investigated that question (Piotrkowski and Crits-Christoph, 1982; Staines and Pleck, 1983; Voydanoff, 1984).

Husbands of women working part time tend to experience higher levels of marital satisfaction than those married to full-time workers or full-time homemakers (Moore and Hofferth, 1979; Rallings and Nye, 1979). Also, these women themselves tend to be particularly happy with their children (Hoffman, 1987). Part-time workers, however, often are poorly paid, receive fewer or no benefits, have less interesting and less satisfying work, and have little opportunity for promotion; Repetti et al. (1989) and Hoffman (1987) find that this may contribute to stress and other negative outcomes.

The amount of time worked does not by itself account for all the effects of work. How the time is arranged—how many hours per day, how many days per week, how many weeks per year, weekdays or weekends, day shift or night shift, regular hours or shifting schedules—and the rigidity of the schedule are also important. According to a national survey, 27 percent of workers claimed that schedules interfered with their family life, and 42 percent complained about such other problems as irregular or unpredictable schedules, early starting time, or late leaving time (Quinn and Staines, 1979). Women were more likely to report problems with schedules; men were more likely to report problems with amount of time worked (Staines and Pleck, 1983).

Research on men working shifts found generally negative effects, both with respect to health and their family life (Pleck, 1983). Night shifts were likely to cause problems with husband-wife relationships; afternoon shifts caused problems with parent-child relationships (Mott et al., 1965). The effects of shift work on families is also influenced by the degree of control people have and the predictability of the schedules. For example, Staines and Pleck (1983) found that the negative relationships between nonstandard work schedules and the quality of family life are strongest when workers have the least control over their schedules—that is, working an afternoon shift decreases time spent with children when they have little control over their schedule, but increases parental time when they have medium and high control. A small study of nurses found unpredictability of schedules to be a problem. Women reported that hours and days off continually changed, with very little advance notice, making care arrangements difficult (Sexton, 1982).

More recent studies show an increase in child care by fathers related to shift work (Presser, 1989). As noted above, parents with young children appear to use shift work in order to provide personal care for their children. Presser finds that this strategy increases positive interaction between fathers and children (Presser, 1988; Presser and Cain, 1983).

Job Demands

Family ties may inhibit geographic mobility, and family members are often negatively affected by a move. A spouse may have to give up a job and may have problems finding an equivalent one in the new location. Children will have to change schools, which is often a painful experience, especially for teenagers. All of them will be uprooted from a familiar community, and they are likely to leave valued friends behind. These are real costs, although difficult to measure. And yet, if earnings increase because of a move, the family as well as the worker benefits.

Frequent job-related travels also are likely to put strains on family life and tend to interfere with regular household responsibilities. Traveling salespersons, long-distance truck drivers, flight attendants, and military personnel are obviously affected, but so are many others, such as public officials and managers in multiplant businesses. Research has been done on how families of corporate executives and military personnel cope under these circumstances. In a review, Voydanoff (1987) concludes that moves and traveling have negative effects, but they are mitigated by factors such as family cohesion before the move, spousal attitude, and coping strategies.

The extent to which the demands and gratifications of a job (both physical and psychological) match the abilities and aspirations of the worker will contribute to work-family satisfaction when there is a good fit and to work-family conflict when there is a bad fit. Only a small minority of workers, mostly highly educated professionals and managers, seem to be more involved in work than in family (Pleck and Lang, 1978). Such high involvement can cause strain in dual-career couples (Bailyn, 1970; Ridley, 1973) and can cause conflict between work and family responsibilities for men (Young and Wilmott, 1973). However, high job satisfaction has also been found to reduce depression and to increase levels of health and energy (Burden and Googins, 1987). This outcome is frequently found for married women and single mothers. Again, however, interpreting the relationship between employment and health requires caution.

More broadly, it is not the number of roles that people are filling—such as worker, homemaker, and caregiver—that causes problems. Several experts have found that multiple roles are beneficial (Baruch et al., 1987;

Epstein, 1987; Gove and Zeiss, 1987; Piotrkowski and Repetti, 1984). For example, a 1978 multistage probability sample of 700 white adults in the Detroit metropolitan area found that the number of roles individuals were involved in did not diminish physical health (Verbrugge, 1987). On the contrary, there was a positive relationship for both men and women between number of roles and health, although the subjective perception of great role burdens had a negative relation to health outcomes. Indicators of the quality of roles, using occupational stressors, such as a heavy workload or lack of control, and home stressors, such as the number of children, have been found to be associated with various physical and mental problems for women (Repetti et al., 1989). For example, longitudinal data from the Framingham Heart Study show that mothers in clerical jobs who have three or more children are at increased risk of coronary heart disease (LaCroix and Haynes, 1987).

Employer Support

In addition to job characteristics, the attitudes and actions of managers and coworkers, perhaps independent of official company policies, may also affect workers and their families. Support includes an understanding environment, as well as specific actions to help solve problems, such as access to a telephone in the afternoon so that parents can be in touch with children after school. Support is part of the workplace culture (discussed in Chapter 6), the set of norms, values, and informal mechanisms that shape day-to-day life in an organization. For example, just being able to discuss a family problem with supervisors or coworkers may provide an environment that people find helpful. Lack of support is illustrated by such behavior as making it clear that personal problems are to be handled away from work or prohibiting the use of leave time for family matters.

In general, lack of social support at work has been associated with depression, hospitalization days, and physical complaints. Supervisors who are not understanding of family problems contribute to increased risk of coronary heart disease for clerical workers (Haynes et al., 1984) and, more broadly, to conflict, stress, and health problems (Galinsky and Hughes, 1987; Galinsky et al., 1987). Increased depression among women bank tellers was related to rigid social climates at work (Repetti, 1987).

In one study probing business changes that would reduce child care problems, 56 percent of respondents identified training to sensitize managers (Galinsky and Hughes, 1987). Lack of employer sensitivity and/or acceptance may reduce the extent to which programs such as parental leave are used. One U.S. study showed that 63 percent of all employers, and 41 percent of those at companies with a leave policy, thought fathers should not have any leave when their wives gave birth (Catalyst, 1986). Pleck

(1988, 1989) and Stoiber (1989) report some negative attitudes among Swedish employers and colleagues toward fathers who take parental leave. This may help explain why relatively few fathers have taken such leaves and the proportion is not increasing more rapidly.

There appear to be differences in corporate support for employees even among companies that are quite similar in their benefits and policies. Burden and Googins (1987), for instance, report that respondents in one company were twice as likely to consider the corporation sensitive to their needs as were those in a second company. The authors attribute the difference to a set of messages that are transmitted through the corporate culture that are more intangible than the policies and programs.

EFFECTS OF FAMILY ON WORK

In the past, researchers paid little attention to the effects of family responsibility on people's performance at work. As more people assume dual responsibilities, however, employers are increasingly concerned with the effects that families have on worker performance, particularly on recruitment, retention, mobility, absenteeism, and tardiness. New research now focuses on the possible conflict for men and women among dependent care, housework, and jobs that may create stress and hence have a negative impact on the discharge of their duties at work.

Stress is defined as "any event in which environmental demands, internal demands, or both, tax or exceed the adaptive resources of an individual" (Monat and Lazarus, 1977). Both major life events, such as the birth of a child (Holmes and Rahe, 1976), and minor events or daily hassles, such as being unable to get the family out the door on time in the morning (Kanner et al., 1981), can tax individuals' resources, leading to anxiety and depression and hence to less than optimal functioning at work and at home. Care for adult dependents, for example, can lead to increased depression and emotional and physical strain (National Long-Term Care Survey, in U.S. Congress, House, 1987; Brody, 1981; McLanahan and Monson, 1989). At the same time, there is also evidence that caring for children, a spouse, or a parent may provide the caregiver with satisfaction, a renewed sense of usefulness, and self-worth (U.S. Congress, House, 1987).

Numerous studies have reported the existence of some work-family interference or conflict that may result in stress. For instance, working long hours limits the time a person is available for family activities; caring for a sick child means there is less time to carry out work responsibilities. Staines and Pleck (1983) found that one-third of both men and women in the 1977 Quality of Employment Survey claimed some or a lot of such interference when asked, "How much do your job and your family life interfere with each other—a lot, somewhat, not too much, or not at all?" Similarly, Voydanoff

(1988), using the same data set, showed that mean interference or conflict, ranging from 1 (low) to 4 (high), was 2.21 for men and 2.22 for women. Reviewing eight company studies, Friedman (1989b) found that the proportion of workers who reported encountering conflict ranged from 23 to 64 percent. In a study of 166 married couples in the Detroit metropolitan area, men and women reported stress on almost one-third of the days worked during a 6-week period (Bolger et al., 1989).

Although people are more likely to report that work interferes with family, they also report that family interferes with work. Among four employer-based studies, estimates of family interference with work ranged from 13 percent of men (Galinsky and Hughes, 1987) to 39 percent of women (Fernandez, 1986). Crouter (1984) found home-to-work negative spillover more likely for wives than husbands. Based on evidence from a national sample of 500 couples, Staines and Pleck (1983), however, reported similar responses for women and men. Burden and Googins (1987) found no sex difference when domestic roles of men and women were held constant. Bolger et al. (1989), using longitudinal data and seven measures of stress, found negative home-to-work spillover significant for men but not for women, even when controlling for work characteristics.

It is clear from these studies that at least some workers perceive a negative impact of family responsibilities on work. There is considerable evidence that the conflict is greater for parents than for people without children at home and especially for single parents, but conflicting evidence whether it is greater for women than for men. Since women do have more family responsibilities, they would be expected to report more such conflict; to the extent they do not, it may be that they have developed better mechanisms for coping with such stress.

Labor Force Participation

There are several indications that men with family responsibilities are more likely to be in the labor force and are more highly motivated. The labor force participation rate of men with children in their household is 96 percent (Hayghe and Haugen, 1987), that of male heads of single-parent families is 88 percent (Norton and Glick, 1986), substantially higher than for all men. Married men are also the group most likely to work overtime and to hold more than one job. The number of hours they work increases with the number of children they have (Smith, 1983). Similarly, a study of white-collar workers found that married fathers and sole male providers are more involved in their work than other men (Gould and Werbel, 1983). It has been suggested that this explains why married men earn more than single men even when a number of characteristics are controlled for (Hill, 1979; Bartlett and Callahan, 1984).

A very different picture emerges for married women, particularly for those with children. Almost none of these women has a spouse who is a homemaker, and although their labor force participation has increased rapidly in recent decades, it nonetheless remains lower than that of other women. Married women with children are also more likely to work part time. This pattern is at times regarded as evidence of their weak commitment to work, but many of them—particularly low-income women—say they would work full time if reliable child care were available (Kisker et al., 1989; O'Connell and Rogers, 1983).

Over the last 20 years the effect of maternity on women's labor force participation has changed considerably. Using data from the national Survey of Income and Program Participation, O'Connell (1990) found that the proportion of women who worked during their first pregnancy rose from 44 percent in 1961-1965 to 65 percent in 1982-1985. Fully 80-90 percent of these women worked full time. Only 28 percent of them quit their job after becoming pregnant in the 1980s, compared with 66 percent during the 1960s, and half of those who quit returned to work within a year after the child's birth.

Teenagers, high school dropouts, and minority women were least likely to be employed when pregnant, and those that were employed were also least likely to return to work within 6 months. The two main factors determining mothers' return to work, however, were how long they had worked before the birth and whether their employers provided maternity leave. Single mothers appear to be strongly motivated to work (O'Connell, 1990), even though very poor mothers of young children continue to be eligible for Aid to Families with Dependent Children.

A number of studies have found that the cost of child care also influences the decision to return to work and the number of hours worked (Presser and Baldwin, 1980; O'Connell and Rogers, 1983; Leibowitz and Waite, 1988; General Accounting Office, 1987b; Blau and Robins, 1986). Several of these studies further showed that cost was especially important for low-income women, single women, and black women. Not surprisingly, availability of child care is an even more serious constraint among young, low-income couples, although it is not uncommon for spouses to work different shifts so that they do not need out-of-home child care (Presser and Cain, 1983; Presser, 1989). Sonenstein and Wolf (1988) also found that some mothers took shift jobs, while their children are cared for by relatives. It is not clear, however, whether they accept shift work in order to accommodate child care or whether those were the only jobs they could find. For nonstandard work hours, there is almost no nonfamily care available (Hayes et al., 1990).

Needless to say, not only the availability of child care but also the availability of jobs determines how much women and men work, for they are not always able to find employment that enables them to work the preferred number of hours. Over the past 20 years the percentage of household heads reporting in the Current Population Survey (CPS) that they would like to work more or fewer hours during the year has remained stable, at approximately 15 percent and 5 percent, respectively (unpublished data, Panel Study of Income Dynamics, 1990). In the 1977 Quality of Employment Survey, however, 53 percent of mothers and 38 percent of fathers claimed they would prefer to work fewer hours even if it meant less income (Moen and Dempster-McClain, 1987). According to Presser (1989), the 1985 CPS data showed that these proportions had become considerably smaller, but the change may have been due to different wording of the question. Also, 17 percent of mothers and 28 percent of fathers who were fully employed indicated they would prefer to work longer hours in order to earn more. On the whole, these findings are consistent with a shift toward greater preference for income at the expense of home time.

Although there is considerably less research on the relationship of employment and providing care for dependents other than children, the data that are available show some interesting correlations. The National Survey of Caregivers found that 9 percent of persons in the sample who had been working full time left the work force to care for a disabled friend or relative: 12 percent of daughters and 5 percent of sons left their jobs to become caregivers. Of the 1 million caregivers who had been employed during the caregiving experience, 20 percent cut back on hours, 29 percent rearranged schedules, and 19 percent took time off without pay (Stone et al., 1987). McLanahan and Monson (1989) found that married women, but not single women, reduced their labor force participation to care for parents.

The fact that married women and those with higher incomes are more inclined than others to drop out of the labor force or to work part time is often taken as showing lack of commitment to work. Moen and Smith (1986), however, argue that behavior is not an appropriate measure of attitude, but that psychological commitment or involvement in work is a subjective orientation measured by questions about continuing to work if there were no financial need. Using data from the 1976 Panel Study of Income Dynamics they found that a majority of women claim they would work even if they did not need the money; commitment is very strong among those who work part time, and even among those who temporarily give up paid employment. Mothers of preschoolers who did work full time often did not show strong commitment but worked for financial reasons. It appears that factors such as other obligations, inability to make satisfactory arrangements for dependents, and cultural beliefs about care, in addition to commitment to work, affect labor force participation.

Absenteeism and Tardiness

Absenteeism and tardiness are two of the most readily measured effects of family on work. Recent studies (e.g., Bonilla, 1989) conclude that gender per se does not influence absenteeism rates. Rather, they are related to children and family responsibilities. Because women are more likely to have these responsibilities, they have increased rates of absenteeism. Three primary sources of family-related absence are illness of another family member, finding care arrangements for dependents, and making alternative arrangements when the usual ones fail.

Overall, the number of days lost for these reasons is small, as reported in national surveys. The reports may be inaccurate, however, because people may falsely report themselves ill in order to care for a family member. While the reported loss is small, the differences by family status are informative. Analysis of data for the period 1979 to 1983 from the Panel Study of Income Dynamics (unpublished data) suggests that workers lose an average of approximately 1 day per year because of the illness of another family member. Only men with a nonemployed wife lost less time; other people with children lost more time. In 1983, the largest losses, almost 4 days per year, were for single women with children under 5. The number of hours lost increased with the number of children. Also, blacks with young children lost more hours due to the illness of others than did other groups. We can only speculate that this difference may be related to poor health, lower income, and less medical care.

Corporate surveys corroborate these findings and provide additional information (for summaries see Creedon, 1989, on elder care; Friedman, 1989b, on child care). In a study of 5,000 employees in five companies, 67 percent reported that child care interfered with work and that absenteeism was one of the main results (Fernandez, 1986). In addition, medical and dental appointments for children were found to be a problem, often resulting in absenteeism. The highest rate of work interference was reported by parents of children ages 2 to 5: 50 percent of women and 26 percent of men reported such interference. In one employer survey, 75 percent of the respondents noted lateness and unscheduled days off among the work-related effects of caregiving (Lucas, 1986).

The illness of dependents, especially children, is likely to cause work interference (Galinsky and Hughes, 1987; Fernandez, 1986). Children's illness was involved for 56 percent of mothers who were absent for 1 to 3 days during the year, 78 percent of those absent 4 to 6 days, and 82 percent of those absent longer than 6 days (Fernandez, 1986). Based on National Health Interview Survey data, the General Accounting Office (1989) estimates that the number of workers eligible to take leave for seriously ill children at 66,000, for seriously ill parents at 182,000, and for seriously ill spouses at 746,000 (firms with 35 or more employees and serious illness defined as 31 or more days of bed rest in a year).

Maintaining child care arrangements is the second major problem related to absenteeism. Of mothers with at least one child under age 15, 5.9 percent reported missing some work during the month prior to the survey as a result of a failure in child care arrangements (Bureau of the Census, 1987). Analysis of data from the 1979 Panel Study of Income Dynamics showed that 3.2 percent of husband-and-wife couples reported that someone had to stay home because child care arrangements broke down in the past year, for an average of 4.1 days. The highest rate of disruptions, 7.8 percent, was found for those who place children in another home as the primary means of care.

Employers who have studied these issues report a higher incidence of child care arrangements failing and affecting absenteeism. In one study, within the 3 months previous to the interview, 40 percent of the parents had experienced a disruption in their child care arrangements, 20 percent of them three or more times. And 39 percent of the parents whose child care arrangements had failed said they had come to work late or left early (Galinsky and Hughes, 1987). Resulting absences were reported more frequently for women than for men and more frequently for families using out-of-home care, with lower incomes, and with fewer children. In larger families, older children may take care of younger ones. Emlen (1987), however, found the greatest number of disruptions for parents at work resulted from children looking after themselves.

The third problem is finding child care. In one study, 25 percent of the women and 10 percent of the men thought that finding quality child care was somewhat of a problem or a big problem (Fernandez, 1986). The *Fortune* study found that people who had a problem finding care were also more likely to be absent (Galinsky and Hughes, 1987). In a survey of 4,000 DuPont employees (DuPont Co., 1989), over 25 percent depended on child care. Although women were only one-third of the sample, they constituted half of the child care users. The substantial number of men using child care, however, suggests that it is not only a concern for women. A majority of the parents reported having difficulties finding child care, particularly for infants, and after-school and summer care for school-age children. In view of all these difficulties, it is not surprising that parents occasionally bring children to work. In one firm, the number of children at work became so numerous that the practice was prohibited (Burden and Googins, 1987).

Other Effects on Work

Family characteristics influence not only labor force participation, absenteeism, and tardiness, but also many other workplace issues, such as unproductive time at work, energy expended on the job, motivation, and geographic mobility. Although relatively little evidence is available on any of these, they should be mentioned.

Unproductive time spent on the job because of responsibility for other family members, especially children, appears to be rather common. Even parents who do not report problems with child care acknowledge interruptions at work. Although these become less frequent as children grow older, 39 percent of women and 17 percent of men with children between ages 15 and 18 still report such interference (Fernandez, 1986). Workers are also likely to spend time worrying about dependents. However, Fernandez points out that people often make up for lost time during lunch breaks, evenings, and weekends.

It has been suggested, most notably by Becker (1985), that women spend less energy on paid work because they use so much energy on their household responsibilities. No proof of this hypothesis has ever been offered, however, and at least one study (Bielby and Bielby, 1985) claimed that the opposite appears to be true. Because their conclusion is based on subjective self-reporting, it is also open to challenge.

Somewhat related to the question of energy is the issue of motivation. Married men, who are generally seen to be the family's primary wage earner, are expected to be more eager to obtain training, to work hard, and to compete for promotions than married women, who are often viewed as secondary wage earners and also likely to spend less time in the labor force. This line of reasoning tends to be part of the traditional explanation of occupational segregation by gender (Polachek, 1979, 1981).

A great deal of the literature in this area has focused on the problems of people in professional or managerial jobs, especially when both spouses are in such occupations. Although such couples may be less in need of assistance than other kinds of families, they are frequently the focus of employer policies. High-level jobs are associated with more intense responsibilities, causing more stress (Shinn et al., 1987; Fernandez, 1986). Very high income, as well as low income, appears to be related to increased vulnerability to stress for women with children. We have not, however, found evidence in the published employer studies of the turnover and resulting costs to employers reported by Schwartz (1989) on the basis of her unpublished work.

In a review of the status of women scientists and engineers, Zuckerman (1987) concludes that marriage and motherhood do not have consistently negative effects on employment status, publication rates, and salaries. While most people with doctoral degrees work full time, a survey of Ph.D.s in science and engineering found that, of those working part time, 37 percent of women, compared with 4 percent of men, gave family responsibilities as the reason (Office of Scientific and Engineering Personnel, 1989).

There also continue to be some differences between women and men in management and the professions in their willingness to permit location of the workplace to determine their residence. Traditionally, men tended to follow jobs, and women followed men. Employers could expect to recruit highly qualified men from throughout the country and to move them to different locations as the occasion arose. In the 1970s, a study of people with Ph.D.s found that, even among this highly educated, professionally oriented group, men were far more likely than women to move, or refuse to move, in order to further their own career rather than that of their spouse (Ferber and Kardick, 1978).

This pattern may have changed somewhat in recent years. From the point of view of business, however, this may not be an improvement, for men would then be less likely to put job before family. Men's decisions are also influenced by other family considerations. Men with school-age children are less likely to move than others (Bureau of the Census, 1983), and among men between the ages of 30 and 39, the probability of moving declines most among married men with children (Sandefur, 1985). Also, in a DuPont survey (1989), 20 percent of child care users said they avoid jobs involving travel or relocation.

Recently, a considerable controversy has arisen because Schwartz (1989), accepting the view that most mothers cannot be expected to make a strong career commitment, proposed a separate family-oriented track, now popularly referred to as the "Mommy track," to avoid possible problems of high turnover of management women in large corporations. Such an approach would require couples to make a choice, and make it very early in their lives, whether the wife should have children or a high-level career. Among the objections that have been raised to this approach are that it perpetuates the traditional notion that only women have family responsibilities and ignores the fact that many women are successfully combining family and high-level careers. Furthermore, there is reason to look askance at a society that divides people into two distinct and separate types, family oriented or career oriented (Spitze, 1988).

Couples in which both partners have careers, however, represent a relatively small proportion of families. In the Quality of Employment Survey they constituted only 13 percent of the sample, compared with 59 percent in which neither spouse was in a professional or managerial job. There is need for more research on single parents, minority couples, and dual-earner couples in which spouses are blue-collar and service workers; such families tend to have far fewer resources either to pay for the care that is available or to buffer the stress that can come from less desirable work (Spitze, 1988; Ferree, 1987; Fernandez, 1986). One British survey of 304 couples with low occupational status, for example, shows that, among other factors, low work commitment and low aspirations were significant predictors of stress

(Lewis and Cooper, 1987). The authors concluded that high-status careers enable people to secure high-quality care for their families and satisfaction from their jobs, which are likely to protect them from pressures. Employer studies in the United States have also found that women in nonmanagement jobs, particularly single parents and low-income women, report more work-family interference with negative consequences on the job. Furthermore, low incomes were related to greater conflict and child-care-related absenteeism for men (Fernandez, 1986; Shinn et al., 1987).

CONCLUSIONS

Early research on work and family focused on the negative effects of women's employment on children and families and emphasized the conflicts for dual-career couples. Newer studies have expanded their focus to investigate both positive and negative aspects of men's as well as women's employment on work and family life; they have shown that the spillover from workplace to family and from family to workplace is complex and that the direction of causality is not always clear. Although there is still much to be learned—particularly about the long-term impact of different types of care on the development of children and on the effect of stress on work performance—several conclusions can be drawn that bear directly on the issues before this panel.

We conclude from the evidence reviewed here that women's influx into the labor force, and the attendant changes in the family and the workplace, have had both positive and negative consequences for all concerned. For women, being employed is related to better physical and mental health (although this correlation may be in part because healthier women are more likely to enter the labor force). In general, favorable effects seem most pronounced when women work by choice. Wives are held in higher esteem by their families, and other family members benefit from the additional income. The effect on the well-being of children depends largely on the care they receive, in or out of the home. Among the negative effects of women's growing labor force participation is that men as well as women increasingly find that work and family responsibilities impinge on each other. Also, when women work because of economic necessity, their pay is usually low, their jobs are frequently not rewarding, and their work and family schedules often conflict. When they have little control over their schedules, they are particularly likely to be subject to considerable stress.

The limited research that has been done suggests that family responsibilities are likely to increase labor force turnover and may have some negative effects on work performance. There is, for instance, evidence of relationships to absenteeism and tardiness, geographic mobility, and disruptions at work. Although problems appear to be somewhat different depending on occupation, they are not confined to any one group. Much more information is needed on both the positive and the negative effects of dual work and family roles for low-income couples, single parents, and members of racial and ethnic minority groups. It is evident that managers, supervisors, and peers play a large part in facilitating or inhibiting the adjustment of workers to their dual responsibilities. Most significantly, permitting employees some choice and some control tends to reduce the negative consequences of combining work and family responsibilities.

4

How Adults Cope:
Dependent Care

For the next generation, two long-term trends in U.S. society will add to the demands on working-age adults in caring for dependents. One trend is the increase in the proportion of elderly people in the U.S. population; the elderly depend to varying degrees on their grown children, especially daughters. The second trend is the steady influx of women into the work force, which reduces the amount of time they have available for the traditional roles of caring for the elderly and for children and creates conflicts for employed women who are responsible for dependents.

As a result, the work-family conflicts experienced by adults of working age in the United States seem likely to grow in the future unless policies are instituted that will help to alleviate them. The costs of care for elderly parents and the cost, quality, and availability of child care are important factors in decisions about work. The mix of costs and benefits available to a given person at a given time—from insurance coverage to public and private subsidies such as employer-subsidized day care—can relieve conflict and stress, or aggravate it. The cost, quality, and availability of care for children and elderly people are therefore among the crucial issues that deserve attention. This chapter reviews who needs care, who provides it, and how it is paid for, to show the range of offerings and apparent shortcomings in the care of dependents that confront working-age Americans.

CARE FOR THE ELDERLY

The increasing numbers of older Americans—absolutely and as a percentage of the total population—have been well documented (U.S. Congress, House, 1987; Rivlin and Wiener, 1988; Gilford, 1988). Between 1950 and

1980, the percentage of people over 65 increased 108 percent, compared with a 62 percent increase for the rest of the population (Taeuber, 1983). The "oldest old," age 85 and over, increased by 281 percent, from 0.6 million in 1950 to 2.2 million in 1980. The Census Bureau projects that the proportion of the elderly (65 and older) in the population will more than double again over the next 50 years, from 11 percent in 1980 (25.5 million) to 22 percent in 2050 (67.1 million).

In 1980 almost half of all the elderly lived in just eight states: California, Florida, New York, Pennsylvania, Texas, Illinois, Ohio, and Michigan. While the elderly population is expected to grow in every region by 2000, growth rates in the South and the West will be dramatically higher than in the Northeast. Projections call for a 60 percent increase in the South and the West compared with 12 percent in the Northeast (Taeuber, 1983). To the extent that the elderly live far from their adult children, they will need more institutional care, and arranging for care will be more complex and expensive for their children. Hence, health care and nursing home facilities are likely to be strained in regions experiencing a heavy influx of older people.

On average, women live considerably longer than men. In 1988 there were approximately 17 million women and 12 million men age 65 and older (Bureau of the Census, 1989d). Because of their greater longevity and because they tend to be younger than their husbands, women are more likely to be left alone: 82 percent of elderly men live in a family setting, 74 percent with their wives; only 55 percent of elderly women live in a family setting, 36 percent with their husbands (Gilford, 1988).

A higher proportion of elderly people are able to live independently longer than ever before (Palmer et al., 1988; Preston, 1984). Social Security benefits are the largest single source (40 percent) of their income. Noncash benefits, such as Medicare, Medicaid, food stamps, and subsidized housing, account for an additional 10 percent of income (Gilford, 1988). However, elderly people who are disabled and need long-term care continue to be of concern. Among them is a significant number of the oldest old (age 85 and older), most of them women who live longer and have more multiple chronic health problems than older men (Palmer et al., 1988; Rix, 1984).

While fewer elderly people live in poverty, 12 percent in 1988 compared with 25 percent in 1969, a larger proportion of elderly women (15 percent) are in poverty than men (8 percent). These differences are expected to narrow in the future, because more retired women will be eligible for pensions and Social Security benefits in their own right (Gilford, 1988). In the near term, the number of very old women living alone and in poverty will remain significant. There are also differences in the elderly by race and ethnicity: 6.3 percent of white men, 23.7 percent of black men, and 18 percent of men of Hispanic origin live in poverty. Comparable figures for elderly women are 12.6 percent of white women, 38 percent of black women, and 25.9 percent of Hispanic women (Bureau of the Census, 1989b). Caring for these elderly people is often a key responsibility of relatives, especially their grown children.

Types of Care

The majority of elderly people can take care of themselves and live independently. For others, care is a mix of institutional care, community-based care, and unpaid care by family and friends. Table 4-1 provides an overview of the projected numbers of the elderly using long-term care in nursing homes and paid home care; the number using both types of care is expected to increase markedly. For example, the number of those over 85 in nursing homes will double by 2020.

The problems of caring for disabled elderly people are particularly serious for employed adults. Of the 28.6 million Americans age 65 and over in 1985, 22 percent (6.3 million) were disabled. And 9 percent of the elderly, or 2.6 million, were severely disabled and required assistance with one or more activities of daily living, such as bathing, eating, or shopping. A disproportionate share of the severely disabled are the oldest old; they are most often widows.

The majority of disabled elderly are cared for by their family and friends. In 1985, between 4.6 million and 5.1 million disabled elderly (depending on the definition used) lived in the community and were cared for by family and friends with some community support (Liu et al., 1986; Macken, 1986). Of the 1.2 million "frail elderly" (as defined in the 1982 National Long-Term Care Survey, LTCS), 10.7 percent lived alone, 40 percent lived with only a spouse, and 35.7 percent lived with their children, with or without a spouse. One-third of the disabled elderly reported family incomes in the poor or near-poor category (Stone et al., 1987). These statistics may undercount elderly mentally disabled people who live with their families.

Only 21 percent of the disabled elderly and about 50 percent of the severely disabled are in nursing homes (Stone et al., 1987; Rivlin and Wiener, 1988). Furthermore, nursing home care does not completely relieve family members of care responsibilities. They continue to visit nursing home patients, frequently providing such assistance as doing the laundry, arranging doctor's appointments, shopping, managing financial matters, and monitoring the quality of the purchased care.

Theoretically, the supply of nursing home beds could be expanded to accommodate all those whose physical disabilities are so severe that they can no longer manage independent living. However, nursing home care is very expensive. So pressures exist to expand paid home care given by

TABLE 4-1 The Elderly Population and the Use of Long-Term Care, 1986-1990 and 2016-2020

	1986-1990[a]				2016-2020[a]			
	All elderly	65-74	75-84	85 and over	All elderly	65-74	75-84	85 and over
Number of elderly (millions)[b]								
In the population	31.3	17.5	10.3	3.5	50.3	28.4	14.6	7.2
Age distribution (percent)	100	56	33	11	100	57	29	14
In a nursing home[c]	2.3	0.4	0.9	1.0	4.0	0.7	1.3	2.1
Age distribution (percent)	100	18	40	42	100	16	32	51
Receiving home care services[d]	4.0	1.2	1.7	1.1	6.4	1.8	2.3	2.2
Age distribution (percent)	100	31	43	26	100	29	37	34
Median family income (1987 dollars)[e]	$9,314	$10,806	$8,657	$6,837	$17,210	$23,203	$14,956	$7,999

[a]Five-year averages.
[b]Age 65 and older.
[c]Persons in a nursing home at any time during the year.
[d]Persons using paid home care services at any time during the year, including the nonchronically disabled elderly.
[e]Family income is joint income for married persons and individual income for unmarried persons. Income sources are Social Security, pensions, Supplemental Security Income, individual retirement accounts, wages, and asset earnings. Families and individuals without income are included.

SOURCE: Adapted from Rivlin and Wiener (1988:Table 1-2). Data from Brookings-ICF long-term care financing model. Reprinted by permission.

relatives and nonrelatives. A major conflict in work-family relations is the number of working-age relatives who work part time or do not seek employment because of the need to care for elderly relatives. This problem is likely to grow as the number of employed people with care obligations for elderly relatives increases.

Nursing Home Care

Nursing homes provide the primary form of institutional care for elderly people. Of all expenditures for long-term care, 80 percent is for institutional services (General Accounting Office, 1988). Although long-term care spending is dominated by nursing home costs, there are shortages of nursing home beds, costs are high, and the quality of care is mixed. These are major national issues, now and for the future.

The first national nursing home survey in 1954 identified 9,000 nursing homes: 86 percent were proprietary, 10 percent were nonprofit, and 4 percent were public. Recent estimates place the number of certified nursing homes at approximately 19,000 with 1.6 million beds: 70 percent of the facilities are run for profit, 22 percent are run by nonprofit organizations, and 8 percent are owned and run by governments (Committee on Nursing Home Regulation, 1986; Rivlin and Wiener, 1988). Most experts agree that nursing homes are operating at capacity and that states limit the number of nursing home beds to keep down state Medicaid costs (Rivlin and Wiener, 1988; Committee on Nursing Home Regulation, 1986). This creates a shortage of beds, which is likely to increase with the growing elderly population.

The cost of nursing home care is so high that it rapidly exhausts the resources of all but wealthy families. The average annual cost per person for nursing home care in 1988 was estimated at between $22,000 and $25,000 (Price and O'Shaughnessy, 1988). Slightly over half of nursing home costs are paid for by the elderly and their families; Medicaid pays for most of the remainder. Of the $33 billion annual estimated cost for nursing home care (1986-1990), 43 percent ($14 billion) is paid for by Medicaid, 55 percent ($18 billion) by families, and 2 percent ($0.6 billion) by Medicare (Rivlin and Wiener, 1988).

Medicaid was intended to provide coverage only for poor and near-poor individuals. When nonpoor elderly people deplete their savings and spend most of their income on nursing home or other health care expenses, however, they may eventually qualify for Medicaid; this is called the Medicaid "spend-down." Recent analysis of data from the 1985 National Nursing Home Survey and the 1982-1984 National Long-Term Care Survey shows that a large proportion of the elderly spend down until they reach eligibility for poverty programs such as Medicaid before going to a nursing home (Liu et al., 1990). In other words, many elderly may put off going to a nursing home until they have reached the poverty level and the cost can be covered by Medicaid, even if nursing home care was needed much earlier.

The quality of nursing home care remains a concern, although efforts have been made to improve quality through regulation. Certification is done at the state level, with federal guidelines established in 1974 to control the use of federal monies. Medicaid is jointly financed by federal and state funds and administered by the states. A review of nursing homes by a panel of experts at the Institute of Medicine (Committee on Nursing Home Regulation, 1986) concluded that 10 years of government regulations had improved nursing homes but that quality of care and quality of life in many facilities remained unsatisfactory. The review concluded that poor-quality homes outnumbered very good homes. The report called for more effective government regulation and enforcement and a stronger federal leadership role. It concluded: "Skilled and properly motivated management, well-trained, well-supervised, and highly motivated staff, community involvement and support, and effective consumer involvement all are required" (Committee on Nursing Home Regulation, 1986:24).

Improving the quality of nursing home care is a thorny problem. Increased regulation and enforcement will improve quality but will also increase costs. Regulatory changes commonly lead to the closing of facilities when meeting new standards is prohibitively expensive. Given the shortage of beds, policy makers are reluctant to act except in circumstances in which conditions are so bad as to represent an immediate threat.

There are many parallels between nursing home care and child care. In both instances, competent, trained, and motivated staff are essential to providing high-quality care. Attracting such staff is difficult and expensive. In 1988, "nursing and personal care facilities" employed over 1.3 million people—a number expected to grow by 3.1 percent annually over the next decade (Personick, 1989). Many nursing homes lack the professional staff of doctors, nurses, and therapists to provide high-quality care. They often hold down costs by employing nurse's aides who are poorly trained, inadequately supervised, and underpaid. The staff is typically required to care for too many patients. Not surprisingly, staff turnover ranges from 70 to 100 percent per year, further impairing the quality of care (Committee on Nursing Home Regulation, 1986).

Paid Home and Community Care

For many elderly people, home care might be a lower-cost alternative, one that many of them prefer. An impressive range of noninstitutional services has developed over the last two decades and are now available in many communities. Services include home health aides, homemaker help, personal care, "meals on wheels," respite care, adult day care, telephone monitoring, and special transportation. There are also community-based programs serving both healthy and impaired elderly people, such as senior centers offering congregate meals and other services. The availability and use of such services are increasing. In 1987 approximately one-third of the elderly with functional disabilities used these services (Table 4-2), an increase from 10 to 25 percent reported in earlier surveys (General Accounting Office, 1988). Federal support of community services has expanded over the last decade; funds are available from Medicare, Medicaid, Title XX, the Department of Veterans Affairs, and under the Older Americans Act.

Of the 5.6 million disabled elderly living at home in 1987, 3.6 million received no formal (i.e., paid) services. The fact that almost 60 percent of those who might benefit from home health services did not receive them could reflect limits of service availability—but it also results from inability to pay. The majority of all noninstitutional care is paid for directly by recipients or by their relatives. Federal and state support for noninstitution-

TABLE 4-2   The Elderly Population with Functional Disabilities Using Paid Home and Community Services, 1987

Population Characteristic	Population (thousands)[a]	Percentage with Service		
		At Home	In Community	Both
Total	5,619	22.4	9.9	4.0
Age in years				
65-74	1,993	18.4	8.2	5.4
75-84	2,315	22.8	9.3	3.9
85+	1,310	27.7	13.3	2.0[b]
Male	1,788	14.3	8.6	2.5[b]
Female	3,830	26.2	10.5	4.6
Functional status				
IADL only	2,261	17.3	9.6	3.3[b]
1-2 ADLs	2,108	21.3	12.2	4.5
3 or more ADLs	1,061	38.5	4.1[b]	4.5[b]
Lives alone	2,364	29.5	13.0	6.9
Lives with others	3,255	16.9	7.4	1.7[b]

[a]Estimates include the population with walking difficulties except where the level of Activities of Daily Living/Instrumental Activities of Daily Living (ADL/IADL) difficulties is specified.
[b]Relative standard error equal to or greater than 30 percent.
SOURCE: Agency for Health Care and Policy Research. National Medical Expenditure Survey—Household Survey, Round 1.

al services is limited but growing. Medicare spent $2.3 billion on home care in 1985 (General Accounting Office, 1988), but Medicare services are limited to treatment of acute conditions that have previously been treated in a hospital or skilled nursing facility. Medicaid coverage of a broader range of in-home services is slowly expanding. The Omnibus Budget Reconciliation Act of 1981 offered states the opportunity to apply for waivers from federal regulations governing Medicaid programs in order to provide a wide range of services to impaired beneficiaries. Medicaid expenditures for home and community-based services were about $0.5 billion in 1985 (General Accounting Office, 1988).

Congress has been considering legislation that would expand services: the 1987 Omnibus Budget Reconciliation Act (U.S. Congress, House, 1988) provided additional Medicaid waiver authority specifically for the elderly, and a 1987 amendment to the Older Americans Act (Title III-D) created a separate authorization for in-home services for the frail elderly. Finally, the Veterans' Benefits and Services Act of 1987 directs the Department of Veterans Affairs to emphasize community services instead of nursing homes. Although these trends are hopeful, the fact that only 2 million disabled elderly out of 5.6 million received paid services indicates that the programs have a significant distance to go to meet all genuine needs.

Supporters argue that paid home care will substitute for nursing home or hospital care and, because they are less expensive, reduce the overall costs of long-term care to individuals and society. However, home-based programs appear to have had little effect on nursing home or hospital use. Data from 15 home care demonstration projects, such as the Chicago Five Hospital Home-Bound Elderly Program, show paid home care has been a complement to, not a substitute for, institutional care, and it actually increases total expenditures (Rivlin and Wiener, 1988).

Opponents of paid home care also argue that it will substitute for the current unpaid care by relatives. While the substitution effect has not been extensively studied, there is some evidence from the demonstration programs that paid home care appears to enable unpaid caregivers to provide additional specialized services rather than reducing the amount of unpaid care (Rivlin and Wiener, 1988). Hence, expanded paid home care offers an opportunity to improve the morale, well-being, and life satisfaction of the elderly themselves while giving limited relief to unpaid caregivers. It also offers some financial relief for out-of-pocket expenses for the elderly and their families (Rivlin and Wiener, 1988).

One variation on paid home care services is to pay family members who provide care. At present, Medicaid rules and regulations in several states prohibit paying family members for providing personal care prescribed by a physician. Yet a survey of 46 states, the District of Columbia, and 3 territories found that 35 of the responding jurisdictions provided for some form of family caregiver payment. Although these are small, limited programs, they represent an alternative that deserves further exploration (Linsk et al., 1988).

Tax incentives are another means of subsidizing paid home care. Tax credits and deductions are easy to administer, involve cost sharing with caregivers, and increase consumer choice. Unless refundable, however, tax credits and deductions will not benefit the many elderly people who are members of low-income families. Some relief is now provided through the federal dependent care tax credit, but less than 10 percent of this tax benefit is estimated to help the elderly (most of it is used for child care). Five states also encourage family care through the tax code, but utilization is low. In both cases, restrictions on eligibility and newness may limit use (Rivlin and Wiener, 1988).

Unpaid Home Care

The extent and market value of unpaid home care are hard to quantify. Partly this is because it is an extension of normal family and community relationships; in addition, important unpaid care by relatives such as emotional support eludes attempts to value it. Despite its being hard to quantify, support provided by family, friends, and neighbors is the critical underpinning of independent living for frail or disabled elderly. However, the long-term demographic changes in the United States will certainly strain and could erode substantially relatives' ability to provide this essential care. These changes include the increase in numbers of dependent elderly people, higher percentages of working-age women entering the work force, and geographic mobility separating elderly parents from their adult children. The decline in availability of family-provided care can be offset to some extent by new types of living arrangements, such as senior apartments or other types of congregate housing offering meals, emergency medical care, transportation, and other services. Even so, many elderly will not have money to substitute these forms of purchased care for unpaid care.

Most of the elderly are tenaciously independent, preferring to live at home rather than have any kind of institutional care (McAuley and Blieszner, 1985). When they can no longer live unassisted and independently, most older people prefer living at home with some assistance from relatives and friends. Elderly persons with relatives who can provide home care are least likely to enter institutions. In a study that controlled for severity of disability, Smyer (1980) found that the best predictor of institutionalization was the family's self-reported ability to provide home-based care. In other words, most elderly people will avoid nursing home care as long as possible, regardless of physical condition or family finances. Supporting this observation are two studies showing that elderly people who have family support enter institutions with much higher levels of impairment than those without family support (Barney, 1977; Dunlop, 1980).

These findings suggest that helping relatives maintain support for frail and disabled elderly people should be an important public policy goal. Absent such support, far larger numbers of elderly people will require institutional care. There are not sufficient nursing home beds to meet current needs, and significant expansion of such facilities is unlikely.

Who cares for the elderly? At present, according to the National Long-Term Care Survey, approximately 2.3 percent of the U.S. population (4.2 million persons) actively provide unpaid assistance to disabled elderly in the community. The amount and duration of care given depends on the older person's level of disability. Women (2.6 million) are more often caregivers than men (1.6 million), and children (2.7 million) more often than spouses (1.5 million). Wives and husbands are most often the sole caregivers for their spouses, 60 percent and 55 percent, respectively. Caregivers are of working age; their average age is 57 years. And 30 percent of caregivers reported their incomes in the poor or near-poor category; one-third rate their own general health as no better than fair or poor (Stone and Kemper, 1989b).

Care can include: emotional support with visits and telephone calls; assistance with daily living such as transportation, shopping, meal preparation, and financial management; and more personal forms of care for the most severely impaired (e.g., bathing, feeding, dressing, toileting, and medical assistance) (Stone et al., 1987; Soldo and Manton, 1985). In the National Informal Survey of Caregivers (part of the National Long-Term Care Survey), 60 percent of the caregivers reported related expenses: 31 percent for travel, 25 percent for phone bills, and 24 percent for special diets or paid medicine for elderly dependents. On average, a frail or disabled elderly person living at home requires 1 to 4 years of care; 80 percent of caregivers provide care 7 days a week.

Because the majority of working-age unpaid caregivers are women, their increasing entry into the labor force raises questions about who will care for the growing elderly population in the future. Table 4-3 shows that almost 11 percent of full-time workers now or will soon face elder care decisions and that almost 2 percent of full-time employed workers are active caregivers: over 500,000 (or one-third) full-time workers have primary responsibility for elderly dependents. Approximately 12 percent of women who work full time are active or potential caregivers (i.e., have a very old parent who might suddenly need care) (Stone and Kemper, 1989a). McLanahan and Monson (1989) found that 3.5 percent of women and 2 percent of men have obligations for both an elderly parent and a child. Almost 200,000 daughters are "women in the middle," caring for young children as well as

TABLE 4-3   Potential and Active Caregivers to the Elderly Age 16 and Over Who Are Employed Full Time (thousands)

	Potential Caregivers	Active Caregivers[a]		
		Primary	Secondary	Total
Men				
Number	4,418	168	523	691
Percent, employed men[b]	9.2	.3	1.2	1.5
Women				
Number	2,952	409	425	834
Percent, employed women[b]	9.2	1.3	1.3	2.6
Total				
Number	7,370	577	948	1,525
Percent, employed[b]	9.2	.7	1.2	1.9

[a]Does not include caregivers of disabled elders in institutions.

[b]Potential and active caregivers as a percentage of U.S. population employed 30 or more hours for each gender and total.

SOURCE: Stone and Kemper (1989a:Table 6). Data from 1984 National Long-Term Care Survey; March 1984 Current Population Survey. Reprinted by permission.

parents. Almost 1 million women employed full time are potential caregivers for both a child and an elderly parent (Stone and Kemper, 1989b).

Surveys of employers and other small, nonrandom samples using broader definitions of care than the national surveys provide additional information on the prevalence of care by employees (Creedon, 1989; Friedman, 1988; Brody, 1985). For example, the Travelers' Companies and IBM report that 30 percent and 20 percent, respectively, of their employees over age 30 provide care for an elderly person. Caregivers are reported to spend from 12 to 35 hours on elder care each week, the amount of time determined mainly by the level of dependence of the person cared for (Creedon, 1989). At Travelers, women reported 16 hours of elder care per week; of those, 31 percent were also caring for young children (The Travelers' Companies, 1985).

CARE FOR CHILDREN

As Chapter 3 explained, American workers' choices of employment—their choice of shift jobs, part-time work, or not working at all—are influenced by family duties: by the need to care for both elderly relatives and children. Satisfactory, affordable child care arrangements can relieve stress, reduce absenteeism and tardiness, and increase worker satisfaction. Conversely, the absence of affordable child care that conforms to parents' values and the failure of child care arrangements can increase stress, absenteeism, and tardiness or can lead to the decision to work fewer hours or not to work at all. Understanding national patterns and trends in child care is therefore critical to a clear understanding of the relationship between work and family.

Parents with children under 18 constitute approximately 37 percent of the work force, and those with children under 6 constitute more than 16 percent (calculated from unpublished data tables, March 1988 Current Population Survey). Between 1960 and 1988, the proportion of married women in the work force, with husbands present and children under age 6, rose most dramatically, from 19 to 57 percent. As shown in Figure 4-1, in the last 10 years, the greatest increase has been in the number of working women with very young children.

As a result, the percentage of children under age 13 cared for by nonem-

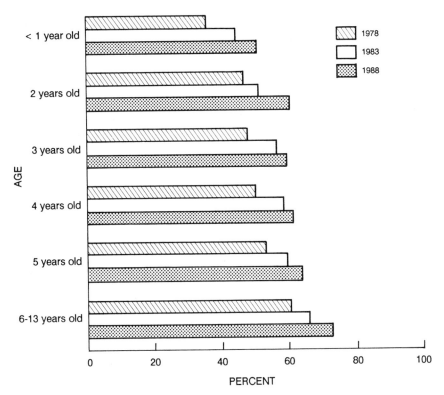

FIGURE 4-1 Labor force participation rate of mothers by age of youngest child, 1977–1988. SOURCE: Data from Bureau of Labor Statistics, *News*, September 7, 1988. Reprinted in Hayes et al. (1990).

ployed mothers at home has declined to about 40 percent, far smaller than 20 years ago, and is expected to decline further. In 1988, of the approximately 65 million children under age 18, about 69 percent were under age 13 and 29 percent were under age 6.

At any given time, the majority of American children live in two-parent families, but at some point in their lives almost half of all children will live in a single-family home (Garfinkel and McLanahan, 1986). Single parents face particular problems in securing appropriate child care arrangements. In effect, it is a vicious cycle: single-parent families tend to have low incomes and a higher proportion of children living in poverty. They also have greater difficulty finding or paying for quality child care that would enable them to go to work or to work more productively. The proportion of children under 18 living in poverty increased from 15 percent in 1970 to 20 percent in 1987.

The fact that one American child in five will spend part of his or her childhood in poverty is startling, and the proportion is far higher among some minority groups. In single-parent, female-headed families, poverty rates are 46 percent for white children, 68 percent for black children, and 70 percent for Hispanic children (Bureau of the Census, 1989b). Overall, children today have the highest poverty rate of any age group; black and Hispanic children are two to three times more likely to live in poverty than white children. Estimates of the number of homeless children range from 100,000 to 500,000 (U.S. Congress, House, 1989).

Many parents of poor children experience extreme work-family stress. Not all poor families are out of the labor force or receiving income support from government programs. In 1988, about 59 percent of poor families included at least one person who worked in that year; 18 percent included two or more workers. In 42 percent of poor female-headed families, the mother worked. Almost 10 percent of poor female householders worked year round, full time. And 65 percent of the poor female householders not in the labor force cited family responsibilities as the reason (Bureau of the Census, 1989b).

Although the focus of this section is on the care of young children before they enter school, as well as their care before and after school, it is important to note that the business community has expressed concern about the quality of public school education, its effect on future workers, and the appropriate role for employers in that system. The severe problems in public education have been extensively documented. Well over one-quarter of the nation's young people do not finish high school. Nearly 13 percent of all 17 year olds enrolled in school are reported to be functionally illiterate and 44 percent to be only marginally literate. Test scores confirm deficiencies in U.S. precollege education, particularly in math, science, and literacy (Kutscher, 1989).

Employers are already starting to experience the effects of a poorly educated labor force. Business leaders have called for a stronger role for business in education, through such activities as private-public partnerships (Committee for Economic Development, 1985), and programs have been initiated in several cities. In Chicago, for example, corporations have joined together and established a corporate community school for low-income children (Corporate/Community Schools of America, 1989; see also Weiner, 1989, and Will, 1989).

Yet even more notable than employers' concerns about education has been their increased interest in providing child care directly or through indirect subsidies. Recognizing the link between child care and employment, many companies have become concerned about the larger forces affecting the present and future work force, such as poverty, and deficiencies in the education system and health care of workers and their families. Although employer involvement has increased in some areas, there is no general agreement on the appropriate ongoing role employers should play in organizing and financing family services.

Types of Child Care

Much of the care for children of working parents is arranged informally: some of it is unpaid care by family members, and some of the paid care is unlicensed. Employed parents pay for most child care. However, there is a growing mix of publicly and privately subsidized centers, including nursery schools, prekindergartens, and kindergartens. Schools and religious organizations sponsor child care. Some school systems operate centers. School-based child care programs are growing, including before- and after-school programs and special programs such as Head Start for poor children. Table 4-4 shows care arrangements for children whose mothers are employed. The type of care used varies with the age of the child. Parental care and care by relatives and in-house babysitters or nannies are declining; care in centers and in family day care is increasing, and these trends are likely to continue in the 1990s (Hofferth and Phillips, 1987).

Care by Parents

Even when they are both employed, parents may choose work schedules that allow them to provide a substantial amount of in-home care. More than 9 percent of children with employed mothers are cared for by their fathers. One study found that in about one-third of young families (parents ages 19 to 27), the spouses worked different shifts (Presser, 1988). Such parents are able to care for their children themselves, but there is a toll on their ability to interact with each other and to be together as a family.

TABLE 4-4 Primary Child Care Arrangements Used by Employed
Mothers of Children Under 15, 1984-1985 (percentage)

Type of Child Care Arrangement	Total	Under 1 year	1 and 2 years	3 and 4 years	5 to 14 years
Care in child's home	17.8	37.3	32.7	27.0	11.8
By father	9.4	18.2	16.2	14.3	6.6
By grandparent	2.7	7.4	6.4	4.5	1.3
By other relative	3.0	3.2	4.5	3.3	2.7
By nonrelative	2.6	8.5	5.7	5.0	1.1
Care in another home	14.4	40.6	41.9	31.0	4.3
By grandparent	4.3	12.6	11.0	8.5	1.7
By other relative	1.8	5.1	4.0	4.7	0.5
By nonrelative	8.3	23.0	26.8	17.7	2.1
Organized child care facilites	9.1	14.1	17.2	32.2	2.8
Day/group care center	5.4	8.4	12.3	17.8	1.6
Nursery school/preschool	3.7	5.7	5.0	14.4	1.2
Kindergarten/grade school	52.2	—	—	1.7	75.2
Child cares for self	1.8	—	—	—	2.7
Parent cares for child	4.7	8.1	8.2	8.1	3.2
Total	100.0	100.0	100.0	100.0	100.0
Total number of children (thousands)	(26,455)	(1,385)	(3,267)	(3,516)	(18,287)

NOTE: Includes mothers working at home or away from home.
SOURCE: Bureau of the Census (1987:Tables B and D).

Another 4.7 percent of children of working parents are cared for by
parents, mainly working mothers. Some work at home; others provide telephone access, most often to school-age children. The Bureau of the Census
(1987) reports that 2.7 million children, most of them of elementary and
junior high school age, care for themselves or are "latchkey" children before and after school. The U.S. Department of Labor (1988) concludes that
care for this group may well be the largest shortage.

Relative and Nanny Care

Another 11.8 percent of children are cared for by relatives, most often
grandmothers: 5.7 percent in the child's home and 6.1 percent in the home
of the relative. Relative care is most often used by low-income families.
Some research suggests that relatives are preferred caregivers because of
the low costs as well as common cultural values (Waite et al., 1988). Other
research finds that low-income mothers using relatives are dissatisfied or
would prefer another arrangement (Kisker et al., 1989; Sonenstein and

Wolf, 1988). But they have difficulty using alternative services because of the hours they work, the cost, or the unavailability of such services in their neighborhoods. In fact, relative care has declined from 68 percent of all care in 1970 to 40 percent in 1985. Care by relatives is expected to decrease further as more working-age women who are grandmothers stay in the paid labor force.

The use of nannies or in-home babysitters is also declining; they now provide care for about 2.6 percent of children. Nannies are often immigrants or young women from other countries participating in living-abroad programs. They may live with the family and have other housekeeping responsibilities as well. This is the most expensive type of child care (Hofferth, 1988); the majority of such care is unregulated, and little is known about its quality.

Family Day Care

Family day care is the second-fastest-growing form of child care after child care centers. Generally, one woman cares in her home for between two and six children, some possibly her own. Estimates of the number of such homes range from 420,000 to more than 1 million. Whereas only 15 percent of employed mothers used family day care in 1958, 30 percent used it in 1985 (Hayes et al., 1990). It is the least expensive form of care other than that by relatives.

An estimated 60 to 90 percent of family day care is unregulated, and little is known about it (Hayes et al., 1990). In 1988, only 27 states required some form of licensing, 13 offered voluntary registration, and 6 had some form of certification for those seeking federal support (Blank and Wilkins, 1985; Morgan, 1987). Research suggests that women who provide this type of care generally earn little, are often isolated, lack training, and frequently do not do this type of work for very long (Fosberg, 1981; Whitebook et al., 1989). This is a matter of concern when considering the large proportion of American children who will spend their formative years in family day care arrangements.

Center Care

The fastest-growing type of child care is group care or centers. Overall, 9 percent of children are in center care: 3.7 percent in nurseries or preschools (often part day). For children under the age of 5, centers account for 23 percent of the care (Figure 4-2). In 1984-1985, approximately 14 percent of infants (under age 1) and 17 percent of toddlers (ages 1 to 2) with employed mothers were in organized child care facilities. The largest group in center care are 3 and 4 year olds, for whom preschool programs have become a widely accepted educational and socialization

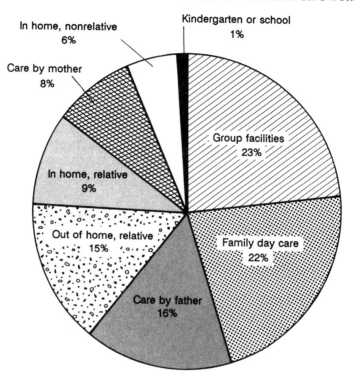

FIGURE 4-2 Primary child care arrangements of employed parents with children under age 5, winter 1984–1985. SOURCE: Data from Current Population Reports Series P-70, No. 9, 1987. Reprinted in Hayes et al. (1990).

process; over 1 million 3 and 4 year olds are in such programs. Almost all 5 year olds are in some type of public school kindergarten, although many are in part-day programs. Children age 6 and older are in school; many up to age 8 are also in after-school center programs.

A 1986 survey estimated that there were 62,989 child care centers, with a capacity for approximately 2.1 million children (Haskins, 1988). This represented an increase of over 200 percent since the mid-1970s. Centers have a growing diversity of programs and sponsorship. There are not-for-profit centers run by government agencies, community groups, employers, and parent cooperatives, as well as for-profit centers, from small "Mom and Pop" operations to large corporate chains. Like nursing homes, centers are regulated by the states, although religious and part-day programs are usually exempt. There is a lively debate about the adequacy, effectiveness, and consequences of regulation, discussed below (Reisman et al., 1988; Blank et al., 1987; Hayes et al., 1990).

Child Care Availability and Need

Women's labor force participation is obviously a major factor driving demand for child care. The availability of acceptable child care also affects women's labor force participation (e.g., Leibowitz and Waite, 1988; O'Connell and Bloom, 1987). Frequent discussions of demand for child care are generally couched in terms of need and disregard the effect of price on demand. Although there appears to be a large unmet demand for free or heavily subsidized child care, there is hardly a shortage in the usual economic sense. Furthermore, the issue often is not that child care is unavailable at affordable prices but that the quality of affordable care is unacceptable.

A recent report of the National Research Council (Hayes et al., 1990) examined the issues of child care availability, affordability, and quality in detail. We note here some of the findings most relevant to this study.

• There appears to be a shortage of quality infant care. Infant care is more expensive than other forms of child care (except care of disabled children); the unavailability of affordable quality infant care causes severe hardship for low-income families, particularly single mothers who must return to work shortly after childbirth.

• Overall, the growth in child care spaces for children ages 3 to 5 has kept pace with the number of such children who have employed mothers, but there remains a serious deficiency in affordable quality care for children from low-income families, children with disabilities, and children whose parents work nonstandard hours.

• The number of latchkey children is increasing, and they could be at greater risk for drug use, violence, and various problem behaviors.

Costs of Child Care

The costs of a parent's staying home to care for children are long term as well as immediate. When a mother leaves her job, she not only gives up current earnings, but she will also, to some extent, reduce her future earnings, especially if she is in an occupation in which experience is highly valued. In addition, she may also lose retirement benefits. In general, the labor market rewards continuity of employment and penalizes interruptions. This long- and short-term earnings reduction contributes significantly to female poverty.

Of an estimated $16 billion spent on out-of-home child care, employed parents spent about half, after tax credits; federal subsidies amounted to almost $7 billion, up from about $2.5 billion in 1980 (Besharov and Tramontozzi, 1988), and state subsidies were about $1 billion (Hayes et al., 1990).

The fastest-growing type of support has been through the tax system, benefiting middle- and upper-income families.

In 1985, among families with employed mothers, 77 percent paid for care for children under age 5, and 57 percent paid for care for those over 5 (Hofferth, 1988). Among families whose youngest child was under 5 and who purchased child care for at least 30 hours per week, the average amount spent has been approximately $1,820 per child per year. According to the Survey of Income and Program Participation, however, 27 percent of families paid more than $50 per week per child (Brush, 1987); similarly, Kisker et al. (1989) report the median total expenditure for those paying for care was $50 per week. Both Hofferth (1987) and Brush (1987) found that families who live in metropolitan areas, have more education, are white, and have higher incomes tend to pay more for care. The average costs in 1987 ranged from $20 a week for a preschool family day care program in Miami to $90 a week for infant center care in New York City (unpublished data, Work/Family Directions, Watertown, Mass., 1987). In general, costs are higher for infants and for children with handicaps (Grubb, 1988; Brush, 1989).

Another way to look at costs is as a percentage of income. Using the 1985 National Longitudinal Survey of Youth, Hofferth (1988) found, on average, that families pay 10 percent of their income for child care. This is comparable to average family food expenditures (Bureau of the Census, 1989f). In both cases, however, they constitute a far larger share of the budgets of low- and moderate-income families. Poor families average 23 percent of their income for child care while other families pay 9 percent. Single parents also pay a higher proportion of their income for child care than do two-earner families. This reflects the lower earnings of single parents and also the fact that single parents have fewer opportunities for shared care arrangements. The dependent care tax credit repays a portion of these costs to families that earn enough to owe taxes.

Child care is often viewed as a cost of women's labor force participation. Waite et al. (1988) calculated that, in middle-income families, child care costs average approximately 25 percent of wives' incomes. Confronted with the same costs, one family might choose eagerly to make the expenditure to allow both parents' careers to progress; another family might bear the expense reluctantly out of financial necessity; while a third might withdraw one parent from the labor force.

Low-income families have fewer choices, and spending over one-fifth of family income for child care presents a serious hardship for them. The proportion is even higher for young families with infants or children with disabilities (Hayes et al., 1990).

Quality of Child Care

As previously noted, the quality of child care is also a matter of serious concern. After a careful review of available research, the Panel on Child Care Policy concluded that, although there are some methodological constraints on the research, quality of care is very important for children's development. For example, children's scores on school readiness and vocabulary tests were related to center group size, teacher qualifications, and center orientation (Ruopp et al., 1979). Howes and Olenick (1986) found that children from low-quality centers were less likely to restrain their behavior in situations in which that would be appropriate. The panel also concluded that much of the care now available is of inadequate quality and that quality varies considerably within and across different types of care and different types of sponsorship.

The report identifies key components of quality. One important measure is the stability of caregivers, yet the wages and benefits of child care workers are very low (Grubb, 1988; Fuchs, 1988; Hartmann and Pearce, 1989), and they have one of the highest turnover rates of any occupation (Eck, 1984). Other measures of quality are staff/child ratios, group size, features of physical facilities, and caregiver training. Although states regulate child care, many states' regulations are inadequate. Children from low-income families are more likely to have poor care unless they are enrolled in programs, such as Head Start, which are of high quality (Howes, in press; Hayes et al., 1990).

Not surprisingly, higher-quality child care usually costs more. Estimates by Clifford and Russell (1989) range from a low of $2,937 per child for what they consider to be the typical existing program (with low salaries and low staff/child ratios) to a high of $5,267 per child for a high-quality program that includes relatively high salaries for staff ($20,000 per year for teachers) and high staff/child ratios (1:4 for infants, 1:6 for toddlers, 1:8 for 3 year olds, and 1:12 for school-age children). Their estimates of the costs of high-quality care coincide with Head Start projections for the costs of quality care for economically disadvantaged children. Because pay for staff amounts to 60 to 90 percent of child care costs, any improvement in wages or staff/child ratios will raise the costs of care.

As with elder care, higher standards and more stringent regulations for child care, while improving quality, are also likely to increase costs and thus decrease affordability. Without subsidies, low-income families are unlikely to be able to afford that care. There is also a question about who should make decisions regarding quality and cost trade-offs for child care. For example, parents might not value quality, as defined by the experts, as much as location, costs, and hours (Waite et al., 1988). Or they simply may not have sufficient information about what experts believe constitutes quality (Grubb, 1988).

A number of government programs provide direct and indirect assistance for child care. Working parents receive subsidies through the tax system and poor families through programs such as Head Start, Aid to Families with Dependent Children, Title XX, and the earned income tax credit. In addition, a small but growing number of employers and unions are addressing problems of child care: some sponsor on-site and consortium child care centers or provide subsidies to employees to reduce the costs of purchasing care elsewhere, through vouchers or tax-based dependent care assistance programs; others sponsor resource and referral programs that offer information and attempt to improve quality.

CARE FOR THE WORKING-AGE DISABLED

In addition to elderly people and children, disabled adults also need care. The 1980 census defined disability as a limitation in the ability to work because of a physical, mental, or other health condition that had lasted 6 or more months. Approximately 13 percent of nursing home residents are under 65 years of age (Committee on Nursing Home Regulation, 1986). The loss of income and the cost of care for people with disabilities are burdens on families. Because these burdens may cause stress for employees, they are also of concern to employers.

Numerous cross-sectional and longitudinal surveys provide an overview of the prevalence and severity of existing disabilities and of the programs and policies to help people and their families. Wide variations in findings are attributed to differences in the wording of questions and interviewer training (Haber, 1989). Among the 19 surveys conducted between 1960 and 1980, estimated rates of disability ranged from approximately 8 to 17 percent of the population. Estimates of severe disability ranged from 2 to 6 percent of the population. The most recent data from the Current Population Survey (CPS) (Bureau of the Census, 1989d) indicate that 8.6 percent of the population have a work disability and 4.8 percent have a severe disability, with similar rates for men and women. In the 1987 CPS, 3.6 percent of working-age men and 2.9 percent of working-age women reported that they had not worked the previous year because of illness or disability (Bureau of the Census, 1989e). Severity is very generally defined, and very little is known about the duration of disabilities. These figures also may somewhat overestimate those in need of care because people who are occupationally disabled—that is, not able to work—may not require the care of family members.

These surveys provide demographic and economic patterns for persons with disabilities. In general, the findings on the relationship of disability to age, education, race, and income have been consistent over time and across surveys. Disability is more common with increasing age, among blacks than whites, among unskilled and semiskilled workers than among skilled and professional workers, among those with less than a high school education than among high school and college graduates, among rural than among urban populations, and among people in the South than in other regions. Because disabled workers tend to have lower earnings than other workers, poverty is not only a predisposing factor, but also a consequence of disability (Haber, 1989; Bureau of the Census, 1989d).

Other sources of information are records on participation in programs established to assist the disabled. As in most industrialized countries, public policies for the disabled in the United States are a mix of income transfer programs and employment programs, but with a much greater emphasis on the former. In 1985 there were approximately 2.7 million people covered by disability insurance programs, 1.9 by the Supplemental Security Income program. Only 200,000 were in narrowly defined job programs, such as sheltered workshops, and 900,000 were in vocational rehabilitation programs. Rehabilitation programs have a success rate of about 30 percent in getting a person back to work (Burkhauser and Hirvonen, 1988).

There is little information on how people with disabilities are cared for and to what extent their caretakers are in the work force (Zitter, 1989; Paula Franklin, Division of Disability Studies, Social Security Administration, personal communication, 1990). According to the 1987 National Survey of Families and Households, during that year approximately 8 percent of women under the age of 65 lived with someone who was chronically ill or disabled. And 3 percent of white women, 2 percent of white men, and 1.3 percent of nonwhite women and men of working age were providing care to spouses in their home (McLanahan and Monson, 1989). Employed women are somewhat less likely to care for a spouse than nonemployed women, even though one early study found that wives of disabled husbands were likely to go to work because of loss of income (Franklin, 1977). Disability insurance, funded through employer and employee contributions, totaling over $18 billion in 1986, and workers compensation, amounting to $32 billion in employer contributions, are major sources of funding for disabled people.

CONCLUSIONS

How dependents are cared for is in large part determined by the resources of individual families and the mix of funding mechanisms available. As we have seen, responsibility for dependents continues to rest primarily on working-age adults in the family. More care is purchased, paid for mainly by families, but partly by governments and employers. Nonetheless, much care continues to be provided by relatives, chiefly women, even though most of them are now in the labor force. Families directly pay for the majority of dependent care. The role of employers in supporting dependent care is influenced by tax policies, government mandates, the demands of employees and their unions, and the needs of business. Employers rarely pay for services directly, but make substantial contributions through taxes and mandated and voluntary insurance systems.

The responsibilities of working-age adults in the United States to care for the elderly, for children, and for disabled friends and family members is bound to increase with time, given demographic trends. Responsibilities tend to change with stages in the life cycle: younger women care for their children; and middle-aged and older women care for husbands after their children have grown; and middle-aged women more than men have primary responsibility for caring for elderly parents. Adults can now expect to spend 28 years with children under 18 and/or parents over 65. The years with parents now exceed those with children (Watkins and Menken, 1987).

The economic status and health of the elderly have improved in recent decades, due in large part to programs such as Social Security and Medicare. The increasing number of elderly, however, means that there is a growing proportion of people in need of care by others. Nursing home care is very expensive, and there are substantial concerns about the quality of care provided. Paid home care services are developing but apparently will not significantly reduce the need for nursing home care.

For children, the use of paid care, particularly center and family day care, has increased rapidly over the last 20 years as the proportion of children in two-earner and in one-adult families has increased. There is evidence that adequate care for infants, for children with disabilities, for economically disadvantaged children, and for children whose parents work nonstandard shifts are in short supply. Very little is known about the care that working-age adults with disabilities now receive.

Inadequate wages, poor training, and high turnover among staff negatively affect the quality of paid care that is available for both children and the elderly. Improved standards and increased regulation of care will increase costs, however, and questions have been raised about the effectiveness of regulations.

The work-family conflicts now experienced by adults in the work force, and the frustrations of those who are not but would like to be, are likely to increase with time. While government policies and programs can play some role in their solution, employers are likely to be called on to play a major role as well.

5

Standard Employee Benefits

Compensation for work consists of wages and salaries as well as non-wage benefits such as health, life, and disability insurance; sick leave; vacations; and holidays. Deferred income—pensions, investment plans, stock options—are also considered nonwage benefits. These benefits form a standard part of total compensation and have increased in both value and importance for some time. They make an important contribution to the well-being of employees and their families. Some benefits are required by federal or state laws; others are offered voluntarily or result from collective bargaining. This chapter reviews the evolution of the most common nonwage benefits; examines why they are offered; and discusses to what extent benefits vary by industry, occupation, wage level, and employment status.

Three types of surveys provide information about employee benefits: (1) surveys of employers, which have samples that are neither national nor random (e.g., U.S. Chamber of Commerce, Wyatt Company); (2) employee surveys that are national but are largely or entirely confined to workers in medium- and large-sized firms (e.g., Bureau of Labor Statistics); and (3) specialized surveys that contain little employer information (e.g., Survey of Income and Program Participation). The data obtained are not comparable and do not provide authoritative information on the scope and availability of many types of benefits. These surveys do, however, give a good picture of the programs overall and a profile of participants.

EVOLUTION OF NONWAGE BENEFITS

Nonwage benefits evolved with the growth of the industrial economy. In the last quarter of the nineteenth century, large, profitable firms began offering pension plans and other benefits, such as paid vacation leave. The American Express Company, for example, established a pension plan in 1875. The concept of welfare capitalism gained a foothold with many large companies in need of skilled workers or hoping to reduce the appeal of labor unions (Brandes, 1976). Managers crafted benefits in growing industries such as steel, electrical products, and automobiles hoping to achieve not only greater productivity, but also such diverse goals as adherence to religious values and literacy (Kamerman and Kahn, 1987; Kanter, 1977b; Schatz, 1983). Benefits offered within a company were not uniform for all employees. Men and women were provided different benefits, reflecting then-current expectations: men would work until old age; women would work until they married and began to raise a family. Thus men were offered pensions and paid vacations; women were offered poetry and cooking classes (Schatz, 1983).

Benefits were generally offered only by large firms seeking workers with special skills. The great majority of working people received few benefits, whether vacations, health care or sick pay. Long hours, hazardous working conditions, and the absence of job security led the emerging labor unions to bargain for better working conditions and support legislative protection for working people. The first state workers compensation laws were enacted in 1911 in response to these pressures. The laws established minimum industrial safety standards and provided compensation in case of job-related death or disability (Berkowitz, 1979). These early laws did not apply to agriculture, which at that time employed the majority of workers, particularly black workers.

During this period, efforts to legislate an 8-hour workday failed. But exposés of brutal industrial and commercial working conditions at least strengthened the movement for reform for women and children. By 1912, 34 states had enacted protective laws limiting women's hours, prohibiting many types of child labor, and protecting maternal roles. Half a century later, 40 states had laws regulating women's employment (Kamerman et al., 1983; Ratner, 1986; Frank and Lipner, 1988; Williams, 1985). It was not until the 1964 Civil Rights Act made these earlier state laws protecting women discriminatory that they were superseded by federal equal employment opportunity laws.

The Great Depression of the 1930s eroded earlier gains in benefits. Employees were grateful for work and made few demands for benefits. The stage was set for government involvement, beginning with the enactment of Social Security legislation in 1935. A cornerstone of the New Deal, it provided for pension benefits, although its coverage in the early years was far from universal. More important at the time were the immediate cash benefits paid to older workers.

Further improvement in benefits occurred during World War II, when labor was in short supply and workers had more leverage with employers. Wartime wage and price controls prohibited bargaining for increased wages, but these controls did not apply to nonwage benefits. Unions successfully negotiated health insurance and pensions. In the years following the war, substantial real wage gains flowed from the growing economy. By 1950, many unions had shifted their priorities somewhat from wages to shorter working hours, vacation leave, and improved health insurance. (See Employee Benefit Research Institute, 1987; Friedman and Gray, 1989; Saltford and Heck, 1989.)

By 1970 a standard benefit package was commonly offered by many medium- and large-sized firms. It consisted of Social Security benefits plus sick leave, a company-supported pension benefit, health insurance, and paid vacations. Although the types of benefits included tended to be similar, the scope and value of offerings varied from firm to firm. In small firms Social Security was frequently the only benefit provided.

As shown in Table 5-1, the aggregate value of benefits grew from a little more than 1 percent of total compensation in 1929 to 10.4 percent in 1969 and 16.2 percent in 1988 (Council of Economic Advisers, 1989). Including benefits such as pay for time not worked (e.g., vacations), 1990 nonwage benefits in private industry accounted for almost 28 percent of total compensation. Growth in all types of benefits did not, however, proceed at an even pace. The long period of expansion of voluntary benefits ended in the 1970s and was followed by a decline in the 1980s. Only increases in benefits required by federal and state governments caused aggregate benefits to increase since 1980. Also, payment for time not worked has de-

TABLE 5-1 Aggregate Value of Employee Nonwage Benefits, 1929-1988

Year	Current Dollars (billions)	Percentage of Total Compensation
1929	$ 0.7	1.3
1939	2.2	4.6
1949	7.3	5.1
1959	21.4	7.6
1969	60.1	10.4
1979	239.5	16.1
1988	464.3	16.2

NOTE: Consists mainly of employer contributions to social insurance and to private pension, health, and welfare funds.
SOURCE: Council of Economic Advisers (1989:Table B-24).

clined. Chamber of Commerce data analyzed by Woodbury (1989) show that payment for days not worked increased during the 1970s and then tapered off. By the mid-1980s it had returned to the approximate level of the 1960s.

The forces causing growth in benefits are complex and do not affect all segments of the economy equally. The factors influencing the provision of voluntary benefits include: tax policy, changes in real wages, employers' efforts to reduce labor turnover and improve productivity, demographic changes, and unionization. And expert views differ regarding the relative contribution of the different factors. But Woodbury (1989) offers convincing evidence that the two most important factors are tax policy and changes in real incomes. The implications of this finding are discussed below.

Federal and state tax policy has explicitly encouraged the growth of many employer-paid benefits by excluding them from taxable employee income while permitting businesses to treat them as a normal business expense. This approach assumes that benefits such as health and life insurance, pensions, etc., are in the public interest and thus merit subsidy through tax expenditures. The exemptions have greater value for the affluent, who are in higher tax brackets. For all income groups the value of exemptions decreases when tax rates decline, as they did in the 1980s. Nonetheless, these exemptions remain very popular. Economists have examined some of the unintended consequences of these exemptions. We have already noted the differential effect by income level. For those with incomes so low that they are not subject to taxes, the exemptions have no value. It has also been noted that government revenues shrink substantially when over one-fourth of employee compensation is not taxed. Munnell (1989) estimates that this loss will amount to $171 billion in 1993. Obviously this means that less money will be available for whatever direct expenditures governments want to make. Some economists also believe that this policy has resulted in excessive resources being allocated to subsidized benefits, for example, health insurance (Feldstein, 1977; Feldstein and Friedman, 1977).

BENEFITS ESTABLISHED BY LAW

Two types of employment-based benefits are established by law: tax-supported benefits managed by public agencies and mandated benefits privately purchased by the employer. Employer contributions for both of these are now 9 percent of total compensation, up from approximately 3.6 percent in 1960 (Andrews, 1988; Bureau of Labor Statistics, 1990a).

Federal Programs

The large federal role in nonwage benefits was established by the Social Security Act of 1935 and its subsequent expansion to include disability and health insurance. This program is funded through a payroll tax on employers, employees, and the self-employed, which is collected and disbursed by federal agencies. Although the federal government also sets standards for unemployment insurance, states may develop their own programs.

Participation in the social insurance programs has expanded steadily since the 1930s and now includes 95 percent of all U.S. workers in private industry (profit and nonprofit), military personnel, federal employees hired since 1984, and about 10 percent of federal workers hired earlier. Some state employees are exempted and covered instead under state programs. Social Security and Medicare provide the foundation of economic support and health insurance coverage for elderly and disabled people, although neither program is intended to cover all needs.

The principal benefits are provided by the Old Age, Survivors, Disability, and Health Insurance (OASDI) program. Retirement benefits account for about 50 percent of Social Security payments. In 1986 approximately 38 million people received OASDI benefits totaling $272 billion (Bureau of the Census, 1989f). In 1990, covered workers and their employers each paid a tax of 7.65 percent on earnings up to $50,400 per individual. The earnings base (income subject to taxation) is indexed to increase with average earnings nationwide.

Medicare Part A (or Hospital Insurance—HI) insures hospital inpatient services and certain follow-up care for people over age 65, those who have been disabled for more than 24 months, and those who suffer chronic kidney disease. In 1989, about 30 million people over age 65 and 3 million disabled people were enrolled in Medicare Part A; expenditures were $60.8 billion (Federal Hospital Insurance Trust Fund, 1990). Individuals eligible for Medicare Part A may elect to enroll in Part B or Supplementary Medical Insurance (SMI), which pays for physician services, outpatient hospital services, and other medical expenses. Premiums paid by enrolled individuals contribute 27.7 percent of all SMI income, while general revenue contributions account for 69.6 percent of income (Federal Supplementary Medical Insurance Trust Fund, 1990). State Medicaid programs pay SMI premiums on behalf of eligible low-income, elderly, or disabled people. SMI expenditures in 1989 were $39.8 billion for benefits to the 32 million people covered by the program.

State Programs

All states have some form of workers' compensation providing benefits for those disabled by work-related injury or illness and for dependents of workers whose deaths resulted from such injury. These programs are generally administered by commissions or by units within state labor departments. They differ greatly in extent of coverage, level of benefits, and the insurance method used to underwrite risks. Underwriting may be through commercial insurance, publicly operated state insurance funds, or self-insurance, primarily by large employers (Nelson, 1989).

About 87 percent of all wage and salary workers were covered in 1986. Employer costs were approximately $34 billion, or slightly more than 1 percent of total payroll (Nelson, 1989). The cost to employers varies significantly depending on industry hazards and the proportion of insured workers in high-risk jobs. Typical benefits cover medical costs and provide two-thirds of gross earnings, up to the average weekly wages in the state. The benefits are tax-free. The tax exemption is of greater value to higher-income workers, although wage replacement ratios are less favorable for workers whose wages exceed the state average and are therefore limited to less than two-thirds of earnings. Many experts recommend reforms in workers' compensation because of escalating costs and inequities between households within and among states (deVol, 1985). Over the last decade more than 1,000 amendments to state workers' compensation laws were enacted in response to problems or perceived inequities (*Business Insurance*, 1989).

Unemployment compensation is another major state program; it provides income to individuals unable to find work. It covers about 97 percent of wage earners. Under the Federal Unemployment Tax Act of 1939 (as amended), employers are taxed 6.2 percent on wages of up to $7,000 per worker, but are allowed substantial credit for payroll contributions paid under state unemployment insurance laws. Thus it is primarily a state program with a small federal component for administrative costs (Hamermesh, 1989). Employer taxes in 1987 totaled $18 billion, about 2.5 percent of total wages. Slightly over 7 million beneficiaries received $14 billion in benefits. Mean weekly benefits were $140, ranging from an average low of $98 in Tennessee to $174 in Massachusetts (Bureau of the Census, 1989f).

Short-term disability programs (discussed below) are legally required in only five states: California, Hawaii, New Jersey, New York, Rhode Island, and Puerto Rico. In each of the plans, employees must contribute to the cost of coverage. Employers in California, New Jersey, New York, and Puerto Rico can purchase coverage from either the state plan or any private plan that meets state requirements, including self-insurance. California and Rhode Island do not require employers to contribute. Hawaii provides only for self-insurance, and Rhode Island has a state plan, with private plans allowed only as a supplement. A summary of the laws is shown in Table 5-2.

Although costs for all states are not available, data from New York provide one example. In 1986 approximately $566 million was paid in benefits: $511 million to compensate for lost wages and $55 million for medical care (State of New York Workers' Compensation Board, 1986). These costs have risen steadily over the last 20 years due to rising wages,

TABLE 5-2 State Nonoccupational Disability Laws, 1989

State Law	Employers Covered	Permissible Plans	Employee/Employer Contributions	Benefit Duration and Benefit Levels	Qualifying Wages or Employment
CALIFORNIA					
Unemployment Compensation Disability Benefits (UCD). Employment Development Dept., Disability Insurance-NIC29, 800 Capitol Mall, Sacramento, CA 95814	Employers of one or more employees when wages paid in a calendar quarter exceed $100.	1. State plan or 2. Private voluntary plan may be insured or self-insured but must equal or exceed state plan.	Employee contributions consist of 0.9% of first $25,149 annual earnings. No employer contributions are mandated; however, employers may elect to pay all or part of employee contribution.	Benefits are based on schedule using quarterly earnings figures. Maximum $226, minimum $50.	At least $300 in the base period, which is a 12-month period determined by the date on which a claim begins.
HAWAII					
Temporary Disability Insurance Law (TDI). Dept. of Labor and Industrial Relations, P.O. Box 3769, Honolulu, HI 96812	Employers of one or more employees. Includes domestics if they earn at least $225 per quarter.	1. No state plan. 2. Private plan may be insured or self-insured and must equal or exceed statutory requirements.	Employees must contribute the lesser of 0.5% of earnings up to a maximum of $2.32 weekly. Employers must pay the balance of costs incurred.	Benefits consist of 55% of average weekly earnings rounded to next higher dollar, maximum $255.	Work at least 14 weeks, 20 hours or more each week. 14 weeks must be in the last 4 completed calendar quarters and person must have earned at least $400 within those 14 weeks.

table continues

TABLE 5-2 *Continued*

State Law	Employers Covered	Permissible Plans	Employee/Employer Contributions	Benefit Duration and Benefit Levels	Qualifying Wages or Employment
NEW JERSEY					
Temporary Disability Benefits (TDI). Dept. of Labor, Disability Insurance Service, P.O. Box CN387, Trenton, NJ 08625-0387	Employers of one or more employees with minimum annual payroll of $1,000.	1. State plan or 2. Private plan may be insured or self-insured, and must equal or exceed state plan. If plan is contributory, majority consent of employees is necessary.	For both employers and employees, the contribution level is 0.5% of first $13,900 annual earnings. Employers who have contributed to the fund during the three prior years are subject to "experience rating." Their contributions may vary from 0.1% to 0.75%.	Benefits consist of 66 2/3% of average weekly earnings to next higher dollar, maximum $261.	At least $99 in each of 20 weeks during preceding year or $6,000 in preceding year.
NEW YORK					
Disability Benefits Law (DBL). Workers' Compensation Board, 180 Livingston St., Brooklyn, NY 11248	Employers of one or more employees. Includes domestics who work at least 40 hours per week.	1. State plan or 2. Private plan may be insured or self-insured and must equal or exceed state plan requirements. No employee consent necessary.	Employee contributions are 0.5% of first $120 of weekly wages. Employers must pay the balance of costs for "standard" plans.	Benefits are 50% of average weekly earnings, maximum $170, minimum $20 or employee's average weekly wage, if less.	Four or more consecutive weeks of covered full-time employment or 25 days of regular part-time employment.

RHODE ISLAND					
Temporary Disability Insurance Benefits (TDI). Dept. of Employment and Training, 101 Friendship Street, Providence, RI, 02903	Employers of one or more employees.	1. State plan only: no private plans allowed, except where private plan is a supplement to the state plan.	Employees contribute 1% of first $22,400 annual earnings. No employer contributions are mandated.	Benefit based on 60% of individual average weekly earnings: maximum $270, minimum $51; additional benefits for dependent children.	At least $85 in each of 20 weeks during the preceding year or $5,100 during the preceding year.
PUERTO RICO					
Disability Benefits Act (DBA). Department of Labor, Disability Dept., Prudential Rivera Martinez Bldg., 505 Munoz Rivera Ave., Rey, Puerto Rico 00918	Employers of one or more employees.	1. State plan or 2. Private plan may be insured or self-insured and must equal or exceed state plan requirements. Majority employee consent needed to set up plan if contributory.	Both employers and employees pay 0.3% of the first $9,000 in wages.	Benefits set at 65% of weekly earnings: maximum $113, minimum $12.	At least $150 per week during the preceding 6 months or more.

SOURCE: Adapted from data from Legal and Research Dept., Foster Higgins & Co., Inc., 125 Broad Street, New York, NY 10004.

increases in statutory benefit rates, extension of the maximum duration of benefits, expansion to additional groups of workers, and repeal of statutory exclusions such as pregnancy-related disability and motor vehicle accidents.

VOLUNTARY BENEFITS

Voluntary benefits are those not required by law that are initiated by employers or provided as the result of collective bargaining. Including the value of pay for time not worked, total benefits account for almost 28 percent of compensation, of which voluntary benefits make up almost 19 percent (Table 5-3). Some voluntary benefits are subject to government regulation, such as the Employee Retirement Income Security Act (ERISA) and the Retirement Equity Act (REA). The seven most common are: pension plans, health insurance, life insurance, long-term disability insurance, vacations, holidays, and sick leave. Others less frequently provided include: subsidized education, discounts on goods and services, job-site cafeterias, parking, and special clothing.

TABLE 5-3 Employer Costs for Employee Compensation in Private Industry, 1990

	Compensation per Hour Worked	% of Total Compensation
Wages and salaries	$10.84	72.4
Benefits	4.13	27.6
Legally required[a]	1.35	9.0
Paid leave[b]	1.03	6.9
Insurance[c]	0.92	6.1
Pensions and savings[d]	0.45	3.0
Supplemental pay[e]	0.37	2.5
Other benefits[f]	g	g
Total	$14.96	100.0

[a]Social security, railroad retirement and supplemental retirement, railroad unemployment insurance, federal and state unemployment insurance, workers' compensation, and other benefits required by law, such as state temporary disability insurance.

[b]Paid vacation, holidays, sick leave, and other leave.

[c]Life, health, sickness, and accident insurance.

[d]Pension and other retirement plans and savings and thrift plans.

[e]Premium pay for overtime and work on weekends and holidays, shift differentials, nonproduction bonuses, and lump-sum payments.

[f]Includes severance pay and supplemental unemployment insurance.

[g]Cost per hour worked is $0.01 or less.

SOURCE: Bureau of Labor Statistics (1990a).

Table 5-4 shows the range of benefits offered in medium- and large-sized firms and the percentage of full-time employees estimated to be eligible for each type of benefit; also shown are differences in rates of participation between employees in private industry and those in state and local government. The most common types of benefits are described below.

TABLE 5-4 Employee Participation in Employee Benefit Programs in Private Industry and Government, 1987 and 1989 (percentage)

Benefit	Private Industry, 1989	State and Local Governments, 1987[a]
Paid time off		
Holidays	97	81
Vacations	97	72
Personal leave	22	38
Lunch period	10	17
Rest time	71	58
Funeral leave	84	56
Jury duty leave	90	98
Military leave	53	80
Sick leave	68	97
Insurance		
Sickness and accident	43	14
Long-term disability	45	31
Health	92	94
Life	94	85
Retirement		
Defined benefit pension	63	93
Defined contribution[b]	48	9

NOTE: Participants are full-time workers in medium- and large-sized firms covered by a paid time-off, insurance, retirement, or capital accumulation plan. Workers eligible for paid or unpaid maternity and paternity leave are also covered. Employees subject to a minimum service requirement before they are eligible for benefits coverage are counted as participants even if they have not met the requirement at the time of the survey. If employees are required to pay part of the cost of a benefit, only those who elect the coverage and pay their share are counted as participants. Benefits for which the employee must pay the full premium are outside the scope of the survey. Only current employees are counted as participants; retirees are excluded.

[a] Most recent year for which data are available.

[b] Plans were counted as retirement plans if employer contributions had to remain in the participant's account until retirement age, death, disability, separation from service, age 59½, or hardship.

SOURCE: Bureau of Labor Statistics (1990a:Table 1; 1988:Table 1).

Pension Plans

There are two major types of retirement plans: defined benefit plans and defined contribution plans. Defined benefit plans provide specified payments beginning at retirement based on a formula tied to the employee's earnings and length of service. In contrast, defined contribution plans do not guarantee a specific retirement benefit amount, but make payments on the basis of the value of contributions made in prior years through such means as profit sharing, thrift savings, employee-owned stock, and employer and employee contributions. In these plans, the exact amount of the retirement benefit depends on the performance of the investment funds into which the contributions have been paid. Since the passage of ERISA in 1974 (following a series of major pension plan failures), the proportion of defined benefit plans has declined from 34.0 percent to 26.7 percent (Employee Benefit Research Institute, 1987), probably because they have become more expensive to establish and maintain. Contributions by private employers to pension and profit-sharing plans rose from $5 billion in 1960 to $51 billion in 1987 (Andrews, 1988).

In 1987 there were approximately 875,000 private-sector pension plans and a range of plans for public-sector employees. The federal Civil Service Retirement System, established in 1920, was one of the first based on employer-employee contributions. Separate plans for state and local government employees also called for employee contributions. Most state and local governments now participate in the Social Security system; annual employer contributions to public retirement plans increased from $4 billion in 1960 to $65 billion in 1987.

Government regulation has strongly affected private pension programs. ERISA sets standards for minimum funding and vesting and requires that employees receive information about their pension fund on a regular basis. It also requires plans to be insured through the Pension Benefit Guaranty Corporation. REA, enacted in 1984, reduced the age for participation and the time needed for vesting and increased the time workers may be away from the job without losing their pension. It also encouraged the provision of joint survivor annuities, which provide not only for retirees but also for their spouses. These provisions are particularly important to women, who are far less likely to have their own pensions. In 1987, roughly 6 percent of women over age 62 received pensions based on their own employment (Saltford and Heck, 1989).

Health Insurance

Health insurance is one of the most important benefits that employers provide, since most working people find it difficult and expensive to purchase adequate health insurance for themselves and their dependents outside employer-based programs (Greenwald, 1987). A 1986 survey by the Small Business Administration found that 44 percent of firms do not offer health insurance to their employees (U.S. Small Business Administration, 1987). The availability of health insurance is closely related to firm size: 54 percent of firms with less than 10 employees and 22 percent of firms with 10 to 24 employees did not offer health insurance. The proportion of employers not providing health insurance varies strongly by industry. Firms in agriculture, personal services, entertainment, retail trade, repair services, and construction are least likely to provide insurance.

Rapidly escalating health costs have pushed total national spending on health to $604 billion or more than 11.6 percent of the gross national product in 1989. These increases have been mirrored in employer spending on health insurance, which increased from 25.9 percent of voluntary benefits in 1960 to 48 percent in 1987. Employers are currently facing premium increases in excess of 20 percent annually for basic group health insurance. As a result, employer spending on health insurance exceeds that for pensions and profit sharing (Andrews, 1988).

Health insurance is subject to federal and state regulation. The Consolidated Omnibus Budget Reconciliation Act of 1985 requires employers with 20 or more employees providing health insurance to offer former employees the option to purchase continued health insurance coverage for up to 18 months after active employment (Employee Benefit Research Institute, 1987). Dependents of deceased workers, divorced spouses, formerly dependent children, and all family members when a worker becomes eligible for Medicare and loses group coverage are entitled to buy up to 36 months of coverage at group rates.

The rapid escalation of health insurance premiums is making retiree participation very costly to employers. In 1986, two-thirds of the participants in health plans in medium- and large-sized firms (see the discussion of size below in the section on coverage of workers) had continued coverage after retirement at age 65, with employers paying the greater share of premiums (Bureau of Labor Statistics, 1987). In the future, retiree health costs will increase as a result of changes in Financial Accounting Standards that will require employers to treat the cost of health insurance benefits promised to retirees (estimated at $68.2 billion by the Employee Benefit Research Institute in 1988) as a liability in their balance sheets. Employers will be required to set aside funds to meet these future obligations, increasing current health-related expenses. It is not surprising that a 1988 Wyatt Company survey found that more than one-third of employers who responded were considering cutting back on retiree health benefits (Wyatt Company, 1988).

Disability Insurance

Disability programs include both short-term and long-term sickness and accident plans, either wholly or partially employer financed. According to the Wyatt Company survey (1988), 58 percent of employers sponsored short-term disability plans, and 58 percent of these plans replaced at least two-thirds of employees' pay. In addition, 91 percent had long-term disability programs, of which 64 percent replaced at least three-fifths of employees' pay. (The Wyatt Company survey does not, however, include an adequate sample of small employers. The coverage figures given do not therefore represent a national sample of *all* employers).

Short-term disability is usually defined as "an employee's inability to perform normal occupation duties" (Employee Benefit Research Institute, 1987). For short-term plans, an employee must generally be out of work a week, during which sick leave at full pay may be paid. Most plans cover workers for 26 weeks, although some do so for up to 52 weeks, generally for one-half to two-thirds of regular pay. These plans are financed through group insurance contracts, employee benefit trust funds established by employers, Taft-Hartley multiemployer welfare funds, or general corporate assets.

Long-term disability plans provide benefits after short-term plans run out. They usually extend up to 2 years and provide 50 to 60 percent of regular pay up to a specified maximum level. Disability beyond 2 years is defined as the "inability to perform any occupation that the person is reasonably suited to do by training, education and experience" (Employee Benefit Research Institute, 1987). In case of permanent disability, an employee may receive an early pension, Social Security, or other retirement benefits.

Life Insurance

Life insurance has become one of the most common components of benefit plans, provided by 95 percent of employers surveyed by the Wyatt Company (1988). Benefits are normally determined by multiplying an employee's annual earnings by 1, 1.5, or 2, paid either as a lump sum or as an income plan. In 1985, there were approximately 642,000 master policy group contracts, providing $2.56 trillion of coverage for workers. Employer contributions for life insurance have increased from $1 billion in 1960 to $10 billion in 1987, but they decreased as a percentage of total contributions for all voluntary pensions and insurance (Employee Benefit Research Institute, 1987; Andrews, 1988).

Paid Time Off

The benefits discussed thus far, whether required by law or provided voluntarily, address employees' financial needs. Employers also provide benefits involving time paid for but not worked, such as holidays, vacations, and sick days as well as lunch periods, rest breaks, and start-up time. The value of these benefits is estimated to be about 9 percent of total compensation, which is more than any other single discretionary benefit (see Table 5-3).

The U.S. Chamber of Commerce (1988) found that 95 percent of employers surveyed provided some paid vacation and 92 percent offered paid holidays, on average about 10 per year. The length of vacations tends to be related to length of service with the employer: employees with 1 year of service average 8.8 days a year, those with 10 years average 15.8 days, and those with 20 years average 20.6 days (Bureau of Labor Statistics, 1987). One-quarter of employers made available some personal days off (e.g., to look after a sick child, attend a funeral, or handle personal business matters), usually 3 or less, and four-fifths of employers allowed some unpaid leave, usually up to 30 days (Wyatt Company, 1988). In addition, a substantial proportion of employees have short-term leaves for funerals, jury duty, and military activities (see Table 5-4).

According to the Wyatt Company survey (1988), 80 percent of employers provide some form of sick leave; about half of the plans are combined with disability insurance. Almost half of them are tied to years of tenure, most often providing 10 days for employees with less than 1 year of service and 15 days for those with 10 or more years. Such leave may now be used for pregnancy and childbirth, but it is not allowed for the purpose of caring for ill family members.

COVERAGE AMONG WORKERS

So far we have reported estimates of the extent to which employers provide benefits. We now turn to the different question of the extent to which workers are covered. In addition to employer surveys, the primary sources of data are surveys of employees, such as the Bureau of Labor Statistics survey of employee benefits. Like employer surveys, they tend to focus on medium- and large-sized firms. There are, however, also national surveys of households, such as the Survey of Income and Program Participation (SIPP), the Panel Study of Income Dynamics (PSID), and the Current Population Survey (CPS), which are not subject to this limitation. It is therefore possible to obtain estimates and to analyze coverage for workers by employment status, occupation, industry, union status, firm size, etc. In-depth studies of particular firms and employees provide additional insights.

Pensions, health insurance, and other voluntary benefits vary considerably across the work force. The primary determinants of coverage and amount of benefits are: size of employing firm, type of industry, wage level of the employee, union membership, and full-time, year-round versus part-time or seasonal employment. As a result, the working people least likely to have benefits are young workers just entering the labor force, women, and minorities. Women raising families alone are particularly likely to be without benefits because their employment is concentrated in small firms and because they frequently have part-time or seasonal jobs (Mitchell, 1989; Spalter-Roth et al., 1989).

Table 5-5 shows the importance of firm size. Small firms with fewer than 100 workers (which employ 37 percent of the labor force) tend to offer far fewer benefits. The data for medium- and large-sized firms (the Department of Labor definition varies, referring to firms employing more than 250

TABLE 5-5 Employee Participation in Employee Benefit Programs by Size of Firm, 1985 (percentage)

Employee Benefit Program	Employees in Medium and Large Firms	Employees in Small Firms
Retirement	91.0	43.3
Health insurance	96.0[a]	74.7
Life insurance	96.0	58.6
Vacations	99.0	80.6
Paid lunch break	10.0	18.6
Sick leave	67.0	45.8
Long-term disability insurance	48.0	25.6
Child care	1.0	4.3
Educational assistance	76.0	23.0
Employee discounts	57.0	34.8

NOTES: Participants are full-time workers covered by a paid time-off, insurance, retirement, or capital accumulation plan. Employees subject to a minimum service requirement before they are eligible for a benefit are counted as participants even if they have not met the requirement at the time of the survey. If employees are required to pay part of the cost of a benefit, only those who elect the coverage and pay their share are counted as participants. Benefits for which the employee must pay the full premium are outside the scope of the survey. Only current employees are counted as participants; retirees are excluded.

Medium and large firms are generally those with at least 100 to 250 employees, depending on the industry. Small firms are those with less than 100 employees.

[a]Includes 0.7 percent of employees in plans that did not offer family coverage.

SOURCE: Small-firm data from tabulations of National Federation of Independent Businesses survey data by the Employment Benefits Research Institute. Medium- and large-firm data from Bureau of Labor Statistics (1985a).

workers in mining and construction, more than 100 workers in manufacturing, and more than 50 workers in some service industries) are taken from a 1985 survey by the Bureau of Labor Statistics. According to this survey, approximately 21 million workers in the 48 contiguous states were covered. The data on employees in small businesses having fewer than 100 employees are taken from a 1985 survey of the National Federation of Independent Businesses. They show substantially lower coverage in smaller firms. Similar findings have emerged from other surveys, such as those by Lewin/ICF, Inc. (1988), the U.S. Chamber of Commerce (1988), and the Wyatt Company (1988). One exception is the insurance industry, in which smaller firms provide more benefits (U.S. Chamber of Commerce, 1988).

There are also substantial differences in benefits by industry. The textile and apparel industry, for instance, spends 27 percent less than average on benefits as a proportion of the payroll, while the primary metals industry spends about 28 percent more than average (U.S. Chamber of Commerce, 1988). As shown in Table 5-6, the hourly cost of benefits was $5.41 in goods-producing industries but only $3.63 in service industries. Among service industries, the transportation industry spent the most on benefits ($6.74 per hour), while retail trade spent the least ($1.90 per hour).

The U.S. Chamber of Commerce study (1988) concludes that businesses more exposed to competition, whether domestic (retailers) or foreign (textile and clothing manufacturers), tend to offer lower levels of benefits than those with more market power. The reason may be that firms in less competitive industries can more easily pass on the costs of benefits to customers through higher prices. There are important differences even among large firms: among the Fortune 500 in 1985, benefits were found to range between 10.7 percent and 34.4 percent of total labor costs (Employee Benefit Research Institute, 1987).

Freeman and Medoff (1984) found that in the manufacturing sector, after controlling for size, occupation, industry, region, demographic characteristics of workers and wages, union firms on average spend 25 percent more on benefits than do nonunion firms. Their analysis of Quality of Employment Survey data also shows that union members receive 8 percent more in benefits. They conclude that unionization has more effect on benefits than on wages.

Low-wage workers are less likely to receive benefits than those with higher wages. In large measure this results from the concentration of low-wage workers in firms that, for the reasons noted above, provide fewer benefits. The greater relative value of tax-free benefits to higher-income workers is also likely to influence decisions about the emphasis placed on benefits rather than wages. Similarly, low-wage workers show less preference for benefits in favor of wages. Woodbury (1989) found the differen-

104

TABLE 5-6 Employer Costs per Hour Worked for Employee Compensation in Private Industry, 1990

Compensation Component	Goods-Producing Industries		Service-Producing Industries					
	Total[a]	Manu-facturing	Total	Transportation and Public Utilities	Wholesale Trade	Finance, Retail Trade	Insurance, Real Estate	Service
Total compensation	$17.55	$17.33	$13.97	$21.48	$17.45	$8.52	$18.04	$14.41
Wages and salaries	12.14	11.86	10.34	14.74	12.65	6.62	13.35	10.75
Total benefits	5.41	5.47	3.63	6.74	4.80	1.90	4.69	3.67
Paid leave[b]	1.19	1.31	0.96	1.77	1.23	0.37	1.49	1.02
Supplemental pay[c]	0.61	0.65	0.28	0.43	0.46	0.16	0.25	0.30
Insurance[d]	1.26	1.37	0.79	1.55	1.12	0.38	1.16	0.74
Retirement and savings[e]	0.61	0.56	0.39	0.93	0.51	0.13	0.54	0.39
Legally required[f]	1.70	1.54	1.21	2.03	1.47	0.86	1.23	1.21
Other benefits[g]	0.03	0.04	h	0.02	0.02	h	h	h

[a]Includes mining and construction, as well as manufacturing.
[b]Paid vacation, holidays, sick leave, and other leave.
[c]Premium pay for overtime and work on weekends and holidays, shift differentials, nonproduction bonuses, and lump-sum payments provided in lieu of wage increases.
[d]Life, health, and sickness and accident insurance.
[e]Pension and other retirement plans and savings and thrift plans.
[f]Social Security, railroad retirement and supplemental retirement, railroad unemployment insurance, federal and state unemployment insurance, workers' compensation, and other benefits required by law, such as state temporary disability insurance.
[g]Severance pay and supplemental unemployment plans.
[h]Cost is $0.01 or less.
SOURCE: Bureau of Labor Statistics (1990a).

tial between occupations within the same industry group to be much smaller than the variations between different industries and sectors of the economy.

Part-time employees are at a disadvantage with regard to benefits, as several surveys document (Kahne, 1988; Kamerman and Kahn, 1987; Levitan and Conway, 1988; Wyatt Company, 1988). This is probably related to the fact that they usually receive lower wages than full-time workers—in 1987 only $4.42 per hour compared with $7.43 (Kahne, 1988). One survey found that only 15 percent of firms provided the same benefits to full-time and part-time workers. The industries most likely to provide equal benefits are those that employ a large proportion of part-time workers, such as hospitals, banks, insurance companies, and publishers. Among the benefits part-time workers are most likely to receive are health insurance and paid vacations (U.S. Chamber of Commerce, 1988). Because health care and paid time off are particularly important to families, we examine their distribution in more detail.

Health Insurance Coverage

Employer-paid health insurance is a very important benefit, not only for employees, but also for their families. The Current Population Survey estimates that 61 percent (40 million) of all children under the age of 18 are covered by employment-based insurance (Moyer, 1989). In addition, 13.9 million employees receive employer group health insurance as dependents: some of these are young people living at home, but 70 percent are women, most often ages 35 to 54, married and working part time (Swartz, 1989).

Cost, Availability, and Participation

As mentioned, rapidly increasing health insurance costs are a growing problem for employers. They have responded with unprecedented cost containment efforts and by shifting more of the costs to employees. In 1980, one survey found that 72 percent of employees had coverage fully paid by employers; by 1986, only 54 percent of employees had fully paid coverage (Wyatt Company, 1988). Comparable figures for the coverage of family members showed a decrease from 51 to 35 percent. Since 1980, 40 percent of the companies with basic medical plans and 60 percent of those with comprehensive plans had raised deductibles for workers by $200 or more. By 1988, one-quarter of the companies with comprehensive plans also had increased maximum out-of-pocket payments for family members to $3,000 or more (Wyatt Company, 1988). A survey of 178 plans, covering nearly 200,000 members of the Service Employees International Union (1989), found that employees' contributions to premiums for family plans had risen by more than 70 percent over 2 years, double the 35 percent increase for employer contributions over the same period.

As mentioned above, increased per capita costs of insurance have called attention to the cross-subsidy that occurs from large to small businesses when employed spouses are insured as dependents rather than covered directly as employees. Large employers, such as Chrysler Corporation and American Airlines, argue that they are carrying too much of the burden for the health insurance coverage of workers' employed dependents (Swartz, 1989).

As is true of benefits generally, the availability of health insurance varies greatly for different groups of workers. In medium- and large-sized firms, 92 percent of employees have access to some coverage, as do 94 percent of employees of state and local governments (see Table 5-4). There are no substantial differences in access to coverage between blue-collar and white-collar workers or, in the public sector, between teachers, police officers, and firefighters (Bureau of Labor Statistics, 1989a). In contrast, as seen in Table 5-5, small firms provide health insurance for only about 75 percent of their full-time employees. Estimates of coverage for all employees in small firms, including those working part time, range from 21 to 37 percent (Chollet, 1987; Swain, 1988; U.S. Chamber of Commerce, 1988).

Small businesses are less likely to provide health insurance than are larger ones. Among the reasons suggested are the marginal financial position of many small firms and the fact that purchasing health insurance is considerably more expensive for small firms than for large ones—according to Swain (1988), as much as 40 percent higher. Insurance costs can be prohibitive if there are one or more high-risk individuals in the group or if the firm is engaged in what insurance carriers judge are hazardous activities. Firms with high employee turnover or in fields with a large proportion of failures may be unable to obtain coverage altogether. Small firms tend to employ a larger number of part-time and seasonal workers than do large firms. High fixed costs for plan administration add further to premium rates. Small businesses that do offer coverage tend to be those that are profitable and growing and that pay higher wages (Lewin/ICF, Inc., 1988).

Table 5-7 shows that many benefits require substantial employee contributions. In medium- and large-sized firms, 48 percent of employees participate in health insurance plans that are wholly employer financed and 44 percent participate in plans only partly financed by employers. And 31 percent participate in wholly employer-financed family plans and 60 percent in partly employer-financed family plans. Optional coverage, copayments, and deductibles are a standard part of insurance plans. They offer workers choice but pose problems for low-wage workers.

In addition to workers for whom no employer-sponsored health plans are available, there are those who do not take advantage of the insurance that is

TABLE 5-7 Participation in Employee Benefit Programs by White-Collar and Production Employees, 1989 (percentage)

Benefit	All Employees	Professional and Administrative	Technical and Clerical	Production
Paid time off				
Holidays	97	97	96	97
Vacations	97	98	99	95
Personal leave	22	28	30	14
Lunch period	10	4	4	16
Rest time	71	57	69	80
Funeral leave	84	87	86	80
Jury duty leave	90	95	92	87
Military leave	53	61	57	45
Sick leave	68	93	87	44
Insurance				
Sickness and accident	43	29	29	58
Wholly employer-financed	36	22	22	51
Partly employer-financed	7	7	7	7
Long-term disability	45	65	57	27
Wholly employer-financed	35	50	43	23
Partly employer-financed	9	15	14	4
Health	92	93	91	93
Employee coverage				
Wholly employer-financed	48	45	41	54
Partly employer-financed	44	48	50	39
Family coverage				
Wholly employer-financed	31	28	25	37
Partly employer-financed	60	64	66	54
Life	94	95	94	93
Wholly employer-financed	82	82	81	83
Partly employer-financed	12	13	14	11
Retirement				
All retirement[a]	81	85	81	80
Defined benefit pension	63	64	63	63
Wholly employer-financed	60	61	61	60
Partly employer-financed	3	3	2	3
Defined contribution[b]	48	59	52	40
Uses of funds				
Retirement[c]	36	43	39	31
Wholly employer-financed[d]	14	15	14	12
Partly employer-financed	22	28	24	18
Capital accumulation[e]	14	18	14	11
Wholly employer-financed[d]	2	1	1	3
Partly employer-financed	12	17	13	8

NOTES: Because of rounding, sums of individual items may not equal totals.

Participants are full-time workers in medium- and large-sized firms covered by a paid time-off, insurance, retirement, or capital accumulation plan. Employees subject to a minimum

table continues

offered. Two recent studies provide some information about those who are offered insurance but do not participate. A 1987 Service Employees International Union survey of low-wage union members, mainly janitors, clerical workers, nurses' aides, and food service workers at 27 sites in 11 states found that, although almost two-thirds of those surveyed were offered insurance, over half of them, most full-time workers, chose not to be enrolled. Roughly half of insured workers with children had no family coverage. The main reasons given for not participating were the high payments required (averaging $130 a month), high deductibles for family coverage (averaging $500), and no coverage for physicians' services. Respondents indicated they would be willing to pay about $24 a month or 5 percent of their take-home pay for coverage.

The second study (Spalter-Roth et al., 1989) confirmed that low-wage workers and workers in low-wage industries are less likely to be covered. More surprisingly, it was discovered that over 50 percent of low-wage workers and 30 percent of those with moderate wages, especially those who did not belong to unions, did not know whether they had health insurance. Possible explanations are that healthy young workers tend to have a cavalier attitude toward health insurance coverage (Chollet, 1988) and that some workers are covered by their spouses' insurance. It may also be that employers do not publicize the availability of coverage to keep costs down (Spalter-Roth et al., 1989).

TABLE 5-7 *Continued*

service requirement before they are eligible for a benefit are counted as participants even if they have not met the requirement at the time of the survey. If employees are required to pay part of the cost of a benefit, only those who elect the coverage and pay their share are counted as participants. Benefits for which the employee must pay the full premium are outside the scope of the survey.

Medium- and large-sized firms are generally establishments with at least 100 to 250 employees, depending on industry.

[a]Includes defined benefit pension plans and defined contribution retirement plans. The total is less than the sum of the individual items because many employees participate in both types of plans.

[b]The total is less than the sum of the individual items because some employees participated in both retirement and capital accumulation plans and in more than one type of plan.

[c]Plans were counted as retirement plans if employer contributions had to remain in the participant's account until retirement age, death, disability, separation from service, age 59½, or hardship.

[d]Employees participating in two or more plans were counted as participants in wholly employer-financed plans only if all plans were noncontributory.

[e]Includes plans in which employer contributions may be withdrawn from participant's account prior to retirement age, death, disability, separation from service, age 59½, or hardship.

SOURCE: Bureau of Labor Statistics (1990a:Table 1).

In summary, although health insurance is a widely available benefit, its coverage is nonetheless incomplete and is least likely to extend to workers in areas of high job growth, namely among small firms in the retail sales and service sectors. Many workers and families without health insurance have low incomes and include a large number of single-adult and minority families.

The Uninsured

There is growing concern about the millions of Americans without any health insurance. As noted earlier, in 1987 an estimated 13 percent (31 million) had no health insurance (Moyer, 1989). The Congressional Research Service (1988) concluded that the increase in the number of uninsured has been caused largely by changes in dependent coverage. It found that fewer people obtained insurance through another family member's employment, for two reasons. First, employers provided less family coverage. Second, children under age 18, most likely to be eligible for coverage, declined as a percentage of the population, and older children are often not eligible for coverage under their parents' policies. The general belief that the increase in the number of uninsured has been caused mainly by the shift in employment from the manufacturing to the service sector appears to be mistaken.

According to a preliminary analysis of the 1988 Current Population Survey, 80 percent of the uninsured are employed or are dependents of employed people. As shown in Table 5-8, half of these families have a full-time, year-round worker. They remain uninsured in part because so many small firms do not offer health insurance: 39 percent of the employed uninsured work in firms of less than 25 employees. As many as 25 percent live in poverty and presumably cannot afford individual insurance: 65 percent are white, 21 percent are Hispanic, and 16 percent are black (Moyer, 1989).

Additional information on the employment status of the uninsured and their dependents comes from the 1987 Current Population Survey (Swartz, 1989; Chollet, 1988). Of the 16.6 million employed uninsured (including 1.8 million people who are self-employed), slightly more than 50 percent were in retail and service trades, and 43 percent were in administrative, sales, and service occupations. Almost two-thirds of the employed uninsured earned less than $5 an hour. Nonetheless, about half of the uninsured families with at least one employed person live in families with an income above 185 percent of the poverty level (Swartz, 1989). We assume that some portion of higher-income workers who do not have health insurance, especially those in large firms, choose not to participate. Almost half of the 10.5 million self-employed workers also are not covered; the other half have individual coverage.

TABLE 5-8   Characteristics of Employed Uninsured People and Their Dependents, 1987

	Uninsured in Employed Families (millions)	Percentage	Percentage of All Uninsured
Work experience of employed person			
Total	25.1	100.0	80.5
Poor	6.1	24.4	19.6
Above 185 percent of poverty	11.4	45.5	36.7
Full-time, all year	13.0	51.9	41.8
Part-time, all year[a]	1.9	7.6	6.1
Full-time, part year	7.6	30.2	24.3
Part-time, part year[a]	2.6	10.3	8.3
Size of employer			
Under 25 employees	9.8	39.0	31.4
25 or more employees[b]	15.3	61.0	49.1
Average hourly wage			
Less than $5.00	12.5	49.9	40.8
$5.00-$9.99	8.8	35.2	28.4
$10.00-$14.99	2.3	9.3	7.5
$15.00 or more	1.4	5.6	4.5
$5.00 per hour or more	12.5	50.1	40.3
Poor	1.4	5.8	4.6
Above 185 percent of poverty	7.5	29.9	24.1

[a]Part-time workers must work 18 hours or more per week.
[b]This category includes all nonrespondents to the question of employer size.
SOURCE: Preliminary tabulations from the March 1988 Current Population Survey, 17 April 1989. Adapted from Moyer (1989:Table 5).

Moyer (1989) estimates that 12 million children are not covered by health insurance. Many of them live in poor, single-parent families without a full-time worker, which nonetheless are not poor enough to qualify for Medicaid. Even in poor, two-parent families with a full-time worker, 43 percent of children are not insured (Chollet, 1988). In 1985 as many as 3.2 million children in families with a worker who had health insurance were not covered.

The uninsured often face daunting financial barriers to obtaining health care or must rely on public providers (clinics, hospitals) having far too few resources. The 1986 Health Interview Survey found that the uninsured see a physician two-thirds as often as the insured and are more likely to rely on emergency room visits for routine care. There are other serious consequences of the absence of universal coverage. Uncompensated care costs the nation's hospitals about $6 billion annually. The lion's share of this burden is borne by public facilities, because the uninsured are more likely to use public clinics and emergency rooms.

Paid Time Off

As we have seen, paid time off is a significant part of employer-provided benefits. Expansion of leave policies to include universal leave for care of infants and ill dependents is proposed by many as particularly important to working families. At present, leave policies in the United States vary considerably by size of firm, occupation, and industry. Apart from holidays and vacations, paid nonwork time is largely limited to sick leave and disability leave. These are available to 68 percent of full-time employees in medium- and large-sized private firms and 97 percent of those in the public sector (Table 5-4), but far less so to workers in small firms (Table 5-5) (Alpert and Ozawa, 1986; Trzcinski, 1988a, 1989). According to one survey of small establishments, 52 percent did not provide paid sick leave, although they were somewhat more likely to provide paid vacations and may be more flexible about informal leaves (U.S. Small Business Administration, 1987).

There are major differences in the availability of sick leave between white-collar and blue-collar workers and among employees in different sectors of the economy (Table 5-7). Among production workers, only 44 percent are allowed sick leave, whereas 93 percent of professional and administrative employees and 87 percent of technical and clerical employees are. In state and local government, 97 percent of employees are allowed such leave (Table 5-4). Among those who are entitled to sick leave, private-sector employees have more days available per year, especially as they achieve seniority. The average is 15 days after 1 year and 41 days after 25 years. The amount of leave varies for different groups of public-sector employees. Teachers average 12 days of sick leave per year, whereas police and firefighters average 18 days per year (Blostin et al., 1988; Wiatrowski, 1988).

Paid time off is especially important to parents with children when the parents work full time. However, Woodbury's findings that overall pay for time not worked has stabilized at approximately the same level as in the 1960s (Woodbury, 1989) suggests that parents still have relatively little flexibility. Woodbury's findings are based on the U.S. Chamber of Commerce time series, *Employee Benefits*. U.S. National Income and Product Accounts do not report payments for time not worked. Because time not worked includes use of sick leave as well as vacations and personal leave, variations in one category may mask changes in another.

CONCLUSIONS

Nonwage benefits for workers have grown in importance since the late nineteenth century and now account for almost 28 percent of total compensation. Benefits established by law amount to 9 percent of worker costs, mainly for Social Security and Medicare at the federal level and unemployment and workers' compensation insurance at the state level. In addition, five states, having almost 25 percent of all employees, require employers to provide short-term disability programs. These benefits, taken as a whole, provide the core of social support programs that have contributed to the reduction of poverty and increased independence among the elderly and have helped unemployed and disabled workers and their dependents.

Other available benefits—including sick leave, health care insurance, and pensions—are provided by employers, as a result of collective bargaining or voluntarily. The costs of almost all benefits are deductible as expenses to employers. With limited exceptions, the benefits are not taxed as income to employees either. This privileged tax treatment makes them an attractive alternative to wage increases, especially for employees in high tax brackets.

Overall, the availability of voluntary benefits is very uneven. More are received by higher-income than by lower-income workers, by employees of medium- and large-sized rather than small firms, by white-collar rather than blue-collar workers, by unionized rather than nonunionized workers, and by those holding full-time rather than part-time jobs. Rapidly growing industries, particularly in the service and retail sectors in which small businesses dominate, are less likely to offer benefits, in part because their costs are higher for small employers. Among workers, minority women and women raising children alone are least likely to receive benefits.

Two benefits of particular importance to families are health insurance and paid time off. An estimated 31 million Americans have no health insurance; 80 percent of the uninsured are employed or the dependents of workers. Up to 12 million children are estimated to be without health insurance. At the same time, rapidly increasing health insurance costs are a major problem for employers; they have responded by increasing worker contributions for health insurance and decreasing their own contributions to dependent coverage. Benefit reductions cause particular problems for low-income workers. These trends are likely to continue unless health insurance costs stop rising at recent rates.

Many employers now provide paid time off, such as vacations and sick leave, and help maintain employees' income through short-term disability programs. The precise terms of these provisions affect how much time employees are allowed for pregnancy, childbirth, and general family care. Availability of paid time off also varies by industry, firm size, unionization, and occupation. Although precise data are not available, there is ample evidence that many employed women have no access to maternity benefits or any paid leave for childbirth. We conclude that, while the current structure of benefits is substantial for many workers, it is inadequate for others.

The outlook for improvements in voluntary benefits is not promising, in part because of two economic developments. One is that tax rates are now lower, so the advantages of receiving benefits rather than wages are no longer as great. Another is the decline in real incomes. In a period of rising real incomes, employees prefer to increase benefits; when real incomes stagnate or decline, employee demand for benefits slackens. Added to the rising costs of some programs, this does not bode well for further increases in voluntary benefits.

We conclude that, although the growth in benefits over the last 50 years has contributed substantially to the security and well-being of workers and their families in this country, millions of Americans lack access to essential benefits. Others have benefits that are inadequate to meet their family needs. Moreover, the near-term outlook for improvements in voluntary benefits is not promising.

6

New Family-Related Benefits

The changing composition of the work force—increased numbers of employees combining family and work responsibilities—has made employers, unions, and elected officials more aware of the severe problems workers often face in fulfilling both job and home obligations. The majority of employers have taken little formal action to reduce this tension by means such as altered work schedules, special leave arrangements, or new types of benefits to purchase services previously provided by family members. However, a small number of firms have pioneered innovative programs and are experimenting with changes in established programs. In addition, federal and state laws enacted over the last decade have created new rights, entitlements, and tax incentives affecting employee benefits. This chapter describes these developments and reviews research assessing the availability, demand for, and impact of such programs.

EMPLOYER-SPONSORED PROGRAMS

Some very innovative work policies and programs designed to ease work-family tensions are the result of employers' increased attention to the problems their employees face in meeting home and job responsibilities. They are quite varied, ranging from flexible work schedules to new flexible benefits that can be tailored to individual family preferences. Table 6-1 shows the types of benefits offered today. Although the adoption of radically new policies and programs is largely limited to a relatively small number of firms, mainly in industries with severe recruitment problems (e.g., hospitals), employer interest in these policies and programs is widespread.

Management literature over the last decade has reflected increasing con-

TABLE 6-1   Life-Cycle Stages and the Range of Employer-Sponsored Policies and Programs Available

Life-Cycle Stage	Financial Assistance	Programs and Services	Counseling and Information	Time
New worker	Health and dental insurance Disability insurance Life insurance Pension and/or other retirement programs Other benefits	Fitness center Employee assistance programs (EAPs) Health risk appraisals	Wellness and health promotion programs EAPs	Holidays Vacations Sick time Disability leaves Leaves of absence (death in family, other)
Marriage	Spouse benefits Flexible benefits Spouse becomes joint annuitant in pension plan	Spouse relocation Job search assistance for spouse	EAPs	Marriage leaves
Pregnancy and adoption	Adoption benefits Medical coverage for prenatal and postnatal care Coverage for delivery at hospital or birthing center Change in beneficiary Coverage for employee benefits		Prenatal courses Information from benefits manager	Parental leaves of absence Maternity disability leaves Use of accumulated sick leaves Alternative work schedules and job arrangements
Childrearing	Medical and dental coverage for dependents Well-baby care Dependent care assistance plans (DCAPs) Vouchers, discounts Life insurance for dependents	On-site child care Family day care School-age care Sick care Breastfeeding on site	Referrals Seminars Support groups Handbooks EAPs	Parental leaves Flexible work hours Use of accumulated sick leaves Earned time-off policies Sick leave for family illness
Divorce	Garnisheeing wages Stepchildren coverage in medical and dental plans Divorced spouse and dependents can continue medical coverage for up to 36 months (COBRA)	Prepaid legal fees EAPs	EAPs	Personal leaves of absence

table continues

TABLE 6-1 *Continued*

Life-Cycle Stage	Financial Assistance	Programs and Services	Counseling and Information	Time
Elder care	DCAPs Long-term care for dependents Respite care	Adult day care Prepaid legal fees EAPs	Referrals Seminars Support groups Handbooks	Family leaves Flexible work hours and job arrangements Use of accumulated sick leave Earned time-off policies
Retirement	Pensions Retiree health and dental care; life insurance Long-term care 401(k) plans and other before-tax savings plans		Preretirement counseling Newsletters for retirees Telephone hotlines	Part-time employment for retirees
Death	Spouse and eligible dependents can continue medical coverage for up to 36 months Beneficiaries receive life insurance and other benefits Spouse receives at least 50% of remaining benefits	EAPs	Grief counseling through EAPs	Funeral leaves Personal leaves of absence

SOURCE: Friedman and Gray (1989:2-3). Reprinted by permission.

cern about work and family issues. A review of the *Periodicals Index* found a gradual decline between 1959 and 1980 in the number of pages devoted to adversarial techniques and organizational loyalty and an increased number dealing with employee motivation and family life (Kanter, 1983). Another indicator of the new concerns is the frequent addition to employer and employee surveys of questions about new benefits (U.S. Chamber of Commerce, 1987; Bureau of Labor Statistics, 1988b, 1989a). These surveys and the studies based on them provide the basis on which we have assessed the availability of new types of programs and the characteristics of the businesses that provide them. The programs discussed include: paid

TABLE 6-2 Family-Related Leaves

Type of Leave	Definition
Maternity	Leave exclusively for women related to pregnancy, childbirth, or adoption but not tied to the actual length of pregnancy-related work disability.
Paternity	Leave during or after childbirth or adoption for the father.
Pregnancy disability	Medical leave for pregnancy- and childbirth-related disabilties. Disability related to normal childbirth is typically 6 to 8 weeks.
Parental or infant care	Leave after childbirth or adoption for mothers and fathers for the purpose of infant care, independent of mother's disability.
Family	Leave for employee care of ill children, ill spouses, ill parents, or other ill or disabled family members.

NOTE: Any of these leaves may either be unpaid or provide partial or total wage replacement and may provide for continuation of some or all benefits (typically health insurance) and a right to return to the same or a comparable job. The wage replacement may be supplied by the employer or by some other source, such as employer insurance or a state fund.

and unpaid leave, alternative work schedules and locations, family support services, and flexible benefit packages.

Paid and Unpaid Leave

As discussed in Chapter 5, paid time off is an important employee benefit, accounting for a major share of total compensation. It includes vacations; holidays; leaves for military duty, jury duty, funerals, disability, and sickness; and, to a limited extent, personal leave. Recently, much attention has focused on a variety of family-related leave policies, defined in Table 6-2. Such leaves, paid and unpaid, are mainly intended to address the need for time off for pregnancy and childbirth as well as care for infants and sick family members (Saltford and Heck, 1989; Trzcinski, 1989; Zigler and Frank, 1988; Ross, 1990; U.S. Chamber of Commerce, 1989). We describe below the need or demand for dependent care leave and current policies and/or programs to meet that need. This section explains the reasons for the attention this subject is receiving and considers possible new approaches to meet the perceived needs of families.

Scope of the Problem

On average, slightly more than 2 million employed women (2 percent of the civilian labor force) give birth to or adopt a child each year (Spalter-Roth et al., 1989). And 51 percent (1.9 million) of all women with infants (up to age 1) were in the labor force in June 1988 (Bureau of the Census,

1989a). Women working full time in medium- and large-sized private firms and in government are usually able to piece together 2 to 4 months of paid leave for pregnancy and childbirth (with access to some benefits) by using combinations of vacation time and sick, disability, maternity, and personal leaves. As we saw in Chapter 5, however, approximately 60 percent of full-time employees are not covered by short-term disability insurance in medium- and large-sized firms, and in small firms 54 percent do not have sick leave.

In 1989, about 40 percent of women in larger firms had access specifically to maternity leave (others, as noted above, use combinations of vacation and sick leave). Only 3 percent of mothers, however, are entitled to paid maternity leave—the remaining 37 percent use unpaid leave (Table 6-3). An analysis of 1981-1985 data from the Survey of Income and Program Participation found that almost 47 percent of employed women who had first births reported having some type of paid sick leave or unpaid maternity leave that included a job guarantee, compared with 16 percent in 1961-1965 (O'Connell, 1990). Despite this increase, of the 54 percent without formal leave, 28 percent quit their jobs, 20 percent had informal unpaid leave but no job guarantee, 2 percent never stopped working, and 4 percent said they lost their job. From these diverse sources, combined with data on women's concentration in part-time jobs, in small firms, and in industries less likely to have benefits (also discussed in Chapters 2 and 5), we estimate that the majority of women (approximately 60 percent) do not have paid leave for pregnancy and childbirth. Many women may not have access to unpaid leave or a job guarantee, but we cannot estimate the proportion on the basis of the available data. This problem is being addressed in some states by legislation.

There are no national legal requirements for employers to offer any kind of leave to any of their employees, not even sick leave; some employers offer none and others offer very minimal leave. However, voluntarily provided benefits are regulated by state and federal laws. According to the current interpretation of the federal Pregnancy Discrimination Act (PDA) of 1978, passed as an amendment to Title VII of the Civil Rights Act of 1964, if employers with 15 or more employees have a sick leave or disability program, then physical problems related to pregnancy and childbirth must be covered like any other sickness or disability. In addition, some city and county jurisdictions have fair employment laws similar to the PDA governing family leave provisions. In some states, fair employment practice laws extend PDA-type requirements to employers of five or more employees (e.g., California). In Puerto Rico and the five states that have short-term disability laws, all employers are covered (Spalter-Roth et al., 1989), although all do not require the employer to guarantee the employee's job. About one-quarter of U.S. workers live in these jurisdictions.

TABLE 6-3 Family-Related Benefit Programs for Selected Full-Time Employees (percent eligible), 1989

Program	Private Medium- and Large-Sized Firms			
	All Employees	Professional/ Administrative	Technical/ Clerical	Production/ Service
Leave				
Vacation	97	98	99	95
Personal leave	22	28	30	14
Sick leave	68	93	87	44
Maternity leave[a]				
Paid	3	4	2	3
Unpaid	37	39	37	35
Paternity leave[a]				
Paid	1	2	1	1
Unpaid	18	20	17	17
Sickness and accident insurance	43	29	29	58
Family benefits				
Employer assistance for child care	5	6	6	3
Adoption financial assistance	5	8	6	3
Elder care	3	4	3	2
Long-term care insurance	3	3	3	2
Health promotion programs				
In-house infirmary	36	40	35	34
Wellness programs	23	30	25	19
Employee assistance programs	49	57	50	44
Flexible benefit plans[b]	9	14	15	3
Reimbursement accounts[c]	23	36	31	11

[a]Paid or unpaid leave provided to new mothers or fathers for the specific purpose of caring for their child during the early days of infancy. This plan is separate from any sick leave, annual leave, vacation, personal leave, or short-term disability plan that the employee may take.

[b]Flexible benefit plans, also known as flexible compensation and cafeteria plans, allow employees to choose between two or more benefits or benefit options, including cash, in determining their individual benefit packages.

[c]Reimbursement (flexible spending) accounts, which are used to finance benefits or expenses unpaid by insurance or benefit plans, may be part of a flexible benefits program or stand alone (free-standing accounts). These accounts may be financed by the employer, employee, or both. The employee contribution is made through a salary reduction arrangement.

SOURCE: Bureau of Labor Statistics (1990a:Tables 1 and 2).

Additional leave to care for an infant, sick child, or other ill family members was rarely available in the past, although some employers have made informal arrangements to grant such leave on a case-by-case basis. Recently, 15 states have passed some form of parental or family leave laws for men and women; these laws generally exempt small employers, however (see Table 6-4).

The probable impact of a mandatory leave entitlement has been a matter of considerable controversy. The General Accounting Office (1989) esti-

TABLE 6-4   Family Leave Legislation Since 1987

State	Weeks per 12-Month Period	Purpose and Eligibility	Employers Covered	Other Provisions
CT	24 max.	Birth, adoption, medical disability, ill child/spouse/parent	Public-sector employees	Health coverage continuous
	16[a]	(as above)	Private sector, 75+ employees	(as above)
ME	8[a] max.	Birth, adoption, seriously ill employee/child/ spouse/parent	Private sector, 25+; city, town, municipal agency, 25+; all other public sectors	Health coverage continuous but at employee's expense
MD	12 max.	Birth, adoption, foster child, ill child/ spouse/parent/dependent	State employees of executive branch	Health coverage suspended unless employee pays
MN	6	Birth, adoption (mothers and fathers can use concurrently)	21+ employees	Health coverage continuous
ND	avg. 16[b]	Birth, adoption, or foster child, child/parent/ spouse with serious health condition	State employees	Health insurance continuous at employee's expense
NJ	12[a]	Birth, adoption, seriously ill child/ spouse/parent	100+ for first year, 75+ for second and third years, 50+ for fourth year	Health insurance continuous
OK	c	Birth, adoption, terminally or critically ill child/dependent adult	State employees	
OR	12	Birth, adoption	25+ employees	Health coverage continuous

TABLE 6-4 *Continued*

State	Weeks per 12-Month Period	Purpose and Eligibility	Employers Covered	Other Provisions
PA	18,[a] 26 max.	Birth, adoption, serious health condition of any family member	10+ employees	Health insurance continuous
RI	13	Birth, adoption, ill child	Private sector, 50+ employees; public sector, 30+ employees	Health coverage continuous
TN	16	Birth, adoption (women only)	100+ employees	Continuous benefits not required
VT	12 max.	Maternity (birth only), ill employee	Private sector, 10+ employees	Health coverage continuous
WA	12[a]	Birth, adoption, terminal illness of child	Private sector, 100+; local government	Continuous benefits not required 100+ employees
WV	12 max.	Birth, adoption, ill child/ spouse/parent	State employees and county school board employees	Health insurance continuous
WI	6 max.	Birth, adoption	50+ employees	Health coverage continuous
	2[d]	Ill child/spouse/parent	50+ employees	(as above)

[a]In a 24-month period.
[b]Length of leave based on hours worked; 16 weeks on average for full-time employees.
[c]Annual leave, enforced leave, leave without pay, sick leave due to pregnancy.
[d]Any 2-week period during the year.
SOURCE: Adapted from Institute for American Values (1989, 1990).

mates that in one year 60,000 employees in firms of 50 or more employees may need time off to care for a seriously ill child, 165,000 for a seriously ill parent, and 676,000 for a seriously ill spouse; few at present have such leave. An estimated 610,000 employees may have a serious illness, and 60 percent do not have short-term disability protection. The numbers would be significantly larger if smaller firms were included.

Even in states in which family leave entitlements are established by law, there are problems in their use. The Equal Employment Opportunity Commission (EEOC), the agency responsible for enforcing the Pregnancy Discrimination Act, reports that during the last 3 years they received a yearly average of 3,400 charges of employer discrimination related to maternity. Of the average 2,500 maternity cases closed each year during this period, 25 percent were settled without a finding of discrimination but usually resulted in some relief granted to the employee. In about 3 percent of cases, the EEOC found reasonable cause to believe the employer discriminated. Although this represents only a little over a quarter of the cases, it demonstrates significant compliance problems. Also, formal complaints are likely to represent only a fraction of the instances in which discrimination may have occurred, since many employees may not have adequate knowledge of the law, may fear reprisal, or may not want to make the effort to bring a complaint. The EEOC also takes maternity cases to litigation: for example, one Title VII suit alleged discriminatory layoffs and discharges for female employees due to pregnancy. In another, a court action was filed against an employer for not reinstating female employees wanting to return to work after pregnancy (Equal Employment Opportunity Commission, 1985).

There is other evidence of compliance problems. O'Connell (1990), using SIPP data that included over 5,000 women and covered the years between 1981 and 1985, found that over 4 percent of the women reported that they were let go from their jobs because of pregnancy. According to another survey, this one of 200 small establishments in two Northeast communities, one-fifth of firms with fewer than five employees did not provide statutory benefits such as Social Security and unemployment insurance (Kamerman and Kahn, 1987). Trzcinski (1989) found that among 600 Connecticut firms a substantial number offered no maternity or parental leave, despite a state maternity leave statute; no follow-up questions were pursued, however, to clarify what appeared to be violations of the law. Such lack of compliance warrants further study.

The availability of family leave affects men as well as women. An estimated 3.2 million employed men have wives who give birth or adopt a child each year. Approximately 19 percent of men in medium- and large-sized firms have access to paternity or parental leave, but only 1 percent have paid leave specifically for these purposes (see Table 6-3). Leaves for fathers are more common for state employees (Makuen, 1988; Pleck, 1988, 1989). Among New York state employees, for example, all parents are entitled to unpaid infant care leave for up to 7 months, and they may receive up to 2 years at the discretion of the supervisor (Makuen, 1988; Cook, 1989).

The use of leave by fathers even when it is available also appears to be rare. One study found that, among 119 firms that offered unpaid leaves, only nine claimed that any fathers used them (Catalyst, 1986). The reason that men do not use such leaves more frequently appears to be related to the often negative attitude of supervisors (reviewed in Chapter 3). A small number of fathers who feel strongly about using their leave entitlements have filed administrative complaints of discrimination when denied leave (Pleck, 1989).

Data on women's use of leave for pregnancy and childbirth are scant. Use is likely to be determined by availability but also by job demands, attitudes of other employees and managers, and whether the leave is paid or unpaid. According to analysis of SIPP data, 47 percent of pregnant workers reported using leave, with either pay or a job guarantee, for a first pregnancy (O'Connell, 1990). Workers using leave were relatively older, college-educated, full-time employees who worked until their last trimester of pregnancy. Women are less likely to be entitled to maternity benefits for second or subsequent pregnancies because, at that stage of their work life, mothers are more likely to be working in part-time and temporary positions than are women without children, and such positions are less likely to provide maternity benefits. Available evidence suggests that having leave—either paid or with a return job guarantee—increases the likelihood of an early return to work following childbirth (O'Connell, 1990). Low-income women, however, find it very difficult to utilize unpaid leave—especially if critical benefits such as health insurance are discontinued.

Without the guarantee of a position at the end of maternity leave, women are faced with the choice of returning to work earlier than they would like to or than is advisable or dropping out of the labor force. Dropping out of the labor force is the preferred choice for some women and their families. However, the economic costs of a break in employment are high. Using projections from the Panel Study of Income Dynamics (1979-1984), Spalter-Roth and Hartmann (1990) estimate that childbirth and adoptions cost women $31 billion in foregone wages annually. In addition, women terminating employment generally forfeit health insurance and reduce their opportunity to earn pension benefits (Spalter-Roth and Hartmann, 1990; Trzcinski, 1988b); the latter exposes them to greater risk of poverty and the need for public assistance in old age. Both lower wages and job loss result in larger numbers of women in need of public assistance and, consequently, in higher costs for income assistance programs. Spalter-Roth and Hartmann (1990) estimate public assistance costs of $108 million annually for employed women who quit work due to lack of maternity leave.

Impact on Employers

Little research has been done in this country to learn how employers manage when they offer maternity or parental leaves. Available evidence suggests that clerical workers are most often replaced by temporary hires, while the tasks of production workers are generally covered by others working overtime. In the case of managers in larger firms, colleagues tend to take on extra work (General Accounting Office, 1987a; Trzcinski, 1989).

Small firms often claim to experience difficulties, for example, not having enough people to share the work of someone who is absent. In a study of 30 small firms in three states, Butler and Wasserman (1988) found that they had financial and operational problems, as well as difficulties with client relationships. The severity of the problems faced by small employers relates to the length of leave used by an employee.

Costs for various types of leave may include wage replacement, continued benefits for workers taking leave, wages and overtime pay for replacement workers, and perhaps reduced productivity. Very few data are available on the costs of current voluntary leave programs beyond those noted in Chapter 5, although there is some information from states that require paid short-term disability leaves (Berman, 1987). Wage replacements in these states are covered from an insurance fund. In two of the states, employers are not required to contribute to the fund, and in all states there is at least a small employee contribution.

In 1985, pregnancy-related disability claims ranged from 11 to 19 percent of total claims, and the average length of leave was about 10 weeks (Berman, 1987). In New York and New Jersey, average total disability benefits paid were lower for women than for men. In New Jersey, women took 3 more days of leave than men, but benefits went primarily to women in lower-wage jobs. Only 3 percent of women taking leave earned $25,000 or more a year. Governor Kean concluded that the New Jersey program is not a major hardship on employers and "fosters economic survival for low and middle income women who wish to have children" (Kean, 1988).

The data and the studies are far too fragmentary to reach firm conclusions about the impact that mandatory unpaid leave would have on employers and on labor markets. Many large employers already provide paid and unpaid leave. Assuming that the length of job-protected leave required does not exceed current norms (6 months or less), there is unlikely to be an adverse impact on larger firms. In smaller firms, or even mid-sized firms primarily employing women, the effects are less easy to predict. Limited research on existing programs that include small firms suggests that such policies are feasible; however, the impact has not been fully explored.

Alternative Schedules and Locations

Time and space—that is, when, how much, and where people work—provides a basic framework for employment and family life. Most employees in industrial economies have traditionally been expected to work for a particular period, usually 9 am to 5 pm, Monday through Friday. As of 1985, however, only 46 percent of women and 42 percent of men in nonagricultural occupations were found to work a 35- to 40-hour, 5-day week. Some—31 percent of women and 14 percent of men—worked fewer than 35 hours a week; others—9 percent and 26 percent, respectively— worked 49 hours or more (Presser, 1989).

Part-time work, shift work, overtime, second jobs, home-based work, and, recently, flexible schedules are growing (Bailyn, 1988). The downsizing and restructuring of many firms, technological changes, and the growth of the service economy are making these changes both possible and necessary. Flexibility appears to be increasingly called for, if not always implemented, in the new corporate world (e.g., Reich, 1987; Kanter, 1989). It is also a way to help workers meet the conflicting demands of work and family, although not all the effects of the nonstandard arrangements are beneficial to employees.

In a Conference Board study of 500 large employers, 90 percent of the firms surveyed offered regular part-time work and 50 percent offered some form of flextime (Christensen, 1989); 35 percent offered a compressed work week, and almost 20 percent offered job sharing, home-based work, and phased retirement. In the financial services and insurance sectors, flexibility is most likely to be in the form of part-time work and job-sharing arrangements. Manufacturing industries are more likely to offer compressed work weeks, phased retirement, and home-based work. In recent years, hospitals have developed some of the most innovative work configurations to cope with severe shortages in nursing personnel. These include special Saturday-Sunday work shifts of 12 hours each day with pay and benefits equivalent to a regular 40-hour work week.

Managerial work is the least amenable to flexible arrangements, while professional positions may allow for more discretion. Most programs involve technical and less-skilled work, and resistance to flexibility remains strong. "Top management is often reluctant to implement changes; unions hesitate to negotiate new arrangements; supervisors find it difficult to manage workers on flexible schedules; and employees who cannot participate in certain arrangements such as flextime resent those who can" (Christensen, 1989:11).

Part-Time Work

We focus on the issues of part-time work, flexible schedules, and alternative work locations because they are a means of accommodating employees with family responsibilities. Part-time work (defined by the U.S. Department of Labor as working less than 35 hours a week), as well as such nontraditional arrangements as temporary and subcontract work, are all increasing (Belous, 1989; Kahne, 1988). As we saw in Chapter 2, their growth has been greatest in the service sector. Several studies found that traditional part-time work appears to be helpful mainly to women living with employed husbands, particularly the wives of skilled blue-collar workers (Blank, 1989; Moen, 1985; Ferree, 1987), although little research has been done on the extent to which shorter or more flexible hours are valued.

Blank (1989) concluded that the impact of part-time work on wages is less important than previously thought when self-selection is taken into account. Other studies, however, have generally found that low wages and sparse benefits are associated with part-time work; it is therefore a poor alternative for single parents or couples who must rely on wives' incomes and benefits in times of recession and layoffs. In 1987 the median hourly earnings for part-time workers were $4.42 an hour, compared with $7.43 for full-time workers, and not all of the difference is accounted for by individual and job characteristics (Blank, 1989). Furthermore, 84 percent of part-time workers do not receive health insurance as an employee benefit. To the extent that they are members of families of workers who receive health insurance for their dependents, this need not be a problem; it is often serious, however, for the families of the 20 percent of part-time workers who are heads of households, many of whom live in poverty (Levitan and Conway, 1988). The absence of health insurance benefits for these families is very significant. Evidence on the relationship between part-time work, lower wages, and lower benefits comes from such sources as employer survey data (e.g., Bureau of National Affairs, 1988a) and multivariate regression estimates (e.g., Ehrenberg et al., 1988).

Evidence suggests that part-time work also has some positive effects on the family stress problems discussed in Chapter 3. For example, in a Swedish study, mothers' reports of daily fatigue and psychological stress related to the birth of a first child were significantly reduced by both leave arrangements and part-time schedules (Moen, 1989). U.S. studies suggest that negative effects of maternal employment on mother-infant relationships are associated only with full-time work (Hayes et al., 1990).

There are few data available on employer motivation for using part-time workers or on the overall costs and benefits. A Bureau of National Affairs (1988a) survey of 223 members and an earlier survey of 68 firms (Nollen, 1982) both concluded that scheduling requirements, particularly large daily or weekly variations in workload, were the primary reason for hiring part-time workers. Employers report some savings related to lower wages, benefits, and overtime, as well as less absenteeism and turnover (Nollen, 1982). Several studies by economists also found the use of part-time workers related to lower wages as well as industry and size of firm (Blank, 1989). At the same time, employers report increases in admini-strative and training costs and managerial problems for those supervising part-time workers.

Recently, what Kahne (1988) calls "new concept part-time work" has become more common: permanent part-time work (with some job security), job sharing (with two people doing one full-time job), work sharing (often the result of production cutbacks), and phased retirement. There is also part-time work as a temporary arrangement for full-time workers, used to accommodate family care needs. This is part of the life-cycle approach to work, outlined in Table 6-1, which recognizes that people may need such an arrangement while children are young or a family member is seriously ill, but they want to maintain their commitment to return to full-time work. For employees, these arrangements tend to provide job attachment, prorated wages, some benefits, and seniority. Employers are more likely to retain an experienced employee and avoid additional recruitment and training costs. Despite these advantages, such arrangements are among the least frequently offered options. The new types of part-time work do not involve savings through lower wages, and costs tend to be higher. Managerial jobs have proved particularly difficult to adapt to part-time status.

Flexible Schedules

Flextime offers another alternative to standard work schedules. It generally means variations in the usual rigidly scheduled workday. Experiments with flextime in the United States began in the 1970s, and by the 1980s about 13 percent of the full-time and 43 percent of the part-time labor force were on some type of flexible schedule (Bureau of Labor Statistics, 1989a). Government and service workers are more likely to have flextime options than other workers (Mellor, 1986). Table 6-5 shows that the likelihood of a firm's offering a flexible schedule policy—formal or informal—differs only slightly by size of firm.

There is a wide range of possible flextime options. Under flextime, employees choose a starting and ending time, work the standard number of hours per day (most often including a core period such as 10 am to 2 pm) and remain with a chosen schedule for a set period of time. Under compressed time, employees work the standard amount of time each week but do so in less than 5 days. Under maxiflex, employees may vary their daily hours as they wish and are not required to be present for any core period. There is some evidence that additional management and scheduling time are required, as well as some concern about potential employee abuses. Yet several studies find that flexible schedules modestly reduce absenteeism and tardiness, as well as somewhat increase job satisfaction and employee morale, at relatively little cost (Nollen, 1979, 1982; Staines, 1989; Christensen and Staines, 1990; Bureau of National Affairs, 1988a). There is a growing interest in alternative schedules, particularly among large employers (Christensen, 1989).

It is widely believed that flextime would be most helpful to women because they continue to be the main providers of care for dependents. One study suggests that it is helpful to women who are married and have school-

TABLE 6-5   Benefits and Work Schedule Policies Aiding Child Care, 1987 (percentage)

Type of Benefit or Policy	Total	Establishments with 10 or More Employees		
		10-49 Employees	50-249 Employees	250+ Employees
Child care benefits or services	11.1	9.0	15.3	31.8
Employer-sponsored day care	2.1	1.9	2.2	5.2
Assistance with child care expenses	3.1	2.4	4.7	8.9
Child care information and referral services	5.1	4.3	6.3	14.0
Counseling services	5.1	3.8	7.6	17.1
Other child care benefits	1.0	.7	1.6	2.9
Work-schedule policies aiding child care	61.2	62.0	58.1	59.4
Flextime	43.2	45.1	37.7	34.9
Voluntary part-time work	34.8	36.0	32.0	25.1
Job sharing	15.5	16.0	13.7	15.7
Work at home	8.3	9.2	5.6	3.8
Flexible leave	42.9	43.8	39.9	40.2
Other leave or work schedule policies	2.1	1.9	2.9	3.1
None	36.8	36.7	38.1	32.5
Total establishments (thousands)	1,202	919	236	47

SOURCE: Bureau of Labor Statistics (1988a:Table 1).

age children (Presser, 1989), but other evidence indicates that it is of limited help. Flextime cannot solve the problem of those who simply do not have enough time for all their responsibilities (Christensen and Staines, 1990). Also, it is often difficult to find child care for nonstandard hours, such as the long hours of compressed work weeks—normally 10 hours for 4 days (Axel, 1985; Presser, 1989; Hayes et al., 1990). Thus it is perhaps not surprising that analyses of the May 1985 Current Population Survey found little difference in the use of flextime between men and women or parents and nonparents (Presser, 1989).

Alternative Locations

Alternative locations, or flexplace, includes traditional home-based work as well as newer arrangements, such as satellite offices and remote or neighborhood centers. There is very little information available on remote centers, however, and home-based work remains the most prevalent alternative location in the United States. Employees doing clerical and high-level professional work are often linked electronically through computers—an innovation called *telecommuting*.

Like part-time work, home-based work has a long history. It was quite prevalent and controversial, for instance, in the garment industry at the turn of the century. Although it is much less common today, it is still controversial. For some it offers flexibility, but for others it has been a source of exploitation. A U.S. Department of Labor regulation prohibiting home-based work in selected garment industries in the 1940s was only recently lifted, and it is still the subject of litigation. New possibilities opened up by computer technology are largely responsible for recently revived interest, and modest growth seems likely (Christensen, 1989; Boris and Daniels, 1989; Bailyn, 1988, 1989).

About half of today's 18 million home-based workers are self-employed, including the two largest categories, farmers and family day care providers. The remainder are employed by the relatively few companies that offer structured home-based programs. In general, advantages for workers in the latter group include greater control over time, savings in time and money by not commuting, and gaining some flexibility for meeting household demands, though many still have to make child care arrangements, and others work late at night (Christensen, 1988). However, the situation is very different for low-level clerical employees and operatives, on one hand, and high-level professionals, on the other (Axel, 1985; Christensen, 1988; Horvath, 1986).

Home-based operatives are typically immigrant women (sometimes illegal), often Hispanic and Chinese, with few skills, who earn little and receive no benefits. There is evidence of employers requiring long hours and paying low wages in violation of wage and hour laws, just as was true for other immigrants in the early part of this century (Boris and Daniels, 1989). However, Fernandez-Kelley and Garcia (1989) caution about generalizing for all minority groups. They found that, for Cuban women, home-based work was often a strategy for reaching a modest standard of living and reconciling conflicts between economic goals such as earning money and cultural norms against women working away from home. For Mexican women, it tended to be a last resort to stay barely a step above poverty, perhaps the only alternative to unemployment.

In general, unions have been strongly opposed to home-based industrial work for operatives and have fought to keep the ban on home-based work in order to improve working conditions. This is understandable, in view of a history of long hours, low wages, poor working conditions, and the use of child labor. Unions have also been concerned with the difficulty of organizing home-based workers. The recent evolution of home-based clerical work utilizing electronic networks raises some of the same concerns for unions. Nonetheless, the American Federation of State, County, and Municipal Employees (AFSCME) and the University of Wisconsin recently negotiated a successful home-based work project (duRivage and Jacobs, 1989). Clerical employees of the University of Wisconsin Hospital work at home, saving the hospital costly new space, and receive the same base pay, benefits, and promotion opportunities as other workers. Both the union and the employer are involved in monitoring the situation, and the union stays in touch with workers through electronic mail and weekly meetings.

High-level professionals have a far more favorable situation (Bailyn, 1988, 1989; Olsen and Primps, 1984). Working at home appears to be of most benefit to higher-income women who can afford to trade income for flexibility. Even so, the impact on these employees of totally meshing home and work life is yet to be seen. It could lead to a new type of workaholic (Foegen, 1984), as well as isolation, lack of career advancement opportunity, and reduced job satisfaction. Some of these managerial and professional women, like many production and service workers, take these jobs whatever the limitations, because the advantages of being able to work at all outweigh the disadvantages of this kind of work (Bailyn, 1989; Olsen, 1985).

Employers benefit by reduced overhead expenses for space, utilities, and parking. There is also evidence that employees who work through telecommuting may be more productive than their counterparts who work in a central location. However, problems of quality control and difficulties for managers who need to communicate with employees remain. Unless new solutions can be found to resolve some of these drawbacks, further expansion of home-based work is likely to be limited (Bailyn, 1989; Silver, 1989). Therefore, predictions of dramatic increases in flexplace arrangements (Ambry, 1988; McGee, 1988) seem unwarranted.

Legal Constraints

In addition to union and employer resistance to more flexible working arrangements, there is a complex set of federal, state, and local laws that have institutionalized the 35- to 40-hour week and the 7- to 8-hour day as full-time work, with important implications for benefit requirements and overtime payments. For example, the Fair Labor Standards Act (FLSA) imposes a requirement that, except for executives and administrators, overtime be paid to most employees working more than 40 hours during a week and to many employees working more than 8 hours a day. The Walsh-Healy Act has a similar provision for employees working on government contracts of more than $10,000. For government employees, however, flex-time and compressed work weeks can be introduced without triggering over-time premiums. Home-based work is also affected by federal, state, and local laws and regulations such as those governing equal employment opportunity, occupational safety and health, workers' compensation statutes, and child labor laws (Elisburg, 1985).

While the simplest forms of flexible schedules pose few problems, greater flexibility makes legal implications more likely. Like the home-based work ban, these laws were originally instituted to protect workers from excessive hours of work, to provide adequate compensation, and to increase the pool of available jobs. These concerns persist and proposed changes will have to address them, requiring cooperation between management, unions, and government at all levels (Staines, 1989).

Family Support Services

Thus far, we have reviewed programs that enable employees to spend more time or more convenient time with infants, children, and other dependent family members. We now focus on programs that help employees who need to make arrangements for the care of family members while they work. Such arrangements include on-site centers, subsidies for other organizations to provide needed services, vouchers for employees, and the provision of information through referral services, seminars, and supportive counseling. Several unions have recently become active in this area, especially those with large female memberships. Most of the programs are directed toward child care; far less is being done to help with care for elderly or disabled family members.

Dependent Care

Child care centers at or near the workplace are not new. Some work-site centers were established as early as the Civil War. During World War II, 2,500 centers, often subsidized by the government, were available in war industries; the centers were dismantled after the war, despite the resistance of many working women (Auerbach, 1988). Interest in employer-sponsored child care reemerged in the 1960s. Between 1964 and 1972, approximately 18 corporate and 70 hospital-based centers opened. In the early 1970s the Amalgamated Clothing and Textile Workers Union negotiated for one of the first centers established through collective bargaining (Friedman, 1985; Kamerman and Kahn, 1987). In 1989 the Conference Board's Work and Family Information Center identified over 1,000 on- or near-site centers (Table 6-6). One of the few programs serving a broader clientele, the Stride Rite Intergenerational Center, which opened in 1990, will eventually provide care for 55 children and 24 elderly persons. In general, on-site programs tend to be of high quality, often serving as a showcase for sponsoring employers and unions.

While the numbers are growing, the capacity of on-site care is very small relative to need. An estimated 11 percent of establishments with 10 or more employees report providing any child care benefits or services. A mere 2 percent report sponsoring child care programs, and half of those are child care centers. Even for establishments with more than 250 employees, the figure is only 5.2 percent (Bureau of Labor Statistics, 1988a). Large firms, governments, and service establishments (especially hospitals) are most likely to have centers. The Conference Board reports even smaller numbers of employers providing services (Table 6-6). The bureau numbers are higher, in part because local branches of large employers are counted as separate establishments, while the Conference Board would report only one employer. Also, unlike the Conference Board, the Bureau of Labor Statistics includes nonprofit organizations such as child care centers.

At present, some government agencies and public-sector unions in particular are expanding or considering expansion of on-site child care (Cook, 1989). The Internal Revenue Service has announced plans to open 10 new centers, and other agencies are undertaking feasibility studies. In New York, the state and four public-sector unions have initiated the Empire State Child Care system, with 30 centers for more than 2,000 children. An experimental 24-hour center is planned. The parents pay a fee and, after start-up, the centers are expected to cover all operating costs except for space, utilities, and maintenance.

TABLE 6-6   Employer-Provided Child Care Services

Type of Service	Number
On- or near-site child care center	1,077
Hospitals	777
Corporations	200
Government	100
Family day care, school-age child care, sick child care	50
Referral services	1,000
Discounts, vouchers	50
Flexible benefits	2,00
Total	4,177

SOURCE: Friedman and Gray (1989:Table 1); data from the Conference Board. Reprinted by permission.

There are several ways that on-site child care programs can be initiated and operated. One way is for employers to own, operate, and perhaps partially subsidize a center. The Bureau of Labor Statistics estimates that, of those establishments that provide centers, 20 percent are free to employees, 40 percent require employees to pay part of the costs, and 40 percent require the full cost to be paid by employees (Bureau of Labor Statistics, 1988, unpublished data). Alternatively, employers contract with an independent operator, provide funds to employees or to labor unions, or hire a local agency to recruit, train, and license family day care providers. An approach seen as particularly helpful for small businesses is a consortium of geographically close employers who provide seed money for a facility, perhaps underwrite operating costs, or provide a partial subsidy for tuition.

Some employers also make provisions for more specialized needs. One of these is care for sick children, which requires establishing infirmaries, sick rooms in existing centers, or subsidization for in-home nursing services. Another is before- and after-school care, often run in collaboration with school districts or community agencies. A third is some arrangement for children during the summer, perhaps a camp, as well as care arrangements for holidays, snow days, and other times when schools—but not workplaces—are closed. There are also a few experiments providing telephone contact arrangements for children who need assistance when they get home from school (Friedman and Gray, 1989). Two airports are establishing 24-hour centers because of the nonstandard hours of their employees (Presser, 1989).

The Conference Board reports that it was able to locate only 50 employers that provide voucher or discount programs for nonemployer-based care of dependents among the medium- and large-sized firms it surveyed (see Table 6-6). In voucher programs, employers subsidize—either directly or by adding the money to employees' paychecks—whatever child care or elder care program an employee chooses. Some employers, for example Polaroid and the Ford Foundation, limit this benefit to lower-income employees (Friedman, 1985). In a discount program, employers negotiate with a specific provider for a reduced fee (usually 10 percent) and guarantee a certain number of places for the children of their employees. Several national for-profit child care franchises offer discount programs (Friedman, 1985). Because the providers often are large, expensive, for-profit chains, it is mainly higher-paid employees who can afford to take advantage of the benefit.

Although there is no comprehensive study of employer motivation for providing child care, a wide variety of sources provide some information. Surveys suggest that the primary reason for employers to offer child care support is to address problems of recruitment, morale, absenteeism, and turnover, as well as public relations. In general, expense, lack of evidence of positive effects, liability issues, concern about paternalism, and reluctance to interfere with employees' personal lives appear to constitute barriers to expansion of such programs. For example, in a survey of over 1,500 human resource professionals conducted by the American Society for Personnel Administrators (1988), expense (77 percent) and insurance liability issues (76 percent) were the most frequently mentioned obstacles to their firms' involvement in child care. Large companies (500 or more) were the most concerned with liability (81 percent).

There are also questions about utilization. Friedman (1985) estimates that less than 5 percent of workers may have children in need of care arrangements, and some of those may prefer other alternatives. Several centers—for example, two opened by AT&T in the 1970s—closed because they were underutilized (Kamerman and Kahn, 1987).

For the present, the only employers with extensive involvement in child care are those who need to attract women with young children into the labor force and whose employees work during hours when other child care is not readily available. This is particularly true of hospitals, but to some extent also of other service industries. To the extent that projected work force shortages materialize, an increasing number of employers may become involved in child care arrangements.

Resource and Referral Services

The number of employers providing resource and referral services for child care and elder care is also small but is growing rapidly. Such services not only help employees locate care, but they also are believed to increase the supply of care available in the community. In addition, they help people to evaluate the quality of available programs and to select those that meet the differing economic circumstances and cultural goals of individual employees. The Bureau of Labor Statistics reports that about 5 percent of establishments offer such services (see Table 6-5). More than 1,000 companies report providing them for child care and 200 for elder care (Friedman and Gray, 1989).

In general, it is far more efficient for employers to help employees find adequate services than for workers to do so on their own. Most individuals do not have the information needed and lack time to acquire it (Grubb, 1988). Employers can establish their own staff or contract with a community resource and referral program. At times, these programs are also directly involved in encouraging new providers to enter the field by subsidizing training and support programs. One example is the California Child Care Initiative, started by Bank of America: 23 employers and foundations and 10 government agencies joined to create a pool of over $3 million for child care, resulting in over 1,600 additional licensed family day care homes (Friedman, 1989a). IBM contracted with Work/Family Directions to provide a nationwide network of referral services to help with both child care and elder care. About 35 other companies now use that service, which directly and indirectly helped to start 45,000 new child care programs (Friedman and Gray, 1989). A similar initiative was part of the recent AT&T collective bargaining agreement.

As with operating centers, employers must also be concerned with liability issues when they recommend other centers. Efforts to minimize the risk include careful selection of the vendor, offering referrals rather than recommendations, explaining that responsibility for the choice lies with parents, and including disclaimers when appropriate. Quality ratings by voluntary organizations, with small user fees, might help address this problem, but an employer's role in such programs and the potential liability involved in their use remain a concern.

Counseling

Some employers provide counseling and related services for child care and elder care, often through Employee Assistance Programs (EAPs), which are a development from alcoholism programs. Such programs are intended to relieve worker stress. The expanded role for EAPs began in the early 1970s when the National Institute on Alcohol Abuse and Alcoholism launched a large-scale initiative to promote employer policies to deal with alcoholic employees. The broader model was developed on the assumptions that (1) employers would more readily adopt programs designed to deal broadly with "troubled employees"; (2) supervisors should not be placed in a position in which they are encouraged to diagnose the problem of a particular worker; and (3) such programs would be more readily supported by workers if they offered access for self-referral of all troubled employees rather than requiring supervisor involvement (Roman, 1988).

Two unanticipated results occurred. First, EAPs have been adopted by employers at a very rapid rate: according to national survey data, more than a third of the U.S. work force in the private sector now has access to EAPs (Bureau of Labor Statistics, 1989b). Second, EAPs have come to devote a considerable proportion of their resources to family issues. A 1984 study of 439 EAPs in private-sector organizations in six states indicated that family-related problems, mainly revolving around marital conflict and often related to work-family issues, constituted about half the typical EAP caseload (Blum and Roman, 1989). A growing number of EAPs are becoming proactive in providing assistance with child care and elder care and in cases of domestic violence (Bureau of National Affairs, 1988b; Googins, 1988). In addition, assistance rendered for employee alcohol and drug problems also has substantial impact on family members.

Other Family-Oriented Policies

Employers are also addressing other family issues, such as relocation and antinepotism rules. Traditionally, relocation policies, if they existed at all, were concerned mainly with managerial and professional employees and tended only to provide assistance with the sale and purchase of homes, moving expenses, etc. Today, they are more likely to include financial incentives, help with schools for children, and counseling and job placement services for spouses, although it has been reported that these programs are often inadequate (Friedman and Gray, 1989).

Many large companies have policies imposing some constraints on hiring members of the same family, particularly in management ranks, because of concern with problems of bias, family fights, and morale. In an American Society of Personnel Administrators survey, 60 percent of 252 responding companies were found to have some such restrictions. But adjustments in these policies are now being made and, increasingly, more couples work for the same organization (Burden and Googins, 1987; DuPont Co., 1989). Universities, where such rules were once pervasive, have virtually abolished them.

Flexible Benefit Programs

A small number of employers have developed flexible benefit packages, usually referred to as cafeteria plans. These cafeteria plans offer employees a degree of freedom in selecting the benefits most useful for their particular situation. Such plans may also reduce benefit costs. In a typical cafeteria plan, the employer provides a set of core benefits (usually including health insurance, life insurance, disability income benefits, vacations, and retirement plans), and the employees choose either additional coverage in some of the basic benefits (often needed by one-earner couples) or other benefits. These may include child or elder care (more likely to be important for two-earner couples and single-adult families), dental care, or legal services. In some plans, employees choose from several packages of benefits, all with the same total value. As is true of benefits generally, the cost may be borne entirely by employers, employees may be required to contribute, or employees may merely be offered the opportunity to participate through a group plan (Employee Benefit Research Institute, 1987; Saltford and Heck, 1989). Approximately 9 percent of employees in large- and medium-sized firms have access to flexible benefit programs, a proportion that grew slowly over the past decade (see Table 6-3).

While reducing costs is often given by employers as an important reason for turning to cafeteria plans, the evidence on savings is far from conclusive. For example, experience under the Federal Employees Health Insurance System, which annually offers a choice among health insurance plans, has shown that employees tend to shift into plans that provide benefits they expect to use in the coming year. Over time, this undercuts the actuarial base of the benefit plan and drives up costs. Estimating costs and benefits is difficult because of the diversity of plans. One difficulty is that some have higher administrative costs, which may be appreciable for smaller firms (Wyatt Company, 1988).

Case studies have produced mixed evidence about the use of flexible benefits by employees (Meisenheimer and Wiatrowski, 1989). In one bank, 94 percent of employees made some change following the introduction of a plan. Employee satisfaction in this instance rose from 39 percent before the plan was introduced to 87 percent 2 years later. In one service organization, however, 88 percent of employees selected a package very similar to what they already had. In any case, the plans do increase employee choice and are likely to be especially helpful to dual-earner families by alleviating the problem of duplicate benefits.

The most recent addition to flexible benefit plans is the Dependent Care Assistance Plan (DCAP). Under the Economic Recovery Act of 1981, DCAPs make it possible for employees to receive up to $5,000 of untaxed income to cover costs of dependent care. Such a plan can be provided as part of a comprehensive cafeteria benefit plan, or it can be a free-standing Flexible Spending Account (FSA) added to a traditional benefit plan. Employers rarely contribute to the costs of DCAPs and have only modest administrative expenses. They may even save money, because they are not required to pay unemployment insurance and Social Security taxes on the portion of the salary that is tax-exempt. Like all special provisions to exempt income from taxation, FSAs and DCAPs reduce revenues and are of greater benefit to families with high incomes. For example, a $5,000 DCAP is worth about $750 to a family in the 15 percent tax bracket and $1,400 to a family in the 28 percent bracket (Robins, 1988).

There are some restrictions on DCAPs and other FSA plans. Employees must specify anticipated expenditures at the beginning of the year and forfeit any portion not spent. In order to use the funds for child care, the children must be 13 or younger, the care provider may not be anyone the employee takes as a personal tax exemption, and documentation is required. To be applicable for the care of elderly or handicapped family members, the relative must be in the employee's home for 8 hours a day and the employee must provide more than 50 percent of the relative's financial support.

A survey of over 2,000 employers found that 19 percent offered some form of cafeteria plan (Wyatt Company, 1988), and almost 75 percent of those offered a reimbursement account (DCAP). Both cafeteria plans and the dependent care option tend to be available in larger firms and in those with relatively more female employees (Bureau of Labor Statistics, 1987; Wyatt Company, 1988). They are also more likely to be offered to professional, administrative, technical, and clerical employees than to production workers (see Table 6-3). FSAs are also becoming popular with employers and are expected to grow rapidly (Besharov and Tramontozzi, 1988).

While more firms are offering the plans, employees are only beginning to use them. Wyatt Company (1988) found that only 7 percent of eligible employees used DCAPs, and the Conference Board found a range of utilization rates for these programs from 2 percent of Mellon Bank employees to 9 percent of employees at Chemical Bank (Friedman, 1985). The utilization rates are much higher, however (e.g., 25 percent in one company), when measured as a percentage of employees with children.

EMPLOYERS WHO PROVIDE BENEFITS

Large national surveys provide data both on employers who offer family-oriented benefit programs and on employees who are eligible to receive them. Case studies provide further insights into the incentives for and barriers to undertaking these programs, and there is some information on the success of these programs in meeting employer goals. All these data have limitations, however, and little sophisticated analysis has been done so far. For example, establishments are not the best unit of analysis, and there is little information on the adequacy of coverage or the utilization of available programs. Still, a general picture emerges.

The employer characteristics that appear to be most closely related to the provision of family-oriented programs are size, type of industry, the proportion of women employees, unionization, and corporate culture. The characteristics are often interrelated.

Employer Size

Definitions of the size of firms vary somewhat. As previously noted, the Bureau of Labor Statistics defines medium- and large-sized firms as those with at least 50 to 250 employees, depending on the industry. But some researchers define as small those with less than 100 employees (Swain, 1988), while employer surveys tend to categorize firms with 500 to 1,000 employees as medium, and very large firms as those with more than 5,000 employees (Wyatt Company, 1988). However size is defined, the evidence suggests that larger firms are more likely than smaller ones to provide some family-oriented programs: certain types of leave, formal flextime, dependent care support services, and flexible benefit plans (Bureau of Labor Statistics, 1989a; Trzcinski, 1989; Axel, 1985; Friedman, 1989b; Kamerman and Kahn, 1987; Wyatt Company, 1988).

This difference can in part be attributed to the fact that large firms offer more benefits in general and can negotiate more advantageous terms in adding additional services. Some programs, such as flexible benefit plans, require additional administrative procedures, which are more easily handled by large firms. Small firms also have special problems with some programs, such as parental leave and, as discussed in Chapter 5, must pay a far higher per capita cost for some benefits such as health insurance. At the same time, small firms may in some cases find it easier to provide flexibility (Kamerman and Kahn, 1987).

These issues are vitally important because the number of small firms is growing and they employ a substantial part of the work force. In 1988 approximately 38 percent of nonfarm wage and salary workers in the private sector, and 45 percent of women, worked for firms with fewer than 100 employees (Piacentini, 1990). Less than 11 percent of today's employees work for Fortune 500 companies, so often highlighted for their innovative work and family programs (Kanter, 1989). Unless ways can be found for small firms to provide family-oriented benefits without placing an unmanageable burden on them, such benefits will not be available.

Industry and Occupation

The availability of family-oriented programs also varies by sector and by industry. Public-sector employers, for instance, have focused to a greater extent on on-site child care centers, subsidies for other child care services, and unpaid maternity and paternity leaves (Cook, 1989). Private industry offers more time and schedule alternatives, dependent care assistance plans, and flexible spending accounts. Within the private sector, service industries, particularly finance, insurance, and health care establishments, tend to provide more nonstandard hours and family-oriented programs than goods-producing industries; retail businesses in particular frequently offer part-time work (Bureau of Labor Statistics, 1988a). As documented in this chapter and in Chapter 5, occupation is a factor as well: managers and professionals are likely to have better benefits in general than clerical, blue-collar, and service workers.

Women Employees

As noted previously, family-supportive policies are most likely to be available in sectors with a large proportion of women employees and where there is a shortage of skilled employees, such as health care, utilities, and finance. However, in female-dominated industries not facing recruitment problems, such as retail trade, firms offer few such benefits.

Unionization

A number of researchers have concluded that unions in the private sector have not been particularly concerned with work and family issues, because unionized firms do not generally have more family-oriented programs than nonunionized firms (Friedman and Gray, 1989; Axel, 1985; Auerbach, 1988). Others report that unionization is positively related to the availability of pregnancy disability and various parental leave policies (Trzcinski, 1989), as well as standard benefits (Freeman and Medoff, 1984). Kamerman and Kahn (1987) found that unionization increased benefits even among the smallest firms. In any case, other factors must be taken into account. For instance, nonunion employees are concentrated in growth industries. Also, union efforts often have focused on federal legislation as a way to resolve these issues, rather than on bargaining. It must be noted, however, that more family-related benefits were negotiated in 1989 than ever before. New or improved plans addressing family care, for example, were adopted in the auto, steel, and telephone communication industries (Ruben, 1989). Public-sector unions, particularly those in state and local governments, have been in the forefront of negotiating innovative programs, such as the Empire State Child Care system discussed earlier. Even unions with a predominantly male membership, such as the United Mine Workers, are beginning to press for such programs (Scott, 1987). A range of collective bargaining initiatives is shown in Table 6-7.

As discussed earlier, unions have generally been opposed to part-time work, home-based work, and flexible schedules in large part because they are concerned about the potential of such options for the exploitation of workers. At the same time, it is increasingly recognized that such programs offer some advantages to employees, and some unions are reconsidering their positions (Cook, 1989).

Workplace Culture

While not readily measured, the set of norms, values, and informal mechanisms that shape day-to-day life in an organization are likely to be important in determining both the availability and the use of benefits. The tone is most often set by the top officials and tends to permeate the entire workplace. On one hand, workplace culture that rewards innovation and change is likely to encourage trying new family policies; on the other hand, even adoption of family-supportive policies may be ineffective when a negative informal culture keeps employees from using the programs. For example, on the basis of several small studies, Pleck (1989) reports that an unsympathetic attitude on the part of managers and coworkers tends to keep men from using family leaves even when they are avail-

TABLE 6-7 Selected Work-Family Bargaining Initiatives by Unions

Unions	Child Care Centers	Resource and Referral	DCAP[a]	Parental Leave	Sick Child Leave	Family Care Leave	Flexible Work Options[b]	Education/Surveys
Service Employees International Union (SEIU)	X	X	X	X		X	X	X
American Federation of State, County, and Municipal Employees (AFSCME)	X	X	X	X	X	X	X	X
American Federation of Government Employees (AFGE)	X							
National Treasury Employees Association (NTEA)	X	X						
Civil Service Employee Association (CSEA)	X	X						
United Mine Workers Association (UMWA)				X	X	X		
United Auto Workers (UAW)		X	X	X	X		X	
Communication Workers of America (CWA)	X	X	X	X		X	X	X
Amalgamated Clothing and Textile Workers Union (ACTWU)	X			X	X		X	X
United Steel Workers				X		X		X

table continues

TABLE 6-7 *Continued*

Unions	Child Care Centers	Resource and Referral	DCAP[a]	Parental Leave	Sick Child Leave	Family Care Leave	Flexible Work Options[b]	Education/ Surveys
United Food and Commercial Workers (UFCW)	X		X					
The Newspaper Guild	X	X	X	X	X	X	X	X
International Ladies Garment Workers (ILGWU)	X			X	X			X
International Brotherhood of Electrical Workers (IBEW)	X	X	X	X		X	X	X
Association of Flight Attendants (AFA)				X				
Oil, Chemical and Atomic Workers (OCAW)								X
Postal Workers/Letter Carriers (APWU/NALC)								X
Amalgamated Transit Workers				X	X			
International Union of Electrical Workers (IUEW)		X	X	X	X	X		

[a]DCAP—dependent care assistance plan.

[b]Includes options for part-time, flextime, job sharing, and flexible excused workday.

able and that men are more inclined to take leave when a child is born if it is not called paternity leave.

There is a small group of innovative firms and unions, unrelated to size, industry, or sex composition of the work force, that appear to have a supportive culture (Kahn and Kamerman, 1987; Berkeley Planning Associates, 1988; Axel, 1985). These establishments range from large, profitable chemical companies, with a predominantly male work force, to small, marginal firms in the garment industry, with a predominantly female work force.

A key element in creating and sustaining a supportive culture appears to be an innovative leader, either a high-ranking officer in the business, most likely the chief executive officer, or a union president. Lack of top management commitment was a barrier to family-related programs mentioned by half the respondents in the survey by the American Society for Personnel Administrators (1988). Having a tradition of supportive attitudes, frequently tied to the philosophy of a company's founder or location of the establishment in a progressive community, also has an influence (Berkeley Planning Associates, 1988; Axel, 1985). So far, the effect of the policies of one firm on others has not been investigated, but there is evidence that, as in the case of technological progress, others often follow once the ice is broken (Kanter, 1989).

Business Conditions

As discussed in Chapter 5, the provision of voluntary benefits is strongly influenced by the general economic climate and by federal and state tax policies. Firms facing strong competition or experiencing financial problems have incentives to reduce compensation costs. Predictably, these companies are least likely to expand benefits and may attempt to reduce previously offered ones (Auerbach, 1988; Axel, 1985), unless they can bring about offsetting gains. Large and small firms with increasing profits and rapid growth tend to offer more generous benefits (Swain, 1988).

Although new types of employee benefit programs may offer some advantage to the community—for example, increasing the supply of child care, reducing traffic congestion, or just being "good for families"—few employers introduce them solely out of a sense of social responsibility. Employers are likely to provide voluntary benefits, standard or innovative, because they are expected to be profitable. Recruitment is generally the primary reason given. Longer-term interests may include the firms' reputation for good citizenship in the community and judgments about employee morale and performance.

As discussed in Chapter 5, a number of businesses have recently reduced rather than increased health insurance benefits because of the rapid escalation in insurance premiums. In the aggregate, voluntary benefits have not expanded significantly since the 1970s. In an analysis based on U.S. Income and Product Accounts data, Woodbury (1989) found that voluntary benefits grew rapidly between 1968 and 1975—at an annual rate of 5.9 percent. However, the rate of growth fell to 3.1 percent in the late 1970s and actually declined at an annual rate of 1.2 percent between 1980 and 1985. Some firms have devised innovative types of benefits and expanded the total nonwage package they offer to employees. This does not reflect the general national picture, and in the near term it appears unlikely that these new types of benefits will be widely adopted.

Two major initiatives deserve attention. In 1988 IBM announced an extension of its unpaid personal leave of absence to 3 years (IBM, 1988a, 1988b). This leave may be taken for any number of personal reasons but was designed to be particularly helpful in meeting family needs. In addition, the IBM sickness and accident program provides 6 to 8 weeks of paid leave for childbirth. In 1989, AT&T, the Communication Workers of America, and the International Brotherhood of Electrical Workers announced a ground-breaking collective bargaining agreement that extends the newborn child leave for mother or father from 6 months to a year and creates a similar leave program for employees who need time off to care for seriously ill family members. The leave is unpaid, but premiums for health care benefits are paid by the employer for the first 6 months and by the employee for the rest of the time; the company also pays the premium on basic group life insurance for the entire leave (Bureau of National Affairs, 1989).

Recruitment is the primary reason given by employers for offering both standard and new types of benefits. Benefits are particularly important in tight labor markets and in industries competing for highly skilled employees. In one study of 204 employers, more of them ranked attracting talented employees first or second among five reasons for providing child care than any other (Magid, 1983). Retaining valued employees is also a consideration in benefit decisions.

Costs and administrative complications are the most frequently cited reasons for not offering benefits (Magid, 1983; Burud et al., 1984; Axel, 1985; Auerbach, 1988; Kamerman and Kahn, 1987). In a survey of over 2,000 employers, for example, complexities of administration (37 percent) and higher costs (22 percent) were the most often identified reasons for not adopting flexible benefit plans (Wyatt Company, 1988). Equity concerns were also mentioned when benefits are limited to one group. This suggests that a general leave policy might be more acceptable than parental leave, for example.

Business organizations (e.g., the U.S. Chamber of Commerce, 1987) and government agencies (e.g., the General Accounting Office, 1987a, 1989) have attempted to estimate the costs of selected new programs, but efforts to estimate the benefits have been left almost entirely to private researchers. So far, the results of both efforts have been quite limited.

Child care and flextime have received the most attention. A small number of studies that investigated the effects of employer-provided child care (e.g., Milkovich and Gomez, 1976; Youngblood and Chambers-Cook, 1984; Ransom and Burud, 1986) found that absenteeism and turnover were lower among parents who used centers than those who did not. Ransom and Burud (1986) also reported a significant effect on job performance, but Krug et al. (1972) and Miller (1984) observed no significant differences between the two groups based on management ratings of workers. Friedman (1989b) reviewed 17 studies of employer-supported child care and concluded that it is almost impossible to prove any direct effect of employer-provided child care on productivity but found some positive effects on related factors.

For flextime, a preponderance of the evidence points toward improved job performance, but some studies find no effects. In a survey of the early literature, Nollen (1979) reports that improvement in various productivity-related behaviors ranged from 0 to 45 percent. In later studies, Harrick et al. (1986) found that workers on flextime used less leave and reported increased satisfaction with their schedules. However, the only study that controlled for workers' demographic characteristics found no effect of true flextime on absenteeism (McGuire and Liro, 1987). It is interesting to note, however, that reports by managers in German and Swedish firms, where they have had years of experience with family-oriented benefits, tend to be more consistently positive than the research results mentioned above (Galinsky, 1989a).

NEW GOVERNMENT PROGRAMS

Government policies are important not only for what they accomplish directly, but also for their symbolic effect, which influences the general climate in the country. Efforts of federal and state governments to establish and promote programs to help families in general, and families in which all the adults are in the labor force in particular, are therefore noteworthy. Since the 1940s, federal and most state tax policies have subsidized families, especially traditional families. This has been accomplished by providing some tax relief to employed persons for each dependent, including full-time homemakers, through personal income tax exemptions and by permitting income splitting. Aid to Families with Dependent Children (AFDC), the main form of public support for the poor, in earlier years enabled poor women with very young children to stay home. More recently, new tax policies such as the earned income tax credit encourage poor heads of households to work.

Tax Credits and Incentives

Federal tax policy recognizes dependent care as a necessary expense of employment and permits a proportion of the costs of purchased care to be deducted from personal income taxes under the Dependent Care Credit (DCC): 30 percent of actual expenses up to $2,400 for one child and $4,800 for two or more children up to maximum credits of $720 and $1,440, respectively. The remaining costs are borne by workers. Use of the DCC increased dramatically along with mothers' employment: from 2.7 million people in 1976 to 8.4 million in 1985. Although no estimates are available of the tax losses of states, losses of the federal government were estimated at $4 billion per year (Besharov and Tramontozzi, 1988). However, to the extent that additional people are in the labor force because of these credits, tax collections will also be larger.

There has been a general policy thrust in the 1980s toward putting more money into the hands of individuals so that they can make their own decisions on how to spend it. Therefore, tax deduction and credit policies are more prevalent, and fewer tax dollars are put into the direct purchase of services. For example, the amount of federal dollars for child care increased from $1 billion in fiscal 1972 to almost $7 billion in 1987, virtually all of it in tax credits (Besharov and Tramontozzi, 1988; Robins, 1988).

Neither the federal tax exemption nor the credit are refundable; thus, they benefit moderate and higher-income workers, but provide no support to the working poor, who do not have an income tax liability (Marr, 1988; Robins, 1988). Only 3 percent of the dependent care tax credit goes to families in the bottom 30 percent of the income distribution. If the credit were refundable to those who work but do not earn enough to pay income taxes, the share going to the bottom 30 percent would increase to 17 percent (Barnes and Giannarelli, 1988).

Employer-Based Tax Incentives

Several initiatives have also been undertaken to encourage more employer involvement in the provision of services, particularly those related to child care. One was an educational campaign. Between 1983 and 1985 the White House sponsored 33 breakfasts for corporate chief executive officers to educate them about child care (Freidman and Gray, 1989). Another was tax incentives for employers. By establishing Dependent Care Assistance Plans (discussed above), employers can shield up to $5,000 of employees' income from taxation. Conservative estimates put the loss of tax dollars for DCAPs at $40 million in fiscal 1987 and $65 million in 1988; a rise to $150 million for 1989 was estimated because of the expanding use of tax credits (Besharov and Tramontozzi, 1988).

Employers can also take tax deductions for child care expenses, such as on-site child care centers, voucher programs, and resource and referral programs. They can make contributions to qualified tax-exempt child care centers, information and referral agencies, and similar organizations and deduct them as charitable contributions. Finally, under Internal Revenue Code Section 502(C)(9), there are tax benefits for money given to child care centers in which employees' children are served and employees have financial responsibility for the program. Munnell (1989) estimated the present revenue loss from income and payroll taxes because of employer-provided child care at $0.3 billion in 1989; she expects it to rise to $1.4 billion in 1993. A number of states also offer tax incentives for employers, but the amount is relatively small. Although helpful, such credits do not appear to play a major role in employers' decisions to provide services.

Proposed Legislative Initiatives

At this writing there are several modest legislative proposals to further increase tax incentives for employers to provide child care support. One calls for annual grants of $25 million (for 3 years) to assist businesses in providing child care services for employees and, when possible, the community. Businesses receiving the grants would have to spend three times the amount of the grant for services; priority would be given to businesses with fewer than 100 employees (Stephen and Stewart, 1989).

There are also proposals for federal programs with universal coverage, such as child allowances, publicly available child care (similar to the public school system), and national health care, and several states are considering paying family members who stay home and care for the elderly (see Linsk et al., 1988). Fuchs (1988), for example, favors universal programs such as the child allowance programs used in Europe and Canada, which are not tied to employment or poverty status. He estimates the cost of providing all families an allowance of $2,000 per child under the age of 12 at $83 billion annually. The net costs to the federal government would be considerably less than this, however, since the allowance would replace the current personal income tax exemption for children, as well as programs such as AFDC, the Dependent Care Credit, and the Earned Income Tax Credit. Fuchs points out that if the program were financed by a proportional tax levied on all nonpoverty households, the net effect would be to increase women's economic well-being and sharply reduce the proportion of children living in poverty. Under current budget constraints, such a proposal is not likely to be adopted.

Hill and Morgan (1990) believe that what is needed is a "child security system" similar to the Social Security system, funded separately by a small income surtax on every parent for 35 years after each birth. The funds would cover health care (or insurance) for all children from prenatal care through adolescence; there might also be some payments to whoever is raising the children. For intact middle-income families, this system would simply ease the money crunch when the children are young but would not reduce lifetime costs of childrearing. One-parent or low-income families would receive a subsidy.

Equal Employment Opportunity and Family Leave

To the extent that the federal government's equal employment opportunity policies are concerned with the treatment of pregnancy and childbirth, they are important for families. The Pregnancy Discrimination Act (PDA) of 1978, discussed earlier, forms the basis of the equal treatment approach, which views pregnancy-related disability the same as other disabilities. At least in part, then, because of passage of the PDA, the five states (California, Hawaii, New Jersey, New York, and Rhode Island) and Puerto Rico that have established state-run, short-term disability programs or mandate that private employers establish such programs do include pregnancy- and childbirth-related disabilities with their coverage. In addition, 11 states now require employers to provide leave in connection with pregnancy, childbirth, and parenting for mothers and fathers (Ross, 1990). According to the National Association of Working Women, 21 state governments provide some parental leave for their employees.

Some states, however, favor policies that treat pregnancy and childbirth differently from other disabilities, on the assumption that special treatment is required in order to afford women equal opportunity. (For a full discussion of the two approaches, see Williams, 1985; Trzcinski, 1989; Piccirillo, 1988; Ross, 1990.) As of 1990, 12 states required employers to provide leave only for pregnancy and childbirth and not for other disabilities. A state's right to pass such laws was upheld by the Supreme Court in 1987, and a wide variety of leave legislation has been passed since then (see Table 6-4). As a result, families face very different policies, depending on where they live.

Broader family leave policies and programs, including mandated leave, are being considered by the federal government. In 1990 there were five bills in Congress that included both parental leave and maternity leave (Gladstone, 1990). A family and medical leave act recently passed by Congress and subsequently vetoed by the President provided unpaid leave— with a job guarantee and continued health benefits—for workers who need time off to care for newborn, newly adopted, or ill children and for seriously ill parents or spouses unable to care for themselves, and unpaid temporary leave for all workers for their own illnesses, including those that are pregnancy related. Employers with fewer than 50 employees were exempt.

Many private groups have also made recommendations regarding parental leaves. For example, the Yale Bush Center Advisory Committee on Infant Care Leave recommends a 6-month leave to care for new infants, with replacement of 75 percent of salaries up to some maximum for 3 months. Alternative financing mechanisms suggested include a federally or state-managed insurance fund modeled on the New York and New Jersey short-term disability programs and employer-selected private insurance programs such as that required by Hawaii's disability law (Zigler and Frank, 1988). The National Research Council's Panel on Child Care Policy, while recognizing problems for small employers, nonetheless recommends up to 1 year of unpaid leave with job guarantees and health benefits, but offers no recommendations on implementation. This panel was primarily concerned with the healthy development of children and therefore disturbed by the lack of affordable out-of-home care of adequate quality for infants (Hayes et al., 1990).

The potential costs of implementing various family leave proposals—to employers, employees, and governments—vary depending on such factors as whether the leave is paid or unpaid, how expenditures are financed, and employer coverage. Costs also depend on the extent to which employees use such leaves. The General Accounting Office (GAO) (1987a, 1989) has projected the costs of mandating up to 10 weeks of unpaid leave with continued health benefits for the care of new infants and for illnesses of children, parents, or the employees themselves. Assuming some restrictions on eligibility and coverage such as minimum tenure in the firm of 1 year and exemption of firms with less than 35 workers, the additional cost to employers would be approximately $300 million annually.

One critical assumption in preparing estimates is how employers organize work to cover an employee's absence. The General Accounting Office (1987a) examined the practices of 80 firms in two cities. They reported that overall about 30 percent of workers were replaced with little overtime or loss of output. Clerical workers were most frequently replaced, while management and professional women were seldom replaced. When replacements were hired, the cost was similar to or less than the cost of the workers on leave. The GAO concluded that the only major cost was for continued health benefits for employees on leave. The U.S. Chamber of Commerce (1987) estimates the costs of the parental leave portion of similar legislation at over $2 billion, in part because it includes what employers are already paying and in part because of its high estimates of worker replacement costs. It assumes that all workers on leave take the maximum time allowed, that they are replaced, that replacement workers are somewhat less productive, and that they receive wages 18 percent higher than the workers on leave. Frank (1988) estimates a range from $1.25 billion for 3 months' leave at 50 percent of wages to slightly over $5 billion for 6 months' leave with full salary (1983 dollars). The U.S. Chamber of Commerce, however, estimates the costs of parental leave at full pay at $75 billion annually. Very little cost analysis is available on the short-term disability available in the five states that provide it, and there appear to be no cost estimates for instituting these programs on the national level.

The cost of parental leave to employers depends very much on how the plan is structured. If the total cost of leave is borne by the individual employer, the burden could be significant, depending on whether the leave is paid or unpaid, the size of the firm, the composition of the work force, the number of employees who elect to use the leave, and the expense and difficulty of providing coverage during an employee's absence. Most of these costs can be mitigated by using broadly based insurance pools (e.g., social insurance, state disability insurance pools) and providing special exemptions for small employers. As discussed in the next chapter, European countries have devised various leave arrangements that are extremely valuable to families and that have proved acceptable to employers. All rely on social insurance funding to spread the costs and avoid disproportionate burdens on individual employers.

Critics agree that family leave is important but argue that it should be provided only on a voluntary basis (U.S. Chamber of Commerce, 1987). In his veto message of the Family and Medical Leave Act of 1990, President Bush said, "I want to emphasize my belief that time off for a child's birth or adoption or for family illness is an important benefit for employers to offer employees. I strongly object, however, to the Federal Government mandating leave policies for America's employers and work force." Critics further argue that mandated leave would be costly for employers, no matter how it is financed, and some combination of higher prices and lower wages would result, possibly accompanied by higher unemployment and discrimination against employees who are more likely to take such leave.

Policies for the Working Poor

As mentioned earlier, public policy has shifted recently from AFDC to programs that encourage, or even require, participants to seek employment. Work incentive programs are based on research showing that prolonged absence from the work force significantly reduces the likelihood that an individual will reenter the labor market. Thus, for instance, the 1988 Family Assistance Act provides for support for services such as child care and requires women with children over age 3 (or, at the discretion of the state, over age 1) to take a job or participate in 20 hours of training per week. Refundable tax schemes and mandated employer health care, which are also being considered, are similarly tied to labor force participation.

The minimum wage is also an important policy intended primarily to help working people to earn enough to avoid poverty. It has not been successful, however, in meeting that objective, as shown by the fact that 44 percent of the heads of poor households (6 million) were in the labor force, about one-eighth of them full time, year round (Hendrickson and Sawhill, 1989). At the same time, a large proportion of people receiving the minimum wage, many of them teenagers, live in households with incomes above the poverty level (Ehrenberg and Smith, 1982). It is further argued that gains to those who receive higher wages may be more than offset by possible losses for workers unable to find jobs. Hence, the minimum wage remains controversial.

However, there is no consensus on the alternatives to a minimum wage in preventing poverty or on the degree to which the minimum wage should be relied on to provide an income floor for full-time employment. "The failure of work to provide an escape from poverty is inconsistent with the belief that any family that makes a reasonable effort to support itself should not be poor" (Hendrickson and Sawhill, 1989:1).

Expansion of the earned income tax credit (EITC) is one alternative to the minimum wage. Under the recently passed Omnibus Budget Reconciliation Act of 1990 (P.L. 101-508), the EITC provides a credit of 23 percent of earnings up to $6,810 (up from 14 percent in prior legislation) for families with one child. For eligible families with more than one child, the credit will be 25 percent. There is an additional 5 percent credit for a child under age 1 and a 6 percent credit for taxpayers purchasing qualified health insurance for their children. The effect is to raise the earnings of people in low-income households with children—generally thought to deserve the highest priority among poor households—and negative employment effects are expected to be minimal (Burkhauser and Finegan, 1989). However, the benefit is small and not sufficient to bring most eligible families above the poverty line. At the same time, the EITC is costly. In 1987, for example, 7.4 million families claimed the credit, on average $433 per family, which reduced federal tax collections by $3.3 billion (Hendrickson and Sawhill, 1989). It has been estimated that the reductions will amount to $18.3 billion over 5 years (1991-1995) (Stewart, 1990).

Costs are also a major barrier to the introduction of general family or child allowances. Unlike the EITC, they might also reduce work incentives, although less so than welfare programs, because payments continue as earnings rise. Family or child allowances are standard throughout Europe and in Canada. Their universality appears to make them more popular and more acceptable politically than benefits narrowly targeted on the needy (Wilensky et al., 1985). In addition, people are not stigmatized as welfare recipients, and administration is far simpler since proof of need is not required.

In the United States, however, government programs for children are directed to the poor, including the new child care legislation, P.L. 101-508, which authorized $4 billion over 5 years. Under the new child care development block grant program, eligible families must have incomes less than 75 percent of the state median income. Under Title IV-A child care grants, they must need child care to enable them to take a job in order to escape poverty (Stewart, 1990).

Health insurance is a matter of particular concern to the working poor and their employers. As discussed earlier, many employers offer health insurance to their employees, and Medicaid covers some of the poor, but more than 30 million people do not have health insurance, the majority in families that include an employed person. One proposal, the Minimum Health Benefits for All Workers Act (Gordon, 1988), attempts to deal with this situation by mandating health insurance coverage by employers. All employers would be required to provide a minimum level of health insurance for all employees who work 17.5 or more hours per week and to include spouses and dependents unless they are covered by another employment-based plan. This would reduce the number of uninsured substantially. Gordon estimates that the bill would affect 58 percent of employees working in firms with less than 25 employees and 19 percent of those in larger firms. At the same time, Gordon suggests that employment might be reduced, and some full-time jobs might be recast into jobs of 17 hours a week or less, especially in low-wage industries.

The additional costs for insurance premiums are estimated at $22 billion annually for employers and $3 billion for employees. A slight decrease in the costs of Medicare, Medicaid, and other government health benefit programs would be expected, but so would a decline of $2.1 billion in personal income taxes and $2.6 billion in Social Security and Medicare payroll taxes, leading to a slight increase of $300 million in the federal deficit. There would also be some loss to states, because employer contributions for health benefits are tax deductible.

States have enacted a wide variety of mandated health coverage laws, 645 between 1968 and 1986. If employers offer health insurance, they may be subject to requirements about services, benefits, time periods, and people covered. More recently, however, states have been developing objective criteria to measure the social and financial impact of new mandates, mindful of the effects many of the requirements are likely to have on costs; Washington, Arizona, Oregon, and Pennsylvania have enacted some form of impact statement (*Employee Benefit Notes*, June 1987).

CONCLUSIONS

Employers and governments (federal, state, and local), separately and in partnership, have undertaken a number of new initiatives to address the dual responsibilities to family and job of an increasingly diverse work force. New types of programs are being considered. In addition to the standard benefits (discussed in Chapter 5), the newer employer programs include several types of family leave, flexible schedules and locations, assistance with dependent care, and increased choice among benefits through flexible benefit programs. Some of these programs, such as traditional part-time work and home-based work, as well as flexible schedules, also respond to employer needs to meet workload variations, to operate at nonstandard hours, and to reduce other costs as well.

To some extent, employers are also assisting employees in finding and paying for dependent care services, some by providing the services directly, others by subsidizing community programs and offering information and counseling services. Flexible benefit plans increase choice among various options, which is often helpful for dual-earner families.

Nevertheless, many unmet needs remain. For instance, although a substantial proportion of women are able to obtain unpaid maternity leave, the majority of employed women do not have access to paid leave for pregnancy and childbirth-related disabilities, and only a small minority of fathers have paid paternity leave. Furthermore, most workers are not entitled to any leave to care for children or ill family members, and a minority of workers lack even sick leave or disability leave for their own illness.

As is true for standard benefits, family leave, direct services, and flexible benefit programs are least likely to be available to those employed in the low-wage service sector, in small firms, to nonunionized workers, and to those working part time. More flexible schedule arrangements are equally likely to be available to employees in small and large organizations, and traditional part-time work is more often provided by small employers and in the service sector. Unions have traditionally been opposed to such arrangements. New programs have been initiated more often in firms that employ substantial numbers of women.

Development and implementation of new programs by employers and unions, as well as utilization of programs by employees, are affected by individual leadership and the informal workplace culture, in addition to cost considerations. There is tentative evidence that new family programs modestly improve recruitment and reduce absenteeism and turnover, all of which reduce labor costs for employers. There is little evidence, however, relating these programs directly to productivity. Lack of better information about the effects of new programs on productivity and costs is frequently reported by employers as a major barrier to new benefit programs. Concerns about liability are mentioned as an additional obstacle for provision of some services.

Employer initiatives are also influenced by governments. For instance, equal employment opportunity laws, such as the federal Pregnancy Discrimination Act, as well as emerging state and local family leave laws, have increased leave availability. Federal and state tax incentives have encouraged the provision of various dependent care assistance and flexible benefit programs, albeit at a substantial cost to the governments in lost revenues. In contrast, regulations such as the wage and hour laws, while providing protection for vulnerable workers, have inhibited the development of more flexible schedules and locations.

Family leaves are helpful to workers with household responsibilities. For example, there is some evidence that family leave policies increase women's labor force participation and reduce the need for expensive out-of-home infant care. Both paid and unpaid leave have economic advantages for families. However, unpaid leaves are of limited benefit for low-income and one-parent families, who in many cases cannot afford to forfeit income for even 3 or 4 months. These are also the families who experience the greatest difficulty in finding adequate infant care.

Based on such information as is available on both current and proposed policies, the panel concludes that providing short-term paid leave related to childbirth and somewhat longer unpaid leave for family care would be very helpful and need not be unduly burdensome for many employers. It is important that alternative ways of sharing costs continue to be explored to find ways of allocating them equitably among employers, employees, and the community. There is similarly a need to explore various ways to share the costs of other employee benefits, including public and private insurance pools, social insurance, and direct government subsidies. It must be expected, however, that the larger the share of costs to be borne by individual employers, the more the business community is likely to resist expanding or even maintaining the present level of benefits and less likely that a majority of workers will have access to benefits that appear very promising for families.

7

Family-Oriented Programs
in Other Countries

As policy makers in the United States consider ways to reduce the tensions between work and family responsibilities, and especially as they consider the question of appropriate roles of governments, employers, and workers, the United States has the advantage of being able to learn from the experiences of other advanced industrialized countries. The panel is well aware of the difficulties inherent in cross-national comparisons, given the multiple historical, economic, cultural, and social differences among countries. Our focus on policies toward workers' family responsibilities necessarily constitutes a relatively narrow slice through a very complex web of arrangements. Despite the inevitable oversimplification that such an effort entails, we believe that the comparative perspective provides useful insights into the issues as faced in the United States. For the most part, we focus on Western Europe and Canada, which have private enterprise economies similar to the United States. Unlike the United States, however, these countries have extensive family-oriented benefit programs. This chapter begins with an examination of differences in the general approach to social welfare issues between the United States, Canada, and Western Europe.

PERSPECTIVES ON SOCIAL POLICY

Social Insurance Provisions

The countries of both North America and Western Europe have policies and programs to protect and assist individuals and families. As Rein (1989) emphasizes, the support comes from employers and governments. On a country-by-country basis there are substantial differences in levels of assis-

155

tance and how it is provided. These differences reflect the unique history and values of each country.

Germany was the first nation to introduce social insurance. The concept originated in Prussia as part of Chancellor Otto von Bismarck's social reforms of the 1870s and 1880s. Social insurance provided ordinary working people with protection against loss of income due to sickness or old age. The institutional form that Bismarck devised—employment-based insurance—has provided the framework for meeting social needs throughout the developed world. The German social insurance model was soon imitated in several other countries. Emerging labor movements created demand for the programs, and strong, centralized bureaucratic governments had the capacity to provide them (Alber, 1981).

The United States and Canada instituted social welfare programs much later than European countries. Of the many possible explanations, an important one is surely the strong American tradition of individualism (Lodge, 1987). American reliance on individual effort rather than collective security has been ascribed to a wide variety of factors, including the absence of a feudal tradition, the emergence of a democratic political system before the emergence of a strong working-class movement, and the relatively high level of per capita income (Kudrle and Marmor, 1981). It has also been suggested that the early union movement in the United States was not very interested in welfare programs because it was dominated by elite skilled workers who could do relatively well by relying on market forces (Quadagno, 1988). The inception of the United States in a revolution directed against a powerful central government whose economic policies were bitterly resented by the colonists may also have had an effect.

The United States and Canada have also been strongly influenced by the frontier tradition. The self-reliance and rugged individualism necessary to survive in the early days of these nations established an outlook markedly different from that of Europe. Medieval serfs were attached to a manorial estate, craft workers of the Middle Ages belonged to guilds, and laborers of the industrial revolution were crowded into communities or company towns surrounding the factories and mines that came to be the focus of their existence. These populations grew up with an acceptance of communal responsibilities that has remained largely foreign to Americans (Alber, 1981).

In addition, there is a widely held belief that the ethnic and racial diversity of the United States has contributed to the country's reluctance to support public welfare programs. People appear more willing to reduce their own standard of living on behalf of their neighbors, or perhaps their neighbor's children, when they share the same language, the same religion, and the same color. Countries that define citizenship by heredity rather than place of birth commonly adopt generous pronatalist policies when faced with declining birth rates and labor shortages, since these countries are not willing to encourage or even permit significant immigration. An exclusionary view of citizenship is the less generous manifestation of such tightly knit cultures. The United States, a nation of immigrants, has accepted immigration from throughout the world and has relied on that flow to sustain its work force. This may explain the absence of significant pronatalist programs in the United States.

Such historic and cultural differences are extremely important in understanding the differences in the auspices and coverage of social welfare policies and programs between the United States and Western Europe. Although there are very significant differences between policies and programs among European nations, a number of common principles distinguish them and Canada from the United States. The most important is the principle of universality. With some exceptions, the major social welfare programs cover everyone in the country with a relatively uniform set of benefits or entitlements. In the United States, only Social Security begins to approach universality of coverage, and even its benefits are limited to subsets of the total population.

Social Welfare Expenditures

Table 7-1 shows social welfare expenditures for seven European countries and the United States. Most of these expenditures in the European countries are provided through government, the revenues coming either from earmarked payroll taxes or general revenues. The first column shows

TABLE 7-1 Social Welfare Expenditures of Selected Countries in the European Community as a Percentage of Gross Domestic Product

Country	Expenditures		
	Mandated	Nonmandated	Total
Belgium	27.9	1.5	29.4
Denmark	27.6	1.1	28.7
Federal Republic of Germany	26.9	2.2	29.1
France	23.1	5.4	28.5
Italy	22.3	1.0	23.3
Netherlands	29.6	4.1	33.7
United Kingdom	19.5	4.6	24.1
United States	14.1	7.5	21.6

SOURCE: Adapted from Rein (1989:Table 1).

that expenditures on programs established by law—including disability, accident, old age, and survivors' insurance and maternity and family allowances—are dramatically higher in Europe than in the United States. For instance, the Netherlands' share of gross domestic product (GDP) spent on their programs is slightly more than twice that of the United States. But looking only at government-financed or required programs underestimates the amount of spending on such social welfare items.

Many programs established under law in European countries, such as health insurance and old age pensions, are often provided by firms on a voluntary basis in the United States. The second column in the table shows that voluntary spending by U.S. firms far exceeds that in European countries. Overall, while the United States still places last in total share of GDP for social welfare programs, the difference is much smaller if voluntary spending is also counted.

A critical difference remains, however. Universal benefits established by law ensure that all residents have at least a minimum set of benefits and generally result in significant subsidization of low-income workers. Voluntary benefits in the United States are provided disproportionately to higher-income workers, leaving millions of low-income families without.

Lower U.S. expenditures for social welfare programs result in lower overall public-sector spending in the United States compared with Canada and Western Europe. This has important effects on the economy, such as permitting lower tax rates and increasing discretionary income for most households. Budget data for 13 advanced industrialized countries are shown in Table 7-2. In terms of expenditures by the central government only, the United States ranks eleventh, lower than all except Canada and Switzerland. When local, state, regional, and provincial governments are included, it ranks thirteenth. As shown in column 4, defense is a larger percentage of government expenditures for the United States than for any of the other countries. U.S. defense expenditures account for about 26 percent of the federal budget—twice as high in the United States as in the United Kingdom. Nondefense expenditures for the other 12 countries average 48 percent of GDP, compared with 31 percent in the United States. Even when higher U.S. defense expenditures are taken into account, total public-sector spending is still lower than in the comparison countries.

The tax structure in the United States differs in some respects from that of the European countries as well. While international comparisons of tax structures are complex (Messere and Owens, 1987), some general comparisons can be made. The U.S. reliance on payroll taxes for about 30 percent of federal revenues is about the same as the average for the other 12 countries. The 9 percent collected from corporate income taxes is marginally above the average of 7 percent. The 43 percent collected in personal income tax, however, is about double the average for the European countries,

TABLE 7-2   Government Expenditures in Western Europe, Canada, and the United States, 1986

Country	Government Expenditures as a Percentage of GDP[a]		General Civilian	Defense as a Percentage of Central Expenditures[b]
	Central[c]	General[d]		
Belgium	4.0 (prelim.)	58.0 (prelim.)	55.0	5.0 (prelim.)
Canada	23.2	47.3	45.4	8.0
Denmark	41.2 (1985)	59.5 (1984)	57.5	5.1
Federal Republic of Germany	30.5 (prelim.)	48.1 (prelim.)	47.2	8.9
Finland	31.4	43.6	40.2	5.3
France	45.1	49.9 (prelim.)	40.9	6.3 (1985)
Italy	51.3	49.8 (1984)	48.3	3.1
Netherlands	53.8	61.9	59.0	5.2
Norway	41.1 (prelim.)	54.1	51.0	8.0
Sweden	45.0	61.7	58.7	6.5
Switzerland	21.4 (1984)	38.0 (1984)	35.9 (1984)	10.3 (1984)
United Kingdom	39.9	43.8	38.6	13.2
United States	25.0	37.4	31.0	25.8
Average, excluding U.S.	39.8	51.3	48.1	7.1

[a]Government expenditures and lending minus repayments.
[b]These expenditures, calculated by subtracting defense expenditures from expenditures as percent of GDP, are not limited to social welfare programs.
[c]From 1988 Yearbook.
[d]Includes central plus local, state, regional, or provincial.
SOURCE: Adapted from International Monetary Fund (1989:58, 92, 94, 112).

although only slightly above the 40 percent collected by Canada. The difference is more than compensated for by the 29 percent of taxes on goods and services and 18 percent value-added taxes raised by the European nations, compared with less than 4 percent in excise taxes in the United States and general sales taxes that vary between 0 and 8 percent among states (International Monetary Fund, 1988). The relatively low level of government expenditures and the reliance on income tax in the United States may be more than coincidental. Wilensky (1976) argues that opposition to government expenditures tends to be greater when a country relies heavily on "painfully visible" taxes, but it is not related to the level of taxation per se.

Overall, taxes as a proportion of the GDP are lower in the United States than in eight of the other countries (except Canada, Finland, Norway, and Switzerland), substantially so in most cases. So even though individual income taxes provide a larger share of revenue in the United States, they do not necessarily constitute as large a burden, especially since the 1986 tax reform, when the top tax bracket was reduced to 32 percent; it is as high as 75 percent in Sweden. Similarly, corporate income taxes and payroll taxes are relatively low in the United States (Pechman, 1988). As for sales and value-added taxes, which in the last analysis are also borne by individuals and businesses, they are very much smaller in the United States as a proportion of total taxes and even more so as a proportion of GDP. Higher total taxes in many of the European countries are in part the result of extensive social welfare and labor market programs. The next section describes specific policies and programs. We return later to the question of the effects of the higher taxes and larger social welfare expenditures on the economy and on the quality of life.

PROGRAMS ESTABLISHED BY LAW

Holidays and Vacations

Working people in Western Europe have more paid time off from work than do their counterparts in the United States. All countries in Western Europe, with the exception of the United Kingdom, stipulate a legal minimum vacation period, usually 3 to 5 weeks starting with the first year of employment. Table 7-3 provides this information for most of the Organisa-

TABLE 7-3 Mandated Public Holidays and Annual Leave in Countries of the Organisation for Economic Cooperation and Development

Country	Public Holidays (1980)	Annual Leave (1983)
Belgium	10	24
Denmark	9.5	30
Federal Republic of Germany	11-13	18
France	10	30
Italy	9-10	20-26 (1978)
Netherlands	8	15-18
Norway	9 (1978)	20
Sweden	10	25
United Kingdom	8	15-20

SOURCES: Data on public holidays, Organisation for Economic Cooperation and Development (1986); on annual leave, Organisation for Economic Cooperation and Development (1983).

tion for Economic Cooperation and Development (OECD) countries. Holidays vary from 8 in the Netherlands and the United Kingdom to 11 to 13 in West Germany (varying by region); annual leave varies from 15 to 18 days in the Netherlands to 30 in Denmark. Collective bargaining agreements often extend vacation time beyond the statutory requirements.

From the point of view of businesses, paying employees for time not worked amounts to an increase in the wage rate, which may or may not be compensated for by increased morale and productivity. Since additional free time, unlike additional income, is not taxed, it is an attractive alternative for employees. Also, when holidays are official nationwide, no one has to worry about competitors staying open.

In comparison, vacations in the United States average 9 days after 1 year of employment, 13 days after 5 years, and 16 days after 10 years (Andrews, 1988). There are no mandatory national public holidays and no legal requirement that employees be given vacation time. Individual states declare public holidays, but this does not mean that all nonessential businesses have to close.

Maternity and Family Leaves

The concept of maternity leave is so widely accepted that, of the 118 countries covered in a survey by the International Labour Organisation (1985), only the United States lacked any national legislation regarding maternity rights and benefits. Maternity leaves date as far back as 1878 in Germany, 1928 in France, and 1937 in Denmark, Finland, and Sweden; other countries instituted them after World War II. Although specific provisions vary from nation to nation, all European plans contain three basic elements: entitlement to a specified period of time away from work before and after the birth, cash benefits payable during the leave period, and protection of job rights.

The European policies were developed in response to varied national concerns, and the policies and programs reflect these differences. Maternity leaves reflect an interest in the well-being of mothers and infants but also, in times of low fertility and labor shortages, an effort to encourage employed women both to have more children and to remain in the labor force. Questions raised by some experts about the effects of full-time day care for infants (and the high cost of such care) have motivated leaves so that parents can stay at home with infants (Kamerman, 1988). Maternal care of infants is so strongly endorsed in the Federal Republic of Germany, for example, that mothers are not only provided with paid leave but are actually forbidden to work in the 8 weeks following childbirth.

While there are significant differences in leave provisions among European countries, in all cases policies are more generous than those in the

United States (Kamerman, 1988; Moss, 1988; Zigler and Frank, 1988). Sweden offers the most extensive leave, with the most generous payments, funded through the social insurance system. When both parents have been gainfully employed at least 180 days, the couple is entitled to share 270 days of leave at 90 percent of their regular pay, an additional 90 days of leave paid at a flat rate by the employer, and up to 18 months of leave without pay. The leave need not be taken all at once; it can be distributed over the first 4 years of a child's life. Upon returning to work, the employee is entitled to the same or an equivalent position (U.S. Department of Health and Human Services, 1985). Parents may also use up to 90 days of leave a year to care for a sick child and 2 days of paid leave to visit a center or school (Galinsky, 1989a).

In the Federal Republic of Germany women are entitled to a paid leave of 6 weeks before and 8 weeks after childbirth, the latter to be extended in case of a premature birth. The health insurance fund pays part of the wage, and employers must contribute the rest, but companies with fewer than 20 employees are reimbursed for 80 percent of the costs (Galinsky, 1989a). An additional 12-month unpaid leave for all parents, with an education allowance paid by the government, was instituted in 1989 (Galinsky, 1989a). Among 11 other European countries, Greece and the Netherlands mandate 12 weeks of maternity leave and Finland provides for 11 months; the eight other countries fall between these two points. Also, the three other Scandinavian countries and the Federal Republic of Germany make the leave available to fathers as well as mothers. Denmark, Italy, and Sweden have some paid parental leave, and several other countries have unpaid parental leave that may be taken by either parent up to some specified age of the child.

In most European countries, maternity and paternity leaves at the time of birth are provided through national insurance, but in some cases they are offered through unemployment insurance or special maternity or employment funds. Thus, employers generally do not pay directly; they pay indirectly by contributing to the funds. Either way, however, some direct expenses are added to the costs related to the absence of workers while on leave. Spreading the cost through social insurance mechanisms shields small employers or those with unusually large numbers of young women employees.

Even so, the policies are costly, especially for small employers who may have difficulty in adjusting workloads. However, studies have documented benefits, such as using the temporary opening to provide on-the-job training for a promising lower-ranking employee; Galinsky (1989a) provides an example of this from a Swedish company. To the extent that costs outweigh benefits, the harm done to individual businesses is mitigated by the fact that not only are others in the same country subject to the same rules, but also competitors in many other countries are subject to similar rules. Maintaining rough equivalence in the costs of nonwage benefits within the European Economic Community is a strong concern to the business community (Stoiber, 1989).

The full impact of parental leave for workers is not clear. So far, even when both parents are eligible, it is predominantly mothers who avail themselves of the opportunity to take leave. They are therefore seen as the chief beneficiaries. It is argued, however, that as long as employers expect women but not men to take time off, they will inevitably prefer to hire and promote those who are less likely to inconvenience them. Beyond that, prolonged absences tend to slow down progress in jobs that have career ladders, when others do not take time off. For example, in Sweden women are concentrated to an exceptional degree in public-sector jobs, where the costs associated with prolonged leaves are more easily managed (Stoiber, 1989).

As Pleck (1989) points out, however, the disparity in the use of parental leaves in Sweden, the country that has had the longest experience with them, has declined over time. By the late 1980s about 85 percent of fathers took an average of 8.5 days of the 10-day postbirth benefit. Roughly 25 percent of fathers took more than a month of the regular and special leave during a child's first year, and in any given year 30 percent of fathers with children under age 12 took an average of 5 "temporary leave days" for child care. Thus, the reality is that relatively few Swedish fathers take long-term leave in lieu of the mother's remaining at home, but a very high proportion take some parental leave. There is also evidence, both in Sweden and the United States, that fathers are considerably more inclined to take leave in order to care for children when it is not labeled *parental* (Pleck, 1989). Fathers and mothers in Sweden are equally likely to avail themselves of leave to take care of sick children, both averaging 6 to 7 days a year.

In Western Europe the elderly receive substantial income transfers, so their economic position has improved in recent years relative to the rest of the population. However, there is a virtual absence of specific policies addressed to helping employees who need to care for older members of the household (Committee on Population, 1987), although workers are generally entitled to some personal leave that may be used for this purpose.

Customs and laws with respect to leaves that are available differ considerably. For instance, France requires employers to allow unpaid leave for personal reasons with entitlement to reemployment and seniority and to permit paid time away from work for routine child care needs, as is true in the Scandinavian countries and the Federal Republic of Germany. Currently the European Economic Community (EEC), which includes Belgium, Denmark, France, Germany, Greece, Holland, Ireland, Italy, Luxembourg, Portugal, Spain, and the United Kingdom, is considering legislation permitting both men and women short periods of leave for "pressing family reasons" (Stoiber, 1989).

Longer vacations and the availability of a wider variety of leave policies enable workers to cope better with family emergencies as they arise, even though that is not always the explicit purpose of those policies. Flexibility is particularly important in the case of needs related to members of the family other than children, because only rarely are there specific arrangements for such problems.

VOLUNTARY PROGRAMS

Part-Time Work

Most businesses in the advanced industrialized countries expect their employees to work a standard week. The number of hours and their scheduling may differ from time to time, from place to place, and by type of industry, but they are generally determined by employers; workers usually have little discretion except perhaps when they initially choose a job that requires a particular number of hours. The average number of hours actually worked in nine Western European countries in 1980 varied from 41 in Spain to 36 in Norway and Sweden, compared with 47 in Japan and 39 in the United States (Organisation for Economic Cooperation and Development, 1986).

The most important exception to this pattern is part-time work, which is growing in most industrial countries, for a variety of reasons. This type of arrangement, which may involve working fewer hours per day, fewer days per week, or fewer weeks per year, is most commonly used because it suits the purposes of the employer and is accepted by workers because it is the best opportunity available given their needs and desires. Recently, such involuntary part-time workers have been a small but growing minority (Organisation for Economic Cooperation and Development, 1986). But there have also always been workers who preferred to work less than full time, such as those who combine work and education, older people in transition to retirement, or men who take a second job. A large proportion of the growing numbers of part-time workers, however, are women, and perhaps even some men, who want to combine holding a job with more time for their family.

Table 7-4 shows the increase in part-time employment in recent years and that in most countries a substantial minority of women are part-time workers. Women constitute a relatively low share of part-time workers in Finland and Italy, where few women work less than full time, and in Canada and the United States (Organisation for Economic Cooperation and Development, 1988).

TABLE 7-4 Part-Time Employment in Europe and the United States, 1979 and 1986

Country	Part-Time Employment as a Proportion of						Women's Share in Part-Time Employment	
	Total Employment		Male Employment		Female Employment			
	1979	1986	1979	1986	1979	1986	1979	1986
Belgium	6.0	8.6[a]	1.0	1.9[a]	16.5	21.1[a]	89.3	86.1[a]
Canada	12.5	15.6	5.7	7.8	23.3	25.9	72.1	71.2
Denmark	22.7	23.8[a]	5.2	8.4[a]	46.3	43.9[a]	86.9	80.9[a]
Fed. Republic of Germany	11.2	12.3[c]	1.5	2.1[c]	27.6	28.4[c]	91.6	89.8[c]
Finland[b]	6.7	8.1	3.2	4.9	10.6	11.5	74.7	68.7
France	8.2	11.7	2.5	3.5	17.0	23.1	82.0	83.0
Italy	5.3	5.3[a]	3.0	3.0[a]	10.6	10.1[a]	61.4	61.6[a]
Netherlands	11.1	24.0[a]	2.8	8.7[a]	31.7	54.2[a]	82.5	76.1[a]
Norway[d]	27.3	28.1	10.6	10.3	51.6	51.3	76.8	79.2
Sweden[e]	23.6	23.5	5.4	6.0	46.0	42.8	87.5	86.6
United Kingdom	16.4	21.2[a]	1.9	4.2[a]	39.0	44.9[a]	92.8	88.5[a]
United States	16.4	17.4	9.0	10.2	26.7	26.4	67.8	66.5

NOTE: Part-time work is defined and measured in different ways and covers different situations in each country; the definitions applied in each country are set out in Annex 1.B of *Employment Outlook* (Organisation for Economic Cooperation and Development, 1987).

[a]1985.

[b]Excludes conscripts but includes people for whom hours of work were unspecified.

[c]1984.

[d]Excludes people for whom hours of work were unspecified.

[e]Starting in 1986 the Swedish data are based on people ages 16 to 64. The data for 1979 have been recalculated to conform to the new age span of the labor force survey.

SOURCE: Adapted from Organisation for Economic Cooperation and Development (1987: Table 1.3).

Increases in the numbers of part-time workers are strongly related to the growing numbers of women in the labor force. Other factors also play a part. When demand for labor is slack, for example, a larger number of people can be employed part time, reducing the number of people who are unable to find any work. Thus, part-time employment increased rapidly in some of the European countries between 1973 and 1983, when full-time employment increased very little and in some instances even declined. The Netherlands has particularly favored this approach, which explains the enormous rise in part-time workers in that country. Policies instituted to ease the transitions of workers into or out of the labor market may also encourage part-time employment; this use is more likely in a tight labor market when employers are eager to hire and retain workers. In Sweden, for instance, parents working in the private sector may reduce their workday from 8 to 6 hours, with a corresponding cut in pay, until their child is 8 years old, while those working in the public sector may do so until the child is 12 (Galinsky, 1989a).

Although many part-time workers in these European countries are now covered by employment protection, they nonetheless face lower wage rates, fewer opportunities for promotion, and fewer or no fringe benefits (Robinson, 1979). In the Federal Republic of Germany, for example, trade unions in the chemical industry are concerned that social insurance is not available for employees working less than 19 hours a week (Galinsky, 1989a). It is therefore not surprising that among adults it is mainly married women with other means of support and a strong commitment to what they perceive to be their family responsibilities who avail themselves of this option. Table 7-5 shows the high representation of married women among part-time compared with full-time workers in several countries. Canada and the United States are the exception because a large proportion of part-time workers are students.

Alternative Work Schedules

As noted above, employees in industrialized countries are generally expected to work at specified times determined by the employer. In recent years, however, there has been a good deal of interest in making different

TABLE 7-5   Percentage of Married Women Among Full-Time and Part-Time Women Workers, 1983

| Country | Percentage of Married Women Among | |
	Full-Time Workers	Part-Time Workers
Canada	60.8	62.4
Federal Republic of Germany	50.7	86.1
France	63.0	79.1
Netherlands	38.0	79.1
Sweden	47.4	73.4 (1979)
United Kingdom	56.0	83.9
United States	55.8	56.0 (1979)

NOTE: Part-time work is defined and measured in different ways and covers different situations in each country.
SOURCE: deNeubourg (1985:Table 9).

options available to workers, and in some Western European countries a number of such programs have been implemented. The specific arrangements vary a good deal. Some offer no more flexibility than permitting the regular workday to start and end a bit earlier or later. At the other extreme, employees are expected to put in a certain amount of time in the course of a month or a year or simply to complete assigned tasks and may do so at their own discretion. Some employers expect a firm commitment to whatever schedule is chosen; others permit variations in this respect as well. All of these arrangements are encompassed under the broad heading of flextime (Owen, 1977). Two forms of flextime have received particular attention in the popular media in the United States but are relatively rare in all countries: the compressed work week and job sharing.

Data on the prevalence of more common flextime arrangements are not available because individual enterprises tend to implement such plans quite informally. The first major program to attract attention was at Messerschmidt Research and Development Center in Germany in 1967 (Owen, 1977). Estimates of the proportion of German workers using flextime ranged from 5 to 10 percent of white-collar workers in the middle 1970s, to as high as 45 percent of the labor force by the early 1980s (Nollen, 1982). The figures for other Western European countries are thought to be substantially lower, especially for blue-collar and service workers. The exception is Switzerland, where flextime has apparently progressed most rapidly and was estimated to cover about one-third of all workers by the mid-1970s (Owen, 1977).

The initial impetus to institute flextime came, to some extent, from concerns about rush-hour traffic in congested urban areas (Racki, 1975). Permitting workers to begin and leave at various times helps to alleviate this problem. Since the traffic advantages would presumably be much the same in the United States, there has been some question why for so long there was considerably higher acceptance of this policy in Europe than in the United States. One explanation appears to be the far more positive attitude of labor unions in Europe toward flextime (Owen, 1977). Another may be early studies among the first firms to implement flextime in Germany, which showed considerable reductions in absenteeism and overtime pay (Wade, 1973).

Alternative Work Sites

The emerging practice of flexplace is considerably more controversial than flextime. One interesting aspect of having employees work at home, or at least close to home, is that it is not at all new. On the contrary, it was rather widespread at one time, and is not uncommon in some countries today where so-called cottage industries still exist. There is some evidence of a renaissance of work in the home, often as an economy measure in response to competition from growing industries in developing countries.

As in the United States, most home-based workers in Europe are unskilled women, often immigrants, although firms are beginning to take advantage of opportunities made possible by new technological developments (Lipsig-Mumme, 1983). In such firms, employees are generally highly skilled. One report (Bailyn, 1988) from the United Kingdom, however, suggests that even highly skilled workers will find home work most useful for jobs for which output is critical and for which periods of extended concentration are necessary, but not for the most creative tasks, which tend to require interaction with other people. Estimates of the number of workers involved range from 100,000 to 150,000 for the United Kingdom to 3 million for Italy (Lipsig-Mumme, 1983), where the practice is in part a continuation of traditional home work.

GOVERNMENT CHILD CARE PROGRAMS

Just as the presence of a growing proportion of mothers of young children in the labor market has brought greater emphasis on family leaves, it has also focused attention on child care; the two issues are to a great extent complementary. In countries in which parents can stay home, say, for the first year of a child's life without much loss of income, fringe benefits, and seniority, there is far less need for purchased infant care. In Sweden, for instance, almost all children under 9 months of age have at least one parent at home (Broberg, 1988). According to some experts, this may be a good solution both for children and parents, although there is some evidence that a long leave may have detrimental effects on a person's career (Hayes et al., 1990; Zigler and Frank, 1988).

In general, efforts to make more and better care facilities available in Europe tend to be concentrated on children over age 1. Progress toward this goal, however, remains uneven; nor is there adequate information to what extent various countries are meeting the demand for child care (Moss, 1988; Kamerman, 1988). Estimating the demand for child care is difficult. We therefore concentrate on an examination of the availability and funding of such care and, to the extent possible, its quality.

A number of European countries have significantly expanded the provision of child care for preschoolers between ages 3 and 5 or 6, when compulsory education begins. Such care is seen as a government responsibility, regardless of families' income and employment status. The proportion of children in this age group cared for in publicly funded institutions is estimated to be as high as 95 percent in Belgium and France, 90 percent in Italy, and 85 percent in Denmark. Under these circumstances, very few employers are involved in child care, except in the Netherlands, where there is little government-sponsored care (Moss, 1988). There is little out-of-home care for toddlers in any of the countries or after-school care for older children (Kamerman, 1988).

The French program of "école maternelle," which dates back as far as the nineteenth century, is perhaps the best known. École maternelle is operated as part of the publicly financed education system. All children from 27 months on are eligible, whether or not both parents are employed, although there are not always enough spaces available for children under age 3. Most children attend all day, but parents have the option of sending them only part time. These preschools are popular and highly regarded, although there are often as many as 25 to 30 children per class with only one teacher, a ratio generally regarded as too high in the United States (Hayes et al., 1990).

Similar though often less extensive programs are operated under the auspices of the education systems in most European countries. In Denmark, Finland, and Sweden, however, child care is offered as part of social welfare. Because it is widely believed that Sweden has very high-quality child care centers (Kamerman, 1988), its approach deserves special attention.

As many as 73 percent of preschool-age children receive out-of-home care in Sweden. About 13 percent of children are in private day care because not enough places are available in the heavily subsidized municipal centers, where preference is given to children of working parents, single mothers, and immigrants. Parents pay income-related fees even in the municipal centers, typically 10 percent of wages (Kamerman and Kahn, 1981). Standards are set by the national government, but costs, which are high, are borne by the municipalities. The groups are small, with a high ratio of staff to children, and the facilities are excellent. There are plans for the further expansion of day care programs so that by the early 1990s all children older than 18 months would be guaranteed a place. Since by then parental leaves are supposed to be extended to 18 months, the goal clearly is to provide quality care for all children until they enter school.

Nonetheless, in Sweden as elsewhere, there is much less organized care available for children between ages 1 and 3 than for older children, and existing programs are aimed mainly at families with working parents. Care for toddlers is provided in a wide variety of ways, including, in some cases, subsidies for in-home care, for cooperative arrangements among families, and for family day care homes, as well as some provision of infant care centers or crèches. Generally this care is not free or even heavily subsidized. Thus, parents tend to have the main responsibility for this early period of children's lives, and care of infants by their own parents is encouraged by the availability of leaves and part-time options.

Less attention has been paid to the needs of school-age children when parents' work hours are longer than school hours, or at times when school is not in session (Moss, 1988). There is, however, growing recognition that parents need to be able to take leave in case of children's illness. The most generous provisions are in Sweden, where parents receive 90 percent of their customary wages for up to 60 days per year when children up to age 10 or their caretakers are ill: wage replacement is through the social insurance system (Stoiber, 1989). In the EEC countries, entitlement is for 5 days per child per year, although some collective bargaining agreements provide far more than this minimum. Beyond explicit arrangements for care of sick family members, workers are likely to take advantage of relatively generous vacations and perhaps leaves intended for other purposes when needs arise such as care for children, elderly parents, or other family members.

The existing programs, financed out of public funds, are expensive, but there are substantially reduced direct costs to parents and few direct costs to employers. It must be emphasized that the indirect costs are shared by all employers and employees through the tax system and that tax rates are considerably higher in Western Europe than in the United States.

ECONOMIC PERFORMANCE AND QUALITY OF LIFE

The various programs discussed in this chapter help workers with family commitments to do justice to both sets of responsibilities. They also entail costs, which may include increased taxes, higher prices, higher unemployment, lower wages, or smaller profits. Thurow (1989) suggests that higher compensation for workers in the service sector in Europe than in the United States has led to greater investment in advanced technology, hence higher productivity and fewer service-sector jobs in Europe. Existing data are not remotely adequate to reliably measure the direct and indirect benefits or costs associated with these programs. However, to the extent we can, it is useful to briefly examine the economic performance and the quality of life attained in the most economically advanced countries of Western Europe and Canada, countries that have relatively generous provisions in some or all of these respects, compared with those in the United States. There is no evidence that either good or bad economic performance is directly linked to the particular programs considered here; many other factors are inevitably involved. It is reasonable to suggest, however, that the programs are at least not incompatible with a creditable economic performance.

Examining the limited information available is particularly important because it is often suggested that extensive nonwage benefits and family-oriented policies will have serious detrimental effects on the economy. Opponents of legally required benefits assert that flexibility is the key for businesses facing pressure from international competition and that the free market approach has encouraged job creation, economic growth, and entrepreneurial activity (U.S. Chamber of Commerce, 1987). They further claim that mandated benefits would force companies to decrease output, go out of business or increase prices (Walker, 1988). Recent high unemployment rates in most European countries are generally cited as supporting evidence.

Economic Performance

Our assessment of economic performance is based on about 25 years' data, a period during which many of the current programs have been in existence. A quarter-century is long enough to avoid undue influence by random short-term disturbances. Table 7-6 shows a long-term perspective on expenditures of the central governments of 13 advanced industrialized countries. Between 1960 and 1987, they amounted to 32 percent of GDP in the United States, compared with an average of 41 percent for the other countries. Only in Switzerland was the proportion lower than in the United

TABLE 7-6 Central Government Average Annual Expenditures in 13 Industrialized Countries, 1960-1987, and Net National Debt, 1988

Country	Total Outlays of Government as a Percentage of Gross Domestic Product	Current Receipts	Surplus/ Deficit	Net National Debt, 1988
Belgium	42.2	37.7	–4.5	124.5
Canada	37.1	33.8	–3.3	39.0
Denmark	44.3	43.7	–0.6	24.2
Federal Republic of Germany	42.6	41.1	–1.5	23.5
Finland	34.3	35.5	1.2	-0.2
France	42.7	40.9	–1.8	25.5
Italy	39.8	32.8	–7.0	92.4
Netherlands	48.9	45.8	–3.1	55.9
Norway	42.5	46.0	3.5	–25.3
Sweden	49.3	49.5	0.2	7.2
Switzerland	25.0	29.2	4.2	—
United Kingdom	41.0	37.6	–3.4	38.4
United States	32.0	29.1	2.9	30.6
Average, excluding United States	40.8	39.4	–1.3	36.8

SOURCE: Expenditures and receipts: Organisation for Economic Cooperation and Development (1989c:Tables 6.5, and 6.6); column 3 is calculated from columns 1 and 2; public debt: Organisation for Economic Cooperation and Development (1989a:Table 34).

States. Also, the net national debt (total federal debt minus the amount held in federal government accounts) in 1988 was 31 percent of GDP in the United States and an average of 37 percent in the other countries. At the same time, the annual U.S. deficit of 2.9 percent of GDP has been substantially larger than the average of 1.3 percent in the other countries. It should be noted, however, that there is a wide range among the latter and the United States ranks sixth among the 13 countries.

Table 7-7 shows several of the most generally accepted indicators of economic performance, frequently used when economists attempt to compare the success of economic systems (Gardner, 1988; Schnitzer and Nordyke, 1983). The first of these is per capita GDP, widely regarded as the best single measure of economic success; estimates, however, tend to be unreliable. Apart from the general problems of unreliable valuation of government services and of the output of the informal sector of the economy, there are additional difficulties when all data have to be expressed in terms of a common currency in order to make comparisons possible. Moreover, there are substantial differences depending on which measure is used: gross national product (GNP) is the value of new goods and services produced by domestic factors of production, and gross domestic product (GDP) is the value of new goods and services produced within the country. Thus, for instance, the United States ranks second in GNP per capita, behind Switzerland (International Bank for Reconstruction and Development, 1988), but fifth in GDP per capita, as shown in the table.

Other indicators are also of some interest. The United States had a higher level of unemployment than any of the other countries except Canada and Italy between 1960 and 1987, but it has been about average in this respect between 1980 and 1987. The United States has done even better in terms of job creation, in part related to its large population increase. The United States ranked tenth in growth of hourly earnings in manufacturing. The annual rate of inflation between 1960 and 1987 in the United States of 5.1 percent compares very favorably with the average of 6.4 percent in the other countries. Because opponents of more generous social welfare programs tend to emphasize the importance of international competitiveness, it is particularly noteworthy that the United States had a less favorable balance of trade than all but two of the other countries.

Quality of Life

Quality of life is even more difficult to gauge than economic performance; nonetheless, it is instructive to look at some widely used indicators. Table 7-8 provides ownership data for three items that are likely to be representative of consumer durables in general, as well as data on hours worked per week. As the table shows, the United States ranks high in

TABLE 7-7 Selected Economic Performance Indicators in 13 Industrialized Countries

Country	GDP per Capita (U.S.$), 1987	Growth in Real GDP per Person Employed		Growth in Hourly Earnings in Manufacturing, 1979-1987	Unemployment Rate		Rate of Inflation, CPI		International Trade Balance as a Percentage of GDP	
		1960-1987	1979-1987		1960-1987	1980-1987	1960-1987	1980-1987	1960-1987	1980-1987
Belgium	14,071	3.0	1.8	5.5	5.5	11.2	5.2	5.5	0.4	0.9
Canada	16,019	1.8	1.1	6.4	6.8	9.7	5.6	7.0	0.9	2.2
Denmark	19,730	2.2[a]	1.0	7.6	3.9[b]	8.3	7.6	7.4	-1.2	0.6
F.R. Germany	18,280	3.1	1.5	4.3	3.1	6.9	3.6	3.1	2.3	2.6
Finland	18,151	3.3	2.4	9.8	3.4	5.1	7.8	7.6	-0.2	0.9
France	15,818	3.4	1.9	9.5	5.0[c]	8.9	7.0	8.4	0.3	-0.2
Italy	13,185	3.9	1.8	17.8	6.7	9.5	9.4	12.5	0.0	-0.4
Netherlands	14,530	2.4	0.1	3.3	4.5	10.1	4.9	3.3	1.4	3.5
Norway	19,756	3.3[d]	—	10.2	1.7[c]	2.4	7.0	9.0	-0.1	4.9
Sweden	18,876	2.6[e]	—	8.3	2.1	2.7	6.9	8.3	0.4	1.4
Switzerland	25,848	1.9	1.4	4.2	—	0.7	3.9	3.4	-0.3	-0.3
U.K.	11,765	2.2	1.8	10.5	4.7	10.1	8.1	7.6	-0.2	0.9
U.S.	18,338	1.2	1.0	5.0	6.0	7.6	5.1	5.8	-0.4	-2.0
Average, excluding U.S.	17,169	2.8	1.5	8.1	4.3	7.1	6.4	6.9	0.3	1.4

[a] 1960-1973, 1979-1987.
[b] 1960-1973, 1980-1987.
[c] 1960-1967, 1974-1987.
[d] 1960-1968, 1973-1979.
[e] 1960-1979.

SOURCES: Organisation for Economic Cooperation and Development (1989c): GDP, Table B; Growth in GDP per employed person, Table 3.7; hourly earnings in manufacturing, Table 9.1; unemployment rate, Table 2.15; rate of inflation, Table 8.11; international trade balance, Table 6.14.

TABLE 7-8   Selected Indices of Quality of Life: Hours Worked and Ownership of Consumer Durables

Country	Hours of Work per Week in Manufacturing, 1988	Number per 1,000 Inhabitants:		
		Cars, 1985	Telephones, 1986	TV Sets, 1986
Belgium	33.0	335 (1984)	461	301
Canada	38.0	421 (1982)	769	546
Denmark	32.5	293	818	386
F.R. Germany	40.1	441 (1986)	640	379
Finland	32.2	329 (1986)	617	480
France	38.7	369 (1986)	608	402
Italy	40.1	355	469	255
Netherlands	37.2	341	621	467
Norway	37.2	382 (1986)	622	348
Sweden	38.4	377	890	393
Switzerland	42.4	402	856	411
U.K.	42.2	312 (1983)	524	534
U.S.	41.0	473 (1984)	760	813
Average, excluding U.S.	37.7	361	658	409

NOTE: Year in parentheses denotes that of most recent data available.

SOURCES: Hours of work, International Labour Organisation (1988); cars, Organisation for Economic Cooperation and Development (1989b); telephones, TV sets, Bureau of the Census (1989f).

ownership of consumer durables, especially automobiles and TV sets. The relatively high level of per capita income no doubt largely accounts for this. Hours of leisure time is another aspect of quality of life. As noted above, the United States has a longer work week than 10 of the other countries. And long hours are generally viewed as a burden, particularly by workers with dual responsibilities.

Great emphasis has been placed above on the level of per capita income and how it has changed over time, because income is crucial in determining the well-being of a population. The distribution of income plays an important part as well, particularly in determining quality of life. Table 7-9 shows that the share of income going to the top 20 percent is about the same in the United States as in the other nations, but the U.S. share of the lowest 20 percent of workers is very small: 5.3 percent of income, about one-fifth less than the average of 6.6 percent for the other countries. Although the greater degree of inequality may be related to the regional variations to be expected in a large country, it is not clear that this accounts for all of the difference.

TABLE 7-9 Income Distribution by Quintiles, OECD Countries, 1975-1982

| Country | Year | Income Distribution by Quintiles | | | | |
		I	II	III	IV	V
Belgium	1978-1979	7.9	13.7	18.6	23.8	35.0
Canada	1981	5.3	11.8	18.0	24.9	40.0
Denmark	1981	5.4	12.0	18.4	25.6	38.6
Finland	1981	6.3	12.1	18.4	25.5	37.6
France	1975	5.5	11.5	17.1	23.7	42.2
F.R. Germany	1978	7.9	12.5	17.0	23.1	39.5
Italy	1977	6.2	11.3	15.9	22.7	43.9
Netherlands	1981	8.3	14.1	18.2	23.2	36.2
Norway	1982	6.0	12.9	18.3	24.6	38.2
Sweden	1981	7.4	13.1	16.8	21.0	41.7
Switzerland	1978	6.6	13.5	18.5	23.4	38.0
U.K.	1979	7.0	11.5	17.0	24.8	39.7
U.S.	1980	5.3	11.9	17.9	25.0	39.9
Average, excluding U.S.		6.6	12.5	17.7	23.9	39.3

NOTE: Data are for the most recent year available.
SOURCE: International Bank for Reconstruction and Development (1988).

Other particularly important indicators of quality of life are measures of survival chances, which are not only important themselves, but are also often viewed as closely linked to level of health and general well-being (Kynch and Sen, 1983). Expenditures on health care in the United States were almost 12 percent of GNP in 1989, a larger share than in any of the other countries, which spend an average of under 8 percent (Meyer and Moon, 1988). The United States does well with respect to maternal mortality, but this is related to the fact that mortality rates are far lower for younger mothers (U.S. National Center for Health Statistics, 1984), and the proportion of women over age 30 giving birth is considerably lower in the United States than for most of the other countries (United Nations, 1986). Infant mortality is higher in the United States than in any of the other countries, almost twice as high as in Sweden and Switzerland. Life expectancy is lower than in eight of the other countries, although the differences are small (Table 7-10).

On balance, it would be difficult to conclude that the quality of life in the United States is as high as one would expect from the relatively high per capita income and large expenditures on health care, although this sketchy evidence is no more than suggestive. One way of summing up the situation in the United States compared with other countries is to say that there are trade-offs: people tend to have a higher standard of living on average, but the poor fare considerably worse; workers have higher earnings but less free time; and people pay lower taxes but receive fewer government benefits.

Opinion is divided as to whether, over the long term, the substantially greater worker benefits in other countries, in significant part paid for by the government, tend to inhibit the achievement of a healthy economy. The data reviewed here suggest that economies are not inhibited by generous worker benefits. As for the poorer performance of the European countries in the late 1980s, it is not clear that this shift can be ascribed to differences in social policy that have existed for a far longer time. The long-term record is consistent with the view that generous social programs have not resulted in an inferior economic performance in the Western European countries compared with the United States. On the contrary, European nations appear to be catching up. In terms of quality of life, the nations of

TABLE 7-10 Indices of Quality of Life: Health Outcomes

Country	Life Expectancy 1988	Infant Mortality (per 1,000) 1988	Maternal Mortality (per 100,000) 1980	Suicides (per 100,000) 1986
Belgium	75.4	8	8.3	22.7 (1984)
Canada	77.1	7	5.0	12.8 (1985)
Denmark	75.3	7	5.8	26.9 (1985)
F.R. Germany	75.8	8	17.2	17.0
Finland	n.a.	n.a	4.8	26.3
France	75.7	9	14.7	21.8 (1985)
Italy	76.7	8	15.2	7.3 (1983)
Netherlands	77.1	8	7.8	11.2 (1985)
Norway	n.a.	n.a	6.7	14.2 (1985)
Sweden	77.3	6	5.2	17.2 (1985)
Switzerland	78.0	6	7.8 (1980)	21.4
U.K.	75.1	9	10.3	9.7
U.S.	75.3	11	9.5	12.4 (1984)
Average, excluding U.S.	76.3	8	9.0	17.4

NOTE: Year in parentheses denotes that of most recent data available.
n.a., not available.
SOURCES: Life expectancy, infant mortality, suicides, Bureau of the Census (1989f); maternal mortality, United Nations (1986).

Western Europe are in many respects equal to and in some respects exceed the United States.

It is worth noting that a number of researchers view the performance of the other countries rather more favorably than we do. For instance, Cameron (1982) concluded that European countries had been more successful in enhancing the functioning of the capitalist system. Wilensky (1983) also points out that their good performance after the oil shock of 1973-1974 is particularly impressive in view of the dependence of many of them on oil imports. These evaluations, however, were based on data up to 1980, and the U.S. performance compares more favorably since then.

CONCLUSIONS

The United States has historically offered fewer social welfare programs than many Western European countries. Employees in Western Europe have more holidays and vacation days, and flextime is more prevalent than in the United States. Most of the countries provide family allowances and extensive family leave, as well as more publicly subsidized child care systems. More leave for parents and more child care services are provided in Western Europe, and coverage is far more likely to be universal, rather than restricted to particular employees and their dependents. Even so, provisions for child care are very uneven, and nowhere is good, affordable care available for all children from infancy on. Moreover, evidence suggests that differential use of parental leave by women may diminish employment and promotion opportunities.

Employee benefits, including vacations and leaves, are generally established by law in Europe and account for a somewhat larger share of labor costs there than in the United States. Government expenditures on related employee benefit programs are much higher than in the United States, which contributes to a considerably higher tax burden for individuals and businesses. An assessment of economic performance measures finds that the United States ranks more favorably than most of the European countries on per capita GDP, inflation, job creation, and very recently on unemployment, but less favorably on central government deficit, growth in hourly earnings, and balance of trade. On selected quality-of-life indicators, people in the United States have more consumer goods but longer work hours. The United States fares well on maternal mortality but very poorly on infant mortality and very slightly so on life expectancy.

While cross-cultural comparisons must be made with caution, the extensive social programs provided by governments in Western Europe, including child care and parental leave, and the heavy tax burden they impose on employers and individuals appear to be compatible with vigorous and growing economies. In terms of the standard of living, Western European countries have been catching up with the United States and in some respects have even overtaken it. This conclusion does not imply that blind imitation of their approach is wise; it does suggest that there are models for the successful combination of higher levels of investment in programs supporting working families and healthy and vigorous private enterprise economies.

8

Findings and Conclusions

This report began by outlining the dramatic changes that have occurred over the past four decades in families, the labor force, and the structure of the economy. These changes have been synergistic: increases in the proportion of families with all adults in the labor force have altered the level and pattern of demand for goods and services. The expansion of traditionally female service and clerical jobs has increased job opportunities for women. At the same time, stagnating earnings and the decline in traditionally male manufacturing jobs further increased the impetus for many wives to enter the labor market. Rising divorce rates and declining fertility have also propelled many women into employment who might otherwise have remained full-time homemakers. Demographic changes have also resulted in a more diverse labor force in terms of ethnic and racial composition.

These changes are not likely to be reversed. More families are benefiting from a second income, and the economy is benefiting from a larger labor force. At the same time there are a growing number of workers with obligations to both jobs and families. Many of them are women who are the sole support for their children. With all these changes, however, families remain the basic social and economic unit for the care of dependents. And families still require a good deal of time and energy from their own members if they are to function successfully.

The panel was asked to examine and synthesize the research on employer policies and working families, to evaluate policy alternatives, and to assess the needs for further research. In this report we have reviewed the trends in the labor market and the labor force; the accumulated evidence about the consequences of those trends for families and employers; how workers and employers are coping with those consequences; and the policies that governments, here and abroad, have adopted to help workers and employers in the changed workplace environment. Although research on many of the relevant topics is limited, analysis of the available data and discussions with experts in the field have enabled the panel to draw several conclusions.

As discussed in Chapter 1, the broader range of public policies designed to improve the quality of families' and workers' lives—including provision of economic security, equal opportunity, health care, and care for dependents—are beyond the panel's charge. Also beyond our charge is the subject of a general family policy (and the mechanisms to support it) of the kind most other industrialized nations have developed. Our findings and conclusions focus on the conflict between work and family obligations and possible ways of easing them. They were developed in the context of existing policies and programs, and they are embedded in a perspective that recognizes not only the needs of workers but also the constraints faced by employers in attempting to improve their operations and maintain the financial health of their organizations.

This chapter contains the panel's findings and conclusions. We summarize below the panel's general findings in three areas: the consequences of changed employment patterns for families, the consequences of workers' increased family responsibilities for workplaces, and the responses of employers and governments to these changes. We then present our conclusions, covering four areas: terms of employment, direct provision of services, program implementation and dissemination, and data collection and research. We conclude with a brief discussion of several public policy alternatives.

GENERAL FINDINGS

We estimate that about half of the U.S. work force have dependent care responsibilities, and fewer than one-third of all employees have a spouse at home. At the same time, women remain the primary caregivers for dependents regardless of employment status. Parents comprise the largest group of workers with dependents: 37 percent of the people in the civilian labor force have children under the age of 18. The most rapid increase in labor force participation has been among women with young children. Between 1960 and 1988, the labor force participation rate of married women with children under the age of 6 increased from 19 to 57 percent.

In addition to workers who are parents, approximately 10 percent of full-time employees are active or potential caregivers for elderly relatives, usually their own parents. This group is expected to increase substantially over the next several years, as both the number of elderly and the number of employed working-age women continue to grow. We estimate that at present 2 to 3 percent of employed people are caring for disabled working-age adults. These facts underlie the panel's findings regarding the consequences of combining work and family responsibilities.

Consequences for Families

Overall, research presented in Chapter 3 finds positive effects of combining work and family responsibilities for men and women and for their families. Benefits of employment include income, enhanced life satisfaction, and better physical and mental health. There is also evidence, however, that conflicts between work and family roles increase stress and the risk of depression: for some people, such conflicts reduce satisfaction in measures of well-being. The extent to which these negative effects occur varies by the employee's racial and ethnic background, income and occupation, and stage of the life cycle, as well as by relevant employer policies. Important factors that moderate the negative effects are individual employee preferences and an individual's sense of control.

The research reviewed in Chapter 3 also shows some negative effects on families, particularly those with young children or elderly parents. Stress occurs in families in which both parents must work to obtain an acceptable standard of living, but satisfactory care for children, especially infants, is not available. Because poor-quality care has negative effects not only on children's well-being but also on their development, social problems and a less capable work force are likely to result over the long term. There is a compounding of economic, health, and social problems among the poor; the children of low-income families are particularly at risk of poor care and possible developmental problems.

Changes in public and private policies or programs would mitigate the negative effects on families of combining work and domestic responsibilities. Such changes are especially needed to improve children's development and life chances and to provide adequate care for the elderly. New provisions should involve men as well as women and should offer all families flexibility in deciding how to meet their obligations.

Consequences for Workplaces

Although little research has been done regarding the direct impact of dual responsibilities on workers' productivity, there is some evidence that family responsibilities tend to increase absenteeism, tardiness, turnover, and workplace distractions. At the extreme, some women involuntarily leave the work force to care for infants or elderly parents because no other adequate arrangements can be found. Losing these workers may have negative consequences for employers, especially those facing tight labor markets as well as for the women and their families.

The panel identified several factors associated with such productivity-related problems:

- terms of employment, such as the number of hours and weeks worked, and the degree of flexibility in work schedules and location;
- the availability of services for family members, such as supplementary care arrangements for children and elderly and handicapped family members and short-term care when regular arrangements break down or family members become ill; and
- the extent to which family considerations are recognized as legitimate in the workplace.

As discussed in Chapter 5, many employers currently provide an extensive base of nonwage benefits, accounting on average for about 28 percent of total compensation. They include provision of some short-term protection (such as medical benefits and sick leave) as well as long-term benefits (such as life insurance and pensions). Considerably less progress has been made in offering new types of benefits particularly needed by families without full-time homemakers.

Governments play a major role in determining the availability and distribution of benefits, primarily through the tax system and regulations. Baseline social insurance programs required by federal law since the 1930s include Social Security, workers' compensation, and unemployment insurance. These programs cover all private employers, regardless of size. They have substantially enhanced the economic independence of elderly people and have improved the economic security of unemployed workers and their families. Social insurance programs are financed by employer and employee payroll taxes and general revenues. Employer contributions to these plans account for approximately 9 percent of total compensation costs.

Some types of benefits, such as short-term disability insurance, are not required by law, but federal and state statutes specify that certain provisions must be included if the benefit is provided. An example is the Pregnancy Discrimination Act, which prohibits discrimination in the availability of benefits for pregnancy-related disabilities. Many such regulations exclude very small firms. Both employers and employees receive tax benefits for most voluntarily provided benefits, such as health insurance, qualified pension plans, and the recently introduced dependent care assistance programs. The costs of all these provisions are eventually borne in varying proportions by employers, consumers, employees, and taxpayers.

Voluntarily and as a result of collective bargaining agreements, many employers offer both standard benefits, such as health insurance and sick leave, and some innovative programs, such as family leave and flexible spending accounts. As Chapters 5 and 6 show, however, the availability of voluntary benefits, which account for approximately 19 percent of total compensation, is uneven, varying by industry, occupation, unionization, and particularly by firm size. Because small firms, many of them in the retail trade and service sectors, often operate on a slender financial margin and also tend to be labor intensive, they are in many instances exempt from government regulations. They also generally pay lower wages and provide fewer voluntary benefits. And yet small firms are more likely than large firms to offer flexible part-time employment and nonstandard hours, which are of great benefit to workers trying to juggle family obligations.

Small firms employ over 38 percent of all workers and a large proportion of women and minorities, so the absence of employment-related benefits such as health insurance and disability leave places already-vulnerable groups at increased risk. For instance, it appears that, on the basis of the data arrayed in Chapter 6, the majority of employed women are without any paid leave for pregnancy or childbirth. Only 45 percent of employees in small firms have paid sick leave, compared with 67 percent in large firms. In retail trade, total benefits account for 13 percent of compensation, compared with 31 percent in manufacturing. Of the approximately 25 million people, including an estimated 12 million children without health insurance who live in families with an employed person, 39 percent are employed in firms with fewer than 25 employees.

Decisions about benefits are influenced by a variety of factors. When total compensation is rising, employees tend to be more interested in receiving at least some of it in the form of additional benefits than if they could obtain them only at the expense of reduced wages. Similarly, when income taxes are high, incentives are strong for employees to prefer untaxed benefits over taxable wages. Also, labor unions have often succeeded in bargaining for more benefits. Thus, if recent trends of stagnant wages, lower taxes, and declining union membership continue, this would suggest that in the short term benefits will not increase and may decline. For example, there has been a decrease in employer-provided health insurance coverage for dependents.

Although employers and governments have to some extent responded to the nation's demographic and economic changes, current policies and programs appear to be inadequate, especially for low-income workers and their dependents. The panel urges researchers and policy makers to break out of the unproductive cycle that has characterized discussions of how to provide important benefits to employees of marginal firms (large or small). New concepts are necessary to meet the needs of workers without destroying the economic viability of businesses.

CONCLUSIONS

Meeting the needs of today's diverse work force and enhancing the health of the economy are the panel's two goals in suggesting how the structure and management of the workplace should be shaped. The crucial assumption underlying the panel's conclusions is that employers should be expected to share the responsibility of making it possible for workers to do justice to both their jobs and their families. As we have seen, there is already a base of family-related employee benefits and government supports; further improvements in this existing structure would bring about a better match between institutional practices and present as well as projected social and economic conditions. On the whole, we outline broad directions for policies and programs, rather than detailed prescriptions. Nor do we suggest when it is most appropriate for federal, state, or local governments to take action in cases that do require intervention.

When government intervention appears indicated, action at the federal level is appropriate if competition among political subdivisions is to be avoided; however, centralization may lead to top-heavy bureaucracy. Also, other levels of government are closer to local concerns and can more readily adjust to local conditions. How to balance these considerations will differ for various programs. It is beyond the scope of this report to attempt to determine this case by case, but, in general, we believe minimum standards and regulations are most appropriately set at the national level, while their administration and the provision of services are best left to state and local governments.

Our conclusions concern four broad topics: (1) terms of employment, (2) direct provision of services, (3) program development, and (4) data collection and research. Unfortunately, cost and benefit analyses of alternative employee benefit programs are inconclusive, and their implications are in dispute. For the most part, therefore, the panel discusses alternative policy approaches rather than presenting definitive recommendations. Because more and better information and analysis would be expected to resolve some of the issues, suggestions for collecting additional data and further research are offered.

Terms of Employment

Terms of employment establish the parameters of work for individual employees. They are shaped by laws, regulations, and negotiations but finally are implemented by employers, and they determine working conditions for employees. Research confirms that such factors as how much time people spend on the job, their work schedule, and how much discretion they have in adjusting it are important determinants of employee well-being.

They may also influence some aspects of job performance, such as absenteeism and tardiness, particularly for workers who also have family responsibilities.

Because flexible policies and choices among a variety of programs are likely to reduce work and family tensions, openness to experimentation on the part of both managers and workers is important in solving existing problems and in meeting constantly changing conditions. Because private initiatives are frequently inadequate, government can perform an important function by providing tax incentives and other supports.

Leave Policy

The availability of leave is critical for workers with family responsibilities. As described in Chapters 4 and 6, the most obvious case is the loss of family income and benefits due to an employee's illness. For women such losses can also occur because of disability related to pregnancy and childbirth. In addition, caring for newborn or newly adopted children, or for disabled adults, is stressful for both employed women and men (although more women are affected because they continue to be primary caretakers). The difficulty of finding supplementary care arrangements, such as high-quality infant care and home health care for elderly and disabled family members, contributes to the stress. Short-term care for dependents, needed when the usual arrangements break down or in case a family member becomes ill, is also costly and often difficult to find.

Although researchers disagree on the long-term effects of nonmaternal care of infants on later development, there is consensus that poor-quality care has negative effects. Researchers also agree that employment and care arrangements consistent with parents' preferences contribute to both parents' and children's physical and psychological well-being.

Leaving the work force to care for dependents has a particularly negative impact on low-income women and single mothers. They are most in need of the wages and benefits that employment provides, and they are least likely to have access to quality alternative care. Several recent studies suggest that leaving the work force has negative effects not only on women's current income (creating for some the need for public assistance), but also on their long-term earnings and benefits. Labor markets reward continuous employment.

Voluntary provisions for paid leave for a worker's own illness (sick leave or short-term disability) are generally part of standard benefit packages (discussed in Chapter 5). Under federal statute, when such leave is offered, it must include leave for pregnancy- and childbirth-related disabilities. Under this system, the majority of women working in medium and large firms can generally piece together 6 to 8 weeks of paid leave by using disability and sick leave, plus vacation time. At the discretion of their employers, women may be able to expand this by 3 to 4 months of unpaid leave with a job guarantee and either continued paid benefits or the option to purchase some of them. These opportunities are much more limited in small and labor-intensive firms, because providing them is likely to be a much greater burden, especially in terms of the reallocation of tasks. Men rarely are able to take any formal leave related to the birth or adoption of a child into the family. Very few women or men can take leave to care for sick family members. Research from European countries suggests that the provision of leave benefits only or chiefly to women may lead to employer discrimination against women.

There is general agreement among researchers, policy makers, and interest groups that some form of family leave is important. Major points of disagreement are whether leave should be negotiated through the labor-management process or required by the government and what priority family leave should receive at a time when employers are concerned about rising costs of existing benefits and are, to some extent, cutting back on them.

More than 20 states across the country have enacted some form of family or maternity leave legislation; the limited data and equally limited analysis of these programs as well as those in other countries (described in Chapters 6 and 7) informed this debate for the panel. Even without legislation, employers facing labor shortages, particularly those whose labor force is predominantly female, are likely to offer some paid or unpaid leave in order to improve recruitment and retention. Hospitals recruiting nurses are an obvious, although not the only, example. By contrast, businesses facing severe economic constraints, as is frequently the case for small businesses, are unlikely to offer such leave. The result is that low-wage workers in greatest need of income and benefits and with the least bargaining power are least likely to have family leave; many do not have sick leave. Neither federal nor state laws guarantee leave, however, and there are compliance problems.

Requiring employers to expand existing leave policies to include infant care and care for other family members in case of illness or breakdown of the usual care arrangements would be an incremental change for many large employers and unlikely to cause serious dislocation. It would, however, impose substantial additional costs on many others. The fact that many large firms and a few small firms already provide such leave voluntarily suggests that the provision of paid leave is nonetheless feasible. The limited data from states with short-term disability programs or required leave policies (described in Chapters 5 and 6) also indicate that such programs are economically feasible. Analyses of economic performance and quality-of-life indicators in West European countries with extensive family benefits (discussed in Chapter 7) further indicate that such policies are not related to poor economic performance.

The costs of unpaid leave with job assurances and access to health benefits are obviously lower than those for paid leave, but they would still be a significant burden for many small firms. Unpaid leave offers more parental choice than no leave, but it is of less value to low-income families that cannot afford to lose a parent's earnings, although some may be able to combine unpaid leave with part-time work. Nevertheless, the alternative to giving up earnings often becomes placing a child or an elderly or disabled relative in inadequate care.

It is critical to note that requiring firms to provide leave need not mean that the entire cost must be absorbed by employers. Not only may businesses compensate to some degree by raising the prices of their products or by keeping wages lower than they otherwise might have been, but also the costs can be covered in a variety of other ways. Several different models, involving employee, employer, and government contributions, are currently being used in the United States and Europe to finance work-related benefit programs. For example, payroll taxes are used to fund existing state disability insurance programs. And in Germany small employers are provided a direct government subsidy.

The panel concludes that, for the economic, physical, and psychological well-being of employees and their dependents, some form of paid sick leave, including paid leave for medical disabilities related to pregnancy and childbirth, and some form of family leave, to care for infants and ill family members, are essential. The panel urges policy makers to explore various approaches to financing and phasing in such benefits so as to minimize economic disruption, spread costs equitably among the community at large, and prevent discrimination against those who use such leave.

Part-Time Work

Businesses have always hired some part-time workers and have been doing so increasingly in recent years: the number of part-time employees more than tripled between 1955 and 1987, from 6 million to 19 million. According to employer surveys, scheduling and workload variations are the primary reasons for hiring part-time workers, usually to do very restricted or routine tasks; most managerial positions are explicitly excluded. Also, part-time employees tend to receive lower wages and particularly lower benefits.

Currently, 27 percent of employed women and 11 percent of employed men work part time, the latter including mainly students and older workers.

While the number of involuntary part-time employees is growing, the majority who work part time do so by choice. Women—many of them with young children and, increasingly, those caring for elderly relatives—account for almost two-thirds of the part-time work force. Reduced work hours clearly help them meet their family responsibilities. But this approach is possible only for families that can afford the diminished income.

Recent research suggests that, when all differences between workers are taken into account, part-time employees may not be at as much of a disadvantage as previously thought. But the evidence also shows that part-time jobs usually pay less and provide fewer benefits than comparable full-time jobs, particularly for low-wage employees in clerical, sales, service, and operative occupations. Managers and professionals are more likely to be at a disadvantage because of limited job choices and fewer opportunities for promotion.

The panel finds that employers and employees are only beginning to explore the possibilities of using part-time work as a transition into or out of the labor market during different stages of the life cycle. Temporary reductions in work time could be particularly helpful when workers have young children, when they have elderly parents to care for, or when their retirement is near. Especially in light of the finding that part-time workers do not lack commitment to their jobs, part-time work should be considered a legitimate option and not be penalized. Providing prorated wages for part-time employees and prorated benefits to those who want them would eliminate existing inequities and reduce the incentive to substitute part-time workers for full-time workers as a way of reducing wage rates and benefit costs.

The panel concludes that increasing part-time work options for those who want them is highly desirable for both hourly and salaried employees. Wages proportional to hours worked and, when feasible, equivalent promotion opportunities and prorated benefits are appropriate.

Statutes governing the hours of work, such as the Fair Labor Standards Act (discussed in Chapter 6), although they safeguard workers against some kinds of exploitation, may impede flexibility by reinforcing distinctions between full-time and part-time work. Federal and state governments, in consultation with employers, employees, and unions, should be encouraged to review the wage and hour laws with a view toward modifications that would permit desired changes while maintaining necessary protection for workers.

Flexible Schedules

Lack of flexibility and unpredictability in work schedules are documented sources of work and family conflict. One solution is flextime, which can vary from permitting small alterations in starting and stopping times each day, to contracting for total time per week, per year, or even over an employee's career. Formal policies of flexible scheduling have made relatively little headway in the United States: it is estimated that in the mid-1980s only 13 percent of full-time workers had such options, although the proportion may have increased somewhat since then. Interestingly, small firms appear to offer this benefit more often than do large firms.

Limited evidence on flextime shows modest positive effects on performance-related factors such as recruitment and absenteeism, as well as employee satisfaction. There is evidence that more flexible schedules often ease the stress felt by those combining work and family obligations, and they are desired by a wide range of employees regardless of family status. Flexible schedules also contribute to an atmosphere that suggests that employee concerns about family are legitimate. However, research also shows that some flexible schedules, particularly when they are not very extensive, provide little help to employees. And many people are simply short of time, no matter how a fixed number of hours is adjusted over a week or even a year. Employers report some problems in managing and administering flextime programs and, occasionally, increased costs, but there is some evidence of overall savings due to factors such as reduced overtime costs.

What degree of flexibility is feasible will vary among different establishments as well as for various jobs. The same kinds of regulations and traditional thinking that have constrained opportunities for part-time workers also appear to have inhibited the spread of flextime. In a number of European nations, a far more substantial proportion of workers now have the opportunity to choose their own schedules, albeit within limits (discussed in Chapter 7). Expansion of flextime may have been influenced by such studies as one by a German firm that found a majority of jobs studied were amenable to flexible arrangements. The same study also found that flexible schedules work best when there are a variety of options rather than only one model.

The panel concludes that policies that seem to work well elsewhere, with modest benefits for both employers and employees, are at least worthy of serious consideration here. Large and medium firms, following the experience of both European employers and of smaller firms in this country, should consider initiating more flexible schedule arrangements for their workers. Government review of the relevant regulations, as was discussed for part-time work, is also appropriate here.

Flexible Locations

Flexibility in location is also thought to be a way to reduce work and family conflict for employees, and it has at times been used by employers to reduce the cost of production. Since the Industrial Revolution, people have tended to think of work as something done in a central place of employment, yet there is a long tradition of paid work performed in the home. More recently, neighborhood centers, satellite offices, and other similar arrangements have also emerged, and interest in these alternatives has been increasing, particularly in view of such innovations as computer-based "telecommuting." A small but growing proportion of employees today work in such settings.

There are documented advantages and disadvantages to alternative work sites. Employers save money by providing less costly space and, at times, by hiring workers on more favorable terms; at the same time, necessary interactions between employees may become difficult, and managers have to learn new techniques of supervision. Employees tend to gain more control over conditions of work and save time as well as money by not commuting. But working at home does not solve most child care problems and results in lack of contact with fellow workers and, in some cases, violation of wage and hour laws. Negative effects are more likely to dominate in the case of workers with few skills and little bargaining power, such as immigrant women in large urban centers. Positive effects are likely to dominate for well-educated, skilled employees in high-technology industries.

In the past, there has been much opposition to home-based work, particularly from labor unions, so that legal bans in selected industries have only recently been lifted. The complexities of this situation and the fact that many types of work cannot be done at home or in neighborhood centers make it unlikely that work in alternative locations will become widespread. Nonetheless, such options may be useful in some cases and should be considered along with other ways of providing greater flexibility.

The panel encourages employers to explore the possibilities of home-based work and other options for alternative locations for employees who would prefer such arrangements, without penalizing them with regard to pay, benefits, or promotions. Ensuring that negative effects do not occur when work is done in alternative workplaces, particularly production or clerical work, is essential.

Direct Provision of Services

We have concluded that employers should consider adopting policies that enable workers to better manage their dual responsibilities by offering more flexible terms of employment. We now consider services that are important for employees with family responsibilities, such as various forms of dependent care. Employers can often efficiently gather and disseminate information about the availability and quality of such services. In other instances, employers can either efficiently provide services or support them indirectly when they are provided by governments, community organizations, and for-profit establishments. Employers can also offer indirect support for services through a flexible benefits system, thus increasing employee choices.

Information and Counseling

In several surveys, as described in Chapter 4, a substantial number of workers report that child care is hard to find, particularly for infants and for children during school vacations and holidays. They also express interest in having more information about the availability and the quality of care for their children and elderly family members. When employees cannot find or afford dependent care services of acceptable quality, absenteeism and tardiness increase. Employers could alleviate these problems by providing resource and referral programs, either using their own staff, joining with other businesses, or contracting with community organizations that offer such services. Employer-supported programs could incorporate or encourage the spread of publicly available quality ratings of care services, which in turn may improve the supply, competitiveness, and quality of services.

In a 1988 survey, 4 percent of small firms and 14 percent of large firms reported providing resource and referral services. Although the evidence is mainly anecdotal, these services appear to help employees find programs that meet their economic circumstances and cultural goals, generally for modest costs. To the extent that employer practices encourage the development and expansion of information services, they are also likely to be helpful in increasing the supply and improving the quality of care available. Caution must be exercised, however, to ensure that dependent care services meet existing state regulations, at a minimum, and that liability issues are resolved (discussed in Chapter 6). We have already noted the need for consideration of improved standards and regulations.

Providing dependent care information may be part of more comprehensive counseling and education services or employee assistance programs. More than one-third of the U.S. work force in the private sector now has access to employee assistance programs, which have in many instances expanded their original focus on alcohol problems to include family-related issues. Additional resources and training may be needed to support this expanded role.

Information and counseling services contribute to a family-friendly environment and also tend to generate goodwill toward employers. The fact that a growing number of companies now provide these services suggests that they are cost-effective.

The panel encourages employers to support development and expansion of resource and referral programs for both child care and elder care or, when necessary, to initiate them. Whenever possible, employers can build on present employee assistance programs to provide counseling and education dealing with work and family issues, adding the additional resources necessary to extend the services.

Dependent Care

Affordable, adequate care for children, particularly infants and children with disabilities, is generally difficult to find, especially for low-income families and workers with nonstandard hours. The severity of the child care problem varies by community. The difficulty of arranging child care, as well as the need to look after adult dependents, often makes it difficult for primary caretakers, most often women, to enter and to remain in the labor force. Those who are employed often experience stress and generally have higher rates of tardiness and absenteeism. Given the growing number of elderly people in the United States and the continuing rise in women's labor force participation, dependent-care-related problems are likely to become more numerous in the future.

To address employees' needs for child care services, especially when recruitment and retention are problems and the resources in the community inadequate, employers have for some years experimented with establishing on- or near-site child care centers. One employer recently initiated an intergenerational center to care for both elderly people and children. The costs of providing a center are high, particularly for companies that underwrite start-up costs and subsidize operating expenses. Liability insurance costs are also a frequently cited concern. In addition, unlike flexible schedules, such centers benefit only a small group of employees. Even though the costs may be treated as normal business expenses for tax purposes, there are today few centers except in establishments that employ large numbers of women and experience difficulties in recruiting and retaining them.

Direct employee subsidies are an alternative when the problem is the cost of care rather than its availability. Other approaches include employer contributions to existing centers in return for guaranteed or preferential admissions for their employees, possibly at a reduced price. A few employers are also experimenting with services for sick children and for after-school times, vacations, and snow days. Available evidence suggests that such programs reduce turnover and improve recruitment to some extent, but it is less conclusive on absenteeism. Employers and employees report that users of employer-supported centers experience improved morale, and employees believe that their productivity is improved.

The panel concludes that insofar as economic considerations permit, employers and unions should be encouraged to continue to provide and expand various types of assistance for the care of children and disabled and elderly family members, particularly when community resources are inadequate. In addition, it is important that governments collect and disseminate information about successful employer- and union-sponsored dependent care programs.

Health Insurance

Employer-based health insurance is a major benefit available to the majority of American workers and their dependents, covering approximately 148 million people, or 61 percent of the population. However, it is least available in some of the areas of high job growth, namely, among small firms in the retail sales and service sectors. Many workers and families without insurance are among the most needy, including a large proportion of single-adult and minority families. More than 12 million children lack public or private insurance protection.

The cost of health insurance has risen from one-fourth of voluntary benefits in 1960 to almost one-half today. Health insurance, the most rapidly increasing cost component of benefit packages, now accounts for almost 6 percent of total compensation and slightly exceeds the cost of pensions. Premiums are increasing at a rate in excess of 20 percent annually, making cost containment a high priority for employers. One method of reducing employer costs is to increase employee copayments and deductibles, particularly for dependent coverage. Because of the nature of the health insurance system in the United States, small firms face higher premium costs than large ones; high premiums are the major reason given by small firms for not providing this benefit. Alternative proposals to meet the health care needs of employed uninsured workers and their families include changes in Medicaid to cover more low-wage workers, a universal system of national health insurance, and mandating expansions in employer health insurance coverage.

The panel concludes that employer-provided health insurance, including dependent coverage, is critical to family well-being and that recently observed cutbacks in dependent coverage pose a serious threat to family security. While reorganizing the need for cost containment, we strongly encourage employers who currently provide health insurance for workers and their dependents to maintain coverage. Employers offering very minimal health coverage are encouraged to improve it when possible. Employers and unions are encouraged to support efforts to improve the current health care system, including the public health system, so as to better meet the needs of all workers and their families.

Although the panel considers the problem of ensuring all Americans access to health insurance and health care services to be an urgent national priority, we do not recommend specific policy approaches. Several national commissions have recently, or will shortly, provide detailed analyses of this subject and offer recommendations for action. The panel limits its comments to urging that policy makers place this problem high on the national agenda.

Flexible Benefits

In addition to flexible terms of employment and specific family-related services, some employers offer a variety of other benefits, from discounts for purchases of household items and van pools to free legal services and subsidized education. Clearly, not all such benefits are equally valuable to all workers, due to differences in incomes, family circumstances, and personal tastes. Furthermore, in families that have more than one wage earner, some benefits may be duplicated. Offering employees a choice is one good solution. "Cafeteria plans" and dependent care assistance plans that include flexible spending accounts are gradually being made available by more employers. Currently, approximately 13 percent of employees in medium- and large-sized firms are offered flexible benefit plans, usually including an option for dependent care. White-collar workers are more likely to be offered such plans than production workers. The majority of flexible benefit plans include an option for dependent care.

Cafeteria plans are of limited utility if they include only benefits urgently needed by almost everyone. Employees are confronted with an unhappy choice, particularly difficult for those with low incomes who cannot afford to purchase substitutes on their own. If, however, cafeteria plans offer what are considered luxury options, they amount mainly to a tax advantage for the well-to-do. Cafeteria plans are therefore most useful when the included benefits are important for some but not all employees: for example, child care and elder care.

No matter what items are included, however, some workers will find the choice difficult, while others may not need any of the options very much. Nevertheless, since those who must forgo some needed benefit will be no worse off than if employers or governments determined which programs to offer, and if the majority of employees benefit from having choices, the programs seem worthwhile. Preliminary evidence suggests that eligible employees are only beginning to utilize flexible benefit plans but that employee satisfaction with benefits improves when plans are available.

Reducing the overall costs of benefits is a major reason given by employers for introducing cafeteria plans. At the same time, however, the most common reason given by employers for not offering cafeteria plans is that such plans often involve increased administrative expenses. There may also be increased costs related to adverse selection of benefits (discussed in Chapter 6). One exception is a dependent care assistance plan that allows employees to spend pretax dollars on a variety of services, such as child care or additional health insurance. This type of plan involves only minor administrative costs and may save money because employee contributions to the account are exempted from payroll taxes. Evidence suggests that increasing employee choices among existing benefits is a useful but limited strategy for employers and employees. However, the larger question of the tax-free status of most benefits deserves further attention from policy makers because of the large drain on tax revenues, estimated to reach $171 billion in 1993. There is also some concern about the smaller value that tax-free benefits have for the poor.

The panel encourages employers to review the structure of their current benefit systems, on the basis of needs assessments of current employees and an examination of utilization data on existing benefits. Employers should consider adopting flexible benefit packages, carefully balancing the need for core benefits against the advantages of more choice. Employers should also develop programs to educate employees about new plans.

Program Development, Implementation, and Dissemination

Throughout this report we have emphasized the diversity of the present work force, the positive as well as the negative consequences of combining work and family responsibilities, and the variation in benefits that employees receive depending on size of firm, degree of unionization, and occupation. Considerable differences in the availability of community resources also influence the need for and the costs of programs that employers might provide. Beyond that, as we have discussed, the terms of employment and the services offered by employers have been determined in part by the culture of the workplace, which includes assumptions about families.

Employers and unions are encouraged to reexamine the structure of the current benefit system, and its underlying assumptions, by assessing the needs of current employees, examining the extent to which they use existing benefits, and developing estimates of the short- and long-term costs and benefits of possible new programs. Research has shown that, even when a new program has been adopted, there are often barriers to implementation, as well as sources of support. Among the barriers are usually inertia, ignorance about innovative new policies, and the heavy weight of traditions that developed when conditions were quite different.

Employees report that supervisors and peers who are unsympathetic to family issues contribute to work and family stress. Even when family-supportive policies are in place, a well-understood if unspoken workplace culture suggests that family problems should be left at home. Such negative attitudes tend to inhibit the use of family-related programs. There is evidence in both the United States and Europe that this problem is particularly acute for men. Women are more likely to encounter discrimination in hiring, promotions, and training when policies and programs are available only to or utilized only by them.

Because changes in an established organization, no matter how useful, are likely to meet with resistance, special efforts are necessary. There is a need for education and training workshops, particularly for top management and union leaders, whose active participation in developing and implementing new programs is crucial for their success. These activities can be facilitated by appointing specifically designated "managers of work and family issues."

Universities with extensive facilities for education and training can play a constructive role in developing and staffing such workshops, in disseminating information, especially to students who will be business and union leaders. Business schools in particular could train the next generation of managers to become knowledgeable about family benefits and their importance for a more diverse work force. Land grant institutions, with a long tradition of successful service to agriculture and, more recently, to other sectors, would find this a logical adaptation of their original mission. Employers may become increasingly interested in such assistance if the predicted labor shortage materializes.

The panel encourages employers and unions, large and small, to conduct assessments of employees' needs and opinions to identify problems and desired solutions, to continue to develop innovative programs as needed, and to facilitate program implementation through training programs for managers and education programs for workers. Family-related benefit programs deserve greater priority in collective bargaining negotiations.

The panel recognizes that some worthwhile programs may be so novel, so high risk, or so expensive to initiate that few firms or unions can undertake them. Examples might be resource and referral services that include quality evaluations of child care and elder care facilities, centers for sick children, or combined centers for children and elderly people. Exhortations and pointing out long-run benefits alone are not likely to prove sufficient incentives to start new programs.

The panel encourages federal, state, and local governments to either implement model programs for their own employees or to help finance

them in the private sector. In some instances, large establishments, perhaps with encouragement and cooperation from labor unions, may be able to bear most of the cost, with only modest contributions from government. Because businesses do not always communicate with each other, governments can also play a part in disseminating information about successful programs.

Data Collection and Research

In the course of our study, the panel reviewed a broad array of primary and secondary data sets, quantitative and qualitative research, and program and policy evaluation reports. In drawing on those sources in this report, we have noted when the evidence is weak or contradictory and when more information is needed. We found many instances in which additional work would be useful. Rather than develop too ambitious an agenda, however, we urge collection and analysis of additional data only when they are necessary for formulating policies and when they are most likely to be cost-effective. A more detailed discussion of data needs appears in Appendix B.

Too often the fact that good research requires good data does not receive adequate attention, nor is it always recognized that research is needed to generate better data. On the basis of our review, it is clear that the federal government could improve data collection in two areas in particular. First, the federal government should institutionalize the current longitudinal panel studies of households, which have proven useful for much policy research but are currently subject to uncertain funding. Their usefulness would be enhanced by developing better measures of time use and additional measures of employee benefits and working conditions. Second, more systematic federal data collection procedures by establishment would be helpful, with greater emphasis on small firms and a focus on benefit utilization as well as availability. Developing appropriate confidentiality safeguards is necessary to ensure employer and union participation.

In addition, the panel urges researchers and those who fund research to include more work on the following topics:

- the long-term effects of various approaches to child care on children's development and the extent to which this is an advantage to employers and the community;
- the use of unpaid family care arrangements for elderly people and people with disabilities;
- the changing roles of men both at home and at work;
- the effects of family responsibilities on work performance, including the development of objective measures, rather than only subjective perceptions, of performance;

• evaluation of new programs, whether voluntary or legally required, and of demonstration projects, focusing on factors that affect their development and implementation as well as the costs and benefits that result from their adoption;

• family-oriented policies and programs as well as their outcomes in other industrialized countries;

• differences in the availability of benefits by occupation, with emphasis on low-income workers; and

• similarities and differences in work and family issues for members of different ethnic and racial minority groups.

Such a diverse but complementary set of data collection and research activities is necessary if satisfactory progress is to be made. For the most part, it is important to build on what has already proven to be fruitful; in that way, the payoff should be high in relation to the relatively modest costs of the activities. In our view, cutting spending for data collection and research is a false economy; the costs of shaping policies without adequate information are likely to greatly exceed any short-term savings.

ALTERNATIVE PUBLIC POLICIES

Although the research base on family and work interaction is not strong, the panel was persuaded over the course of the study that facilitating the combination of work and family increases the well-being of workers and their dependents. It is likely to improve the labor force by increasing employees' commitment and sense of responsibility to their employer—and quite possibly their productivity. To the extent that children get a better start, they are expected to become not only better adjusted, more successful individuals rather than misfits, but also more skilled and productive workers rather than dropouts, and more reliable citizens rather than a burden on the community. Hence, introducing programs that make it easier for workers to do justice both to their job and to their household responsibilities will benefit business and society as well as families. There will, of course, be costs as well.

Evaluating public policies for family-related benefits raises broad questions related to tax and regulatory policies. For example, the tax-free status of most benefits is an issue needing further analysis and consideration. Although the panel encourages voluntary programs, we note the important role for government regulations and standards, particularly of dependent care programs, and for some terms of employment.

The argument for regulation of dependent care programs (discussed in Chapter 4) is that the recipients of such care are frequently not in a position to judge quality. Although family members responsible for children, elderly people, or adults with disabilities may attempt to evaluate institution or program quality, they may lack adequate knowledge and right of entry, just as customers in a restaurant lack the expertise and the right of access of the health inspector. Also, they may have few or no alternatives for care arrangements. Thus, it is not surprising that most states have regulations for minimum standards for nursing homes and child care programs.

The argument for regulating terms of employment (discussed in Chapters 5 and 6) has been that governments should be responsible for safeguarding the rights of those with insufficient bargaining power. Thus, wage and hour laws have long set minimum standards for compensation and regulated the schedule and location of work. More recently, discrimination in employment, including the provision of benefits, has been prohibited, as has work at home in some industries.

Reaching agreement on appropriate regulatory policies, however, is a very difficult task. There are serious questions about to what extent regulators can remain independent of the industry they are regulating. Equally important is the question of who should make decisions with respect to cost and quality trade-offs. Decisions to improve standards must be tempered by the additional costs to institutions in meeting higher standards. It does little good to make standards so high that the resulting cost of the product or service is priced beyond the reach of those who need it.

Nonetheless, regulations are often considered necessary—for example, other studies have proposed national minimum standards for child care, including required ratios of staff to children and specified amounts of training for caretakers, with actual regulation and enforcement to be done at the state level. Care should be exercised that such regulations do not become obstacles to desired flexibility. This may have happened, for example, with some aspects of the wage and hour laws, as noted in Chapters 5 and 6. The panel did not evaluate all types of government regulations relevant to family-related benefits; we did indicate throughout, however, when review of existing regulations or consideration of new standards is likely to be particularly valuable for policy development.

Federal, state, or local governments may require employers to provide certain benefits, for example, leave plans. We are aware that such legally required or mandated programs are controversial (see Chapters 1, 5, and 6). Opponents take the view that programs advantageous for businesses, or at least not harmful to them, will generally be provided either voluntarily or as a result of employee demands. They further argue that very costly regulations are likely to result in hardships, bankruptcies, less competition, and higher unemployment and therefore ultimately may not be good for anyone. Critics also point out that even when all employers are required to offer the same benefits, so that the playing field seems level, this is not really the case. Small businesses that employ more labor relative to other resources, and often employ low-skilled workers, are likely to find the same programs far more burdensome than large, more capital-intensive businesses. Small firms have been the source of a large share of new jobs in recent years.

These objections should not be taken lightly, but neither should the value of required programs be ignored. Proponents emphasize that legally required benefits—either directly provided through government programs or mandated for private purchase—are the only way to ensure that all workers will be covered. In the case of Social Security and unemployment insurance, the need to cover all workers is considered more important than the negative effects of requiring participation. Legally required programs protect workers who may not be able to negotiate on equal terms with employers. The decline in union representation since the 1960s means that the proportion of workers with a formal means of pursuing their demands independently has declined.

It has also been suggested that firms that cannot afford to pay basic benefits may be poorly managed and inefficient. Thus, the economy might benefit if such firms go out of business and release resources for use in more efficient firms. Finally, it is argued that legally established programs do level the playing field to some extent: they at least ensure that all domestic competitors have to offer the same benefits. If the advantages of a legally required program outweigh its disadvantages, it deserves favorable consideration. The evidence from other industrialized countries suggests that they have found a way to support generous benefits without destroying economic competitiveness or healthy growth.

One way of avoiding some of these difficulties is to impose mandates but permit exemptions. This approach is part of recent legislation that extended health insurance coverage to former employees and their dependents but excluded employers with fewer than 20 employees; it is also part of most current family-related legislative proposals. But a mandate with exemptions does not achieve one of its main purposes: to ensure that everyone in the relevant group is covered. This flaw is particularly serious in the area of work and family benefits, because it is small firms that are usually exempted, and they are most likely to pay low wages and offer few benefits. Therefore, the neediest workers would tend to be left out.

It is important to emphasize that there are various ways of financing required programs. As previously noted, legal requirements do not mean that employers have to bear all the costs, nor do individual employers have to bear the actuarial cost of funding benefits for their employees. Social Security is paid for by worker and employer taxes: the costs are spread across the entire work force and are not made firm specific. Workers' compensation and unemployment insurance distribute the costs among employers, workers, and taxpayers. Each of the five states with disability laws that provide all workers with wage replacement does so with a different funding mechanism; two of them require no employer contribution (see Chapters 4 and 5).

There is little agreement on how to weigh the various arguments for and against mandates and regulations, except for the fact that legal requirements should not be imposed lightly, and possible negative effects should be carefully weighed. We believe that mandates should be instituted only when uniform coverage is viewed as crucial. Ultimately, if society believes that every worker should receive some minimum benefit, such as workers' compensation, society must be willing to pay for that benefit, if necessary by providing subsidies to some firms and workers. In the absence of clear evidence pointing toward a best option, the panel has not made recommendations in this area.

SUMMARY

The panel has used available information to determine how best to meet the needs of workers and their families while promoting a healthy economy. We have also suggested where additional information would be particularly useful in helping to make future policy decisions. Taken as a whole, our study offers an ambitious agenda for employers and suggests the need for additional public policies. We note, however, that some employers, particularly large firms, are already doing more than is suggested in this report. New programs would nevertheless increase costs for other firms, especially small and labor-intensive ones, as well as for taxpayers and, most likely, consumers. In return, however, the large and growing proportion of people with dual responsibilities to work and family would be helped to do justice to both.

Greater awareness on the part of all interested parties—workers, employers, governments, and the larger community—of the extent to which their interests coincide is crucial in meeting workplace challenges. Employers need a productive labor force now, which is possible only if workers are able to cope successfully with dual responsibilities to their families and their jobs. Employers will similarly need a productive, educated future work force, which requires that children be adequately cared for today. Workers need jobs, which can be generated only by firms that are successful and competitive. The community is dependent on a healthy economy, which requires government policies that enable it to function both efficiently and equitably. Conflicts are inevitable, but there are also enough common interests that much can be achieved by relying not only on altruism, but also on the far-sighted self-interest of all the parties involved.

References

Alber, Jens
1981   Modernization, democratization and the development of welfare states in Western Europe. Pp. 37-80 in Peter Flora and Arnold J. Heidenheimer (eds.), *The Development of Welfare States in Europe and America.* New Brunswick, N.J., and London: Transaction Books.

Alpert, William, and M. Ozawa
1986   Fringe benefits in nonmanufacturing industries: How they vary. *The American Journal of Economics and Sociology* (April):189-200.

Ambry, M.
1988   At home in the office. *American Demographics* 10:30-33, 61.

American Society for Personnel Administrators
1988   *Employers and Child Care: The Human Resource Professional's View.* Alexandria, Va.: American Society for Personnel Administrators.

Andrews, Emily S.
1988   An Overview of the Employee Benefit System. Paper presented to the National Research Council Panel on Employer Policies and Working Families, Committee on Women's Employment and Related Social Issues (November 11). Washington, D.C.: Employee Benefit Research Institute.

Arrow, Kenneth.
1973   The theory of discrimination. In Orley Ashenfelter and Albert Rees (eds.), *Discrimination in Labor Markets.* Princeton, N.J.: Princeton University Press.

Auerbach, Judith D.
1988   *In the Business of Child Care: Employer Initiatives and Working Women.* New York: Praeger.

Axel, Helen
1985   *Corporations and Families: Changing Practices and Perspectives.* Report No. 868. New York: The Conference Board.

Baca-Zinn, Maxine
  1989   Family, race and poverty in the eighties. *Signs: Journal of Women in Culture and Society* 14(2):856-874.
Baca-Zinn, Maxine, and D. Stanley Eitzen
  1990   *Diversity in Families,* Second Edition. New York: Harper & Row.
Bailyn, Lotte
  1970   Career and family orientation of husbands and wives in relation to marital happiness. *Human Relations* 23:97-113.
  1988   Freeing work from the constraints of location and time. *New Technology, Work and Employment* 3(2):143-152.
  1989   Toward the perfect workplace? *Communications of the ACM* 32(4):460-471.
Barnes, Roberta Ott, and Linda D. Giannarelli
  1988   The Distribution Effects of Alternative Child Care Proposals. Paper presented at the 10th Annual Meeting of the Association for Public Policy Analysis and Management, Seattle, Wash. (October 17-19). Washington, D.C.: The Urban Institute.
Barney, J.L.
  1977   The prerogative of choice in long-term care. *The Gerontologist* 23:300-306.
Bartlett, R.L., and C. Callahan
  1984   Wage determination and marital status: Another look. *Industrial Relations* 23:90-96.
Baruch, Grace C., Lois Beiner, and Rosalind C. Barnett
  1987   Women and gender in research on work and family stress. *American Psychologist* 42:130-136.
Bean, Frank D., and Marta Tienda
  1988   *The Hispanic Population of the United States.* New York: Russell Sage Foundation.
Becker, Gary S.
  1985   The allocation of effort, specific human capital, and differences between men and women in earnings and occupations. *Journal of Labor Economics* 3(1/Part 2):S33-S58.
Belous, Richard S.
  1989   *The Contingent Economy: The Growth of the Temporary, Part-Time and Contingent Workforce.* Washington, D.C. National Planning Association.
Belsky, Jay
  1988   A reassessment of infant day care. Pp. 100-119 in Edward F. Zigler and Meryl Frank (eds.), *The Parental Leave Crisis: Toward a National Policy.* New Haven, Conn.: Yale University Press.
Bergmann, Barbara R.
  1976   Reducing the pervasiveness of discrimination. In Eli Ginzberg (ed.), *Jobs for Americans.* Englewood Cliffs, N.J.: Prentice-Hall.
Berkeley Planning Associates
  1988   Small Business Options for Child Care. Final Report to the Small Business Administration. Contract No. SBA-2056-AER-87 (March 20).

Berkowitz, Edward D.
1979   The American disability system in historical perspective. Pp. 16-74 in Edward D. Berkowitz (ed.), *Disability Policies and Government Programs*. New York: Praeger.

Berman, Melissa A.
1987   What do women get? *Across the Board* (March). (Published by The Conference Board).

Besharov, D., and P. Tramontozzi
1988   *The Costs of Federal Child Care Assistance*. Washington, D.C.: American Enterprise Institute for Policy Research.

Bielby, Denise D., and William T. Bielby
1985   She works hard for the money: Household responsibilities and allocation of effort. Paper presented at the annual meeting of the American Statistical Association.

Blank, H., and A. Wilkins
1985   *Child Care: Whose Priority? A State Child Care Fact Book*. Washington, D.C.: Children's Defense Fund.

Blank, H., A. Wilkins, and M. Crawley
1987   *State Child Care Fact Book 1987*. Washington, D.C.: Children's Defense Fund.

Blank, Rebecca M.
1989   Part-time and temporary work. Pp. 1519-1558 in *Investing in People: A Strategy to Address America's Workforce Crisis*. Commission on Workforce Quality and Labor Market Efficiency, U.S. Department of Labor. Washington, D.C.: U.S. Government Printing Office.

Blau, David M., and Philip K. Robins
1986   Fertility, Employment and Child Care Costs: A Dynamic Analysis. Paper presented at the meeting of the Population Association of America, San Francisco, Calif.

Blau, Francine D., and Marianne A. Ferber
1986   *The Economics of Women, Men, and Work*. Englewood Cliffs, N.J.: Prentice-Hall.
1987   Discrimination: Empirical evidence from the United States. *American Economic Review* 77(2):316-320.

Bloom-Feshbach, Sally, Jonathan Bloom-Feshbach, and Kirby A. Heller
1982   Work, family and children: Perceptions of the world. Pp. 268-308 in Sheila B. Kameman and Cheryl D. Hayes (eds.), *Families That Work: Children in a Changing World*. Panel on Work, Family, and Community, Committee on Child Deveopment Research and Public Policy, Commission on Behavioral and Social Sciences and Education, National Research Council. Washington, D.C.: National Academy Press.

Blostin, Allan P., Thomas P. Burke, and Lora M. Lovejoy
1988   Disability and insurance plans in the public and private sectors. *Monthly Labor Review* 111(12):9-17.

Blum, Terri C., and Paul Roman
1989   Employee assistance programs and human resources management. In K. Rowland and G. Ferris (eds.), *Research in Personnel and Human Resources Management* 7:259-312.

Blumstein, Philip, and Pepper Schwartz
  1983   *American Couples.* New York: William Morrow.
Bolger, Niall, Anita de Longes, Ronald C. Kessler, and Elaine Wethington
  1989   The contagion of stress across multiple roles. *Journal of Marriage and the Family* 51(February):175-183.
Bonilla, Carlos E.
  1989   *Determinants of Employee Absenteeism.* Washington, D.C.: National Chamber Foundation.
Boris, Eileen, and Cynthia R. Daniels, eds.
  1989   *Homework: Historical and Contemporary Perspectives on Paid Labor at Home.* Chicago: The University of Illinois Press.
Brandes, S.D.
  1976   *Welfare Capitalism: 1880-1920.* Chicago: University of Chicago Press.
Brazelton, T.B.
  1986   Issues for working parents. *American Journal of Orthopsychiatry* 56:14-25.
Broberg, Anders
  1988   The Swedish child care system. Unpublished paper (cited in Galinsky).
Brody, Elaine M.
  1981   Women in the middle and family help to older people. *The Gerontologist* 21(5):471-480.
  1985   Parent care as a normative family stress. *The Gerontologist* 25(1):19-29.
Brody, Elaine M., and Claire B. Schoonover
  1986   Patterns of parent care when adult daughters work and when they do not. *The Gerontologist* 26:372-381.
Bronfenbrenner, Urie, and Ann C. Crouter
  1982   Work and family through time and space. Pp. 39-83 in Sheila B. Kamerman and Cheryl D. Hayes (eds.), *Families That Work: Children in a Changing World.* Panel on Work, Family, and Community, Committee on Child Development Research and Public Policy, Commission on Behavioral and Social Sciences and Education, National Research Council. Washington, D.C.: National Academy Press.
Brownlee, W. Elliot, and Mary M. Brownlee
  1976   *Women in the American Economy.* New Haven, Conn.: Yale University Press.
Brush, L.
  1987   Usage of Different Kinds of Child Care: An Analysis of the SIPP Data Base. Paper prepared for the Social Services Policy Division, Planning and Evaluation, U.S. Department of Health and Human Services, October 14.
  1989   Projecting the Costs of Full-Day Child Care from the Costs of Head Start. Paper prepared for the Panel on Child Care Policy, Committee on Child Development Research and Public Policy, Commission on Behavioral and Social Sciences and Education, National Research Council, Washington, D.C.
Burden, Diane S., and Bradley Googins
  1987   *Balancing Job and Homelife Study: Managing Work and Family Stress*

in Corporations. Boston, Mass.: Boston University School of Social Work.

Bureau of the Census

1983   *Geographic Mobility of Labor, March 1980 to March 1981.* Current Population Reports, Series P-20, No. 377. Washington, D.C.: U.S. Department of Commerce.

1986   *Earnings in 1983 of Married Couple Families by Characteristics of Husband and Wife.* Current Population Reports, Series P-60, No. 153 (March). Washington, D.C.: U.S. Department of Commerce.

1987   *Who's Minding the Kids. Child Care Arrangements: Winter 1984-85, Data from the Survey of Income and Program Participation.* Current Population Reports, Series P-70, No. 9. Washington, D.C.: U.S. Department of Commerce.

1989a   *Fertility of American Women: June 1988.* Current Population Reports, Series P-20, No. 436. Washington, D.C.: U.S. Department of Commerce.

1989b   *Money Income and Poverty Status in the United States, 1988.* Current Population Reports, Series P-60, No. 166. Washington, D.C.: U.S. Department of Commerce.

1989c   *Money Income of Households, Families, and Persons in the United States, 1987.* Current Population Reports, Series P-60, No. 162. Washington, D.C.: U.S. Department of Commerce.

1989d   *Population Profile of the United States.* Current Population Reports, Series P-23, No. 159. Washington, D.C.: U.S. Department of Commerce.

1989e   *Poverty in the United States, 1987.* Current Population Reports, Series P-60, No. 163. Washington, D.C.: U.S. Department of Commerce.

1989f   *Statistical Abstract of the United States, 109th Edition.* Washington, D.C.: U.S. Department of Commerce.

1990a   *Money Income and Poverty Status in the United States, 1989.* Current Population Reports, Series P-60, No. 168. Washington, D.C.: U.S. Department of Commerce.

1990b   *Statistical Abstract of the United States, 110th Edition.* Washington, D.C.: U.S. Department of Commerce.

Bureau of Labor Statistics

1983   Monthly Labor Review 106(11).

1985a   *Employee Benefits in Medium and Large Firms, 1984.* Bulletin 2237 (June). Washington, D.C.: U.S. Department of Labor.

1985b   *Employment, Hours and Earnings of the United States, 1909-1984, Volume 2.* Bulletin 1312-12 (March). Washington, D.C.: U.S. Department of Labor.

1987   *Employee Benefits in Medium and Large Firms, 1986.* Bulletin 2281 (June). Washington, D.C.: U.S. Department of Labor.

1988a   BLS Reports on Employer Child Care Practices. News Release 88-7 (January 15). Washington, D.C.: U.S. Department of Labor.

1988b   *Employee Benefits in State and Local Governments, 1987.* Bulletin 2309 (May). Washington, D.C.: U.S. Government Printing Office.

1988c   Employment and Earnings (August), Washington, D.C.: U.S. Government Printing Office.

1989a   *Employee Benefits in Medium and Large Firms, 1988.* Washington,
        D.C.: U.S. Department of Labor.
1989b   Survey of Employer Anti-Drug Programs. Report 760. Washington,
        D.C.: Bureau of Labor Statistics.
1990a   Employer Costs for Employee Compensation, March 1990. News Re-
        lease 90-317 (June 19). Washington, D.C.: U.S. Department of Labor.
1990b   *Employment and Earnings* 37(1). Washington, D.C.: U.S. Government
        Printing Office.
1990c   *Employment and Earnings* 37(3). Washington, D.C.: U.S. Government
        Printing Office.
Bureau of National Affairs
1988a   *Alternative Work Schedules: Changing Times for a Changing Workforce.*
        Special Report #5. The National Report on Work and Family. Wash-
        ington, D.C.: Bureau of National Affairs.
1988b   *Employee Assistance Programs: Focusing on the Family.* Special Re-
        port #6. The National Report on Work and Family. Washington, D.C.:
        Bureau of National Affairs.
1989   Text of family care provisions of the AT&T labor contract. *The Na-
        tional Report on Work and Family.* (June 9):9-10. Washington, D.C.:
        Buraff Publications.
Burke, R.J., T. Weir, and R.F. Duwors, Jr.
1980   Work demands on administrators and spouse well-being. *Human Rela-
        tions* 33:253-278.
Burkhauser, Richard V., and T. Aldrich Finegan
1989   The minimum wage and the poor: The end of a relationship. *Journal of
        Policy Analysis and Management* 8(1):53-71.
Burkhauser, Richard V., and Petri Hirvonen
1988   United States Disability Policy in a Time of Economic Crisis: A Com-
        parison with Sweden and the Federal Republic of Germany. Paper
        prepared for the Milbank Memorial Fund Round Table on Disability
        Policy (November).
Burud, Sandra L., Pamela R. Aschbacher, and Jacquelyn McCrosky
1984   *Employer-Supported Child Care: Investing in Human Resources.* Do-
        ver, Mass.: Auburn House Publishing Company.
Business Insurance
1989   41 States Revise Workers' Compensation Laws (October 16):41.
Butler, Barbara, and Janis Wasserman
1988   Parental leave: Attitudes and practices in small businesses. Pp. 223-232
        in Edward F. Zigler and Meryl Frank, (eds.), *The Parental Leave Crisis:
        Toward a National Policy.* New Haven, Conn.: Yale University Press.
Cameron, David
1982   On the limits of the public economy. *Annals of the American Academy
        of Political and Social Science* 459(January):46-62.
Catalyst
1986   *Report on a National Study of Parental Leaves.* New York: Catalyst.
Cherlin, Andrew
1979   Work life and marital dissolution. In G. Levinger and O.C. Moles (eds.),

Divorce and Separation: Context, Causes, and Consequences. New York: Basic Books.

Chollet, Deborah
1987   Financing retirement today and tomorrow: The prospect for America's workers. Pp. 25-44 in *America in Transition: Benefits for the Future.* Washington, D.C.: Employee Benefit Research Institute.
1988   *Uninsured in the United States: The Nonelderly Population Without Health Insurance, 1986.* Washington, D.C.: Employee Benefit Research Institute, P-42. (October).

Christensen, Kathleen
1988   *Women and Home-Based Work: The Unspoken Contract.* New York: Henry Holt and Company.
1989   *Flexible Staffing and Scheduling in U.S. Corporations.* Research Bulletin No. 240. New York: The Conference Board.

Christensen, Kathleen, and Graham Staines
1990   Flextime: A viable solution to work-family conflict. *Journal of Family Issues.*

Cicirelli, Victor G.
1981   *Helping Elderly Parents: The Role of Adult Children.* Boston: Auburn House.

Clark-Stewart, K.A., and G.G. Fein
1983   Early childhood programs. Pp. 917-999 in P.H. Mussen (ed.), *Handbook of Child Psychology*, Vol. 2. New York: Wiley.

Clifford, R., and S. Russell
1989   Financing programs for preschool age children. *Theory into Practice.* Special Issue 28(1).

Committee for Economic Development
1985   *Investing in Our Children.* New York: Committee for Economic Development.

Committee on Nursing Home Regulation
1986   *Improving the Quality of Care in Nursing Homes.* Report of the Committee on Nursing Home Regulation, Institute of Medicine. Washington, D.C.: National Academy Press.

Committee on Population
1987   *Demographic Change and the Well-Being of Children and the Elderly*: *Proceedings of a Workshop.* Committee on Population, Commission on Behavioral and Social Sciences and Education, National Research Council. Washington, D.C.: National Academy Press.

Congressional Research Service
1988   *Health Insurance and the Uninsured: Background Data and Analysis.* Washington, D.C.: U.S. Government Printing Office (May).

Cook, Alice
1989   Paper prepared for the Panel on Employer Policies and Working Families, Committee on Women's Employment and Related Social Issues, Commission on Behavioral and Social Sciences and Education, National Research Council, Washington, D.C.

Corporate/Community Schools of America
1989   *Progress Report*. Chicago: Corporate/Community Schools of America
(June).
Council of Economic Advisers
1989   *Economic Report of the President*. Washington, D.C.: U.S. Government Printing Office.
Creedon, Michael A.
1989   The corporate response to the working caregiver. *Aging Magazine*.
Crouter, Anne C.
1984   Spillover from family to work: The neglected side of the work-family
interface. *Human Relations* 37:425-444.
Danziger, Sheldon, Peter Gottschalk, and Eugene Smolensky
1989   How the rich have fared, 1973-1987. *American Economic Review* 79(2):310-
314.
Degler, Carl N.
1980   *At Odds: Women and the Family in America from the Revolution to the
Present*. New York: Oxford University Press.
de Neubourg, Chris
1985   Part-time work: An international quantitative comparison. *International
Labour Review* 125(5):559-576.
deVol, Karen
1985   Income Replacement for Short-Term Disability: The Role of Workers'
Compensation. Report No. WC 85-2 (December). Cambridge, Mass.:
Workers Compensation Research Institute.
DuPont Co.
1989   DuPont Corporate News. DuPont External Affairs Department, Wilmington,
Del. (January 5).
Dunlop, B.O.
1980   Expanded home-based care for the impaired elderly: Solution or pipe
dreams? *American Journal of Public Health* 70:514-519.
duRivage, Virginia, and David Jacobs
1989   Home-based work: Labor's choices. Pp. 258-271 in Eileen Boris and
Cynthia R. Daniels (eds.), *Homework: Historical and Contemporary
Perspectives on Paid Labor at Home*. Chicago: University of Illinois
Press.
Eck, A.
1984   New occupational separation data improve estimates of job replacement
needs. *Monthly Labor Review* 107(3):3-10.
Ehrenberg, Ronald G., and Robert S. Smith
1982   *Modern Labor Economics, Theory and Public Policy*. Glenview, Ill.:
Scott, Foresman and Company.
Ehrenberg, Ronald G., Pamela Rosenberg, and Jeanne Li
1988   Part-time employment in the United States. In Robert A. Hart (ed.),
Employment, Unemployment, and Labor Utilization. London: George
Allen and Unwin.
Elisburg, Donald
1985   Legalities. Pp. 59-65 in *Office Workstations in the Home*. Board on

Telecommunications and Computer Applications, Commission on Engineering and Technical Systems, National Research Council. Washington, D.C.: National Academy Press.

Emlen, A.C.
1987   Panel on Child Care, Work and Family. Paper presented at the annual convention of the American Psychological Association, New York (August).

Employee Benefit Research Institute (EBRI)
1987   *Fundamentals of Employee Benefit Programs*, Third Edition.   Washington, D.C.: EBRI.

England, Paula
1989   An Overview of Segregation and the Sex Gap in Pay. Paper presented at the meetings of the American Statistical Association, 1989.

England, Paula, and George Farkas
1986   *Households, Employment, and Gender: A Social, Economic and Demographic View.* New York: Aldine Publishing Company.

Epstein, Cynthia F.
1987   Multiple demands and multiple roles: The conditions of successful management. Pp. 23-25 in F.J. Crosby (ed.), *Spouse, Worker, Parent: On Gender and Multiple Roles.* New Haven, Conn.: Yale University Press.

Equal Employment Opportunity Commission
1985   *20th Annual Report, FY 1985.* Washington, D.C.: Equal Employment Opportunity Commission.

Federal Hospital Insurance Trust Fund
1990   1990 Annual Report of the Board of Trustees of the Federal Hospital Insurance Trust Fund. Reprinted in House document 101-174, 101st Congress, 2d session. Washington, D.C.: U.S. Government Printing Office.

Federal Supplementary Medical Insurance Trust Fund
1990   1990 Annual Report of the Board of Trustees of the Federal Supplementary Medical Insurance Trust Fund. Reprinted in House document 101-173, 101st Congress, 2d session. Washington, D.C.: U.S. Government Printing Office.

Feldstein, Martin
1977   The high cost of hospitals—and what to do about it. *The Public Interest* 48(Summer):40-54.

Feldstein, Martin, and Bernard Friedman
1977   Tax subsidies, the rational demand for insurance, and the health care crisis. *Journal of Public Economics* 7(April):155-178.

Ferber, Marianne A., and Betty Kardick
1978   Sex differentials in the earnings of Ph.D.s. *Industrial and Labor Relations Review* 31(4):227-238.

Ferber, Marianne A., and Helen M. Lowry
1976   Women—the new reserve army and the unemployed. *Signs, Journal of Women in Culture and Society* 1(3, Summer):213-232.

Ferber, Robert, and Werner Z. Hirsch
1982   *Social Experimentation and Economic Policy.* Cambridge, U.K.: Cambridge University Press.

Fernandez, John
1986   *Child Care and Corporate Productivity: Resolving Family/Work Conflicts.* Lexington, Mass.: D.C. Health and Company.
Fernandez-Kelly, M. Patricia, and Anna Garcia
1989   Hispanic women and homework: Women in the informal economy of Miami and Los Angeles. Pp. 165-179 in Eileen Boris and Cynthia R. Daniels (eds.), *Homework: Historical and Contemporary Perspectives on Paid Labor at Home.* Chicago: University of Illinois Press.
Ferree, Myra Marx
1987   Family and job for working-class women: Gender class systems seen from below. Pp. 289-301 in Naomi Gerstel and Harriet Engel Gross, (eds.), *Families and Work.* Philadelphia: Temple University Press.
Filer, Randall
1989   Occupational segregation, compensating differentials, and comparable worth. Chapter 7 in Robert T. Michael, Heidi I. Hartmann, and Brigid O'Farrell (eds.), *Pay Equity: Empirical Inquiries.* Washington, D.C.: National Academy Press.
Foegen, J.R.
1984   Telecommuting: New sweatshop at home computer terminal. *Business and Society Review* (Fall):55-95.
Fosberg, S.
1981   *Family Day Care in the United States: National Day Care Home Study,* Volume 1, Summary of Findings. DHHS Publication No. 80-30282. Washington, D.C.: U.S. Department of Health and Human Services.
Frank, Meryl
1988   Costs, financing, and implementation mechanisms of parental leave policies. Pp. 315-325 in Edward F. Zigler and Meryl Frank (eds.), *The Parental Leave Crisis: Toward a National Policy.* New Haven, Conn.: Yale University Press.
Frank, Meryl, and Robyn Lipner
1988   History of maternity leaves in Europe and the United States. Pp. 3-22 in Edward F. Zigler and Meryl Frank (eds.), *The Parental Leave Crisis: Toward a National Policy.* New Haven, Conn.: Yale University Press.
Franklin, Paula A.
1977   Impact of disability on the family structure. *Social Security Bulletin* (May):3-18.
Freeman, Richard B., and James L. Medoff
1984   *What Do Unions Do?* New York: Basic Books.
Friedl, Ernestine
1975   *Women and Men: An Anthropologist's View.* New York: Holt, Rinehart and Winston.
Friedman, Dana
1985   Corporate financial assistance for child care. *The Conference Board Research Bulletin* No. 177.
1989a   Addressing the supply problem: The family daycare approach. Pp. 1477-1518 in *Investing in People: A Strategy to Address America's Workforce Crisis.* Commission on Workforce Quality and Labor Mar-

ket Efficiency, U.S. Department of Labor. Washington, D.C.: U.S. Government Printing Office.

1989b   Impact of child care on the bottom line. Pp. 1425-1476 in *Investing in People: A Strategy to Address America's Workforce Crisis*. Commission on Workforce Quality and Labor Market Efficiency, U.S. Department of Labor. Washington, D.C.: U.S. Government Printing Office.

Friedman, Dana E., ed.

1988   *Issues for an Aging America: Elder Care*. Research Report No. 911. New York: The Conference Board.

Friedman, Dana E., and Wendy B. Gray

1989   *A Life Cycle Approach to Family Benefits and Policies*. Perspectives No. 19. New York: The Conference Board.

Fuchs, Victor, R.

1988   *Women's Quest for Economic Equality*. Cambridge, Mass.: Harvard University Press.

Fullerton, Howard N.

1989   New labor force projections, spanning 1988-2000. *Monthly Labor Review* 112(11):3-12.

Furstenberg, F.

1974   Work experience and family life. In J. O'Toole (ed.), *Work and the Quality of Life*. Cambridge, Mass.: MIT Press.

Galinsky, Ellen

1989a   The Implementation of Flexible Time Leave Policies: Observations from European Employers. Paper prepared for the Panel on Employer Policies and Working Families, Committee on Women's Employment and Related Social Issues, Commission on Behavioral and Social Sciences and Education, National Research Council, Washington, D.C. (July).

1989b   Labor force policies of dual-earner couples and single parents. Pp. 1261-1312 in *Investing in People: A Strategy to Address America's Workforce Crisis*. Commission on Workforce Quality and Labor Market Efficiency, U.S. Department of Labor. Washington, D.C.: U.S. Government Printing Office.

Galinsky, Ellen, and D. Hughes

1987   The Fortune Magazine Child Care Study. Paper presented at the annual convention of the American Psychological Association, New York.

Galinsky, Ellen, M. Love, P.H. Bragonier, and D. Hughes

1987   *The Family Study*. Foundation Report. New York: Bank Street College of Education.

Gardner, H. Stephen

1988   *Comparative Economic Systems*. Chicago: The Dryden Press.

Garfinkel, Irwin, and Sara McLanahan

1986   *Single Mothers and Their Children: A New American Dilemma*. Washington, D.C.: The Urban Institute Press.

General Accounting Office

1987a   *Parental Leave: Estimated Costs of H.R. 925, the Family and Medical Leave Act of 1987*. GAO/HRD-88-34 (November). Washington, D.C.: U.S. Government Printing Office.

1987b   Welfare: Income and Relative Poverty Status of AFDC Families. GAO/
         HRD 88-9. Washington, D.C.: U.S. Government Printing Office.
1988   *Long-Term Care for the Elderly: Issues of Need, Access, and Costs.*
         GAO/HRD-89-4. Washington, D.C.: U.S. Government Printing Office
         (November).
1989   *Parental Leave: Revised Cost Estimate Reflecting the Impact of Spou-
         sal Leave.* GAO/HRD-89-68. U.S. Government Printing Office
         (April).

Gerstel, Naomi, and Harriet Engel Gross, eds.
1987   *Families and Work.* Philadelphia: Temple University Press.

Gilford, Dorothy M., ed.
1988   *The Aging Population in the Twenty-First Century: Statistics for Health
         Policy.* Panel on Statistics for an Aging Population, Committee on
         National Statistics, Commission on Behavioral and Social Sciences and
         Education, National Research Council. Washington, D.C.: National Academy
         Press.

Gladstone, Leslie
1990   Parental Leave: Legislation in the 101st Congress. CRS Issue Brief
         1B86132 (February 14). Congressional Research Service, Washington,
         D.C.

Googins, Bradley
1988   The relationship between work and family. *The Almacan* 18(9):20-24.

Gordon, Nancy
1988   Statement Before the Subcommittee on Health and the Environment,
         House Committee on Energy and Commerce, U.S. Congress (April 15).

Gould, S., and J.D. Werbel
1983   Work involvement: A comparison of dual wage earner and single wage
         earner families. *Journal of Applied Psychology* 68:313-319.

Gove, Walter R., and Carol Zeiss
1987   Multiple roles and happiness. Pp. 125-137 in F.J. Crosby (ed.), *Spouse,
         Parent, Worker: On Gender and Multiple Roles.* New Haven, Conn.:
         Yale University Press.

Greenwald, Matthew H.
1987   Health insurance: The crucial employee benefit. Pp. 73-80 in *America
         in Transition: Benefits for the Future.* Washington, D.C.: Employee
         Benefit Research Institute.

Grubb, W.N.
1988   Choices for Children: Policy Options for State Provision of Early Childhood
         Programs. Unpublished paper prepared for the Education Commission
         of the States. "The New School Finance Research Agenda: Resource
         and Utilization in Schools and School Districts."

Haber, Lawrence D.
1989   Issues in the Definition of Disability and the Use of Disability Survey
         Data. Paper presented at the Workshop on Disability Statistics, Com-
         mittee on National Statistics, Commission on Behavioral and Social
         Sciences and Education, National Research Council, Washington, D.C.
         (April 6-7).

Hamermesh, Daniel S.
1989   Unemployment insurance financing, short-term compensation, and labor demand. Pp. 937-990 in *Investing in People: A Strategy to Address America's Workforce Crisis*. Commission on Workforce Quality and Labor Market Efficiency, U.S. Department of Labor. Washington, D.C.: U.S. Government Printing Office.

Hamermesh, Daniel S., and Albert Rees
1988   *The Economics of Work and Pay*, Fourth Edition. New York: Harper & Row.

Handlin, Oscar, and Liliam Handlin
1982   *A Restless People: Americans in Rebellion, 1770-1787*. Garden City, N.Y.: Anchor Press/Doubleday.

Hareven, Tamara K.
1982   The life course and aging in historical perspective. In T.K. Hareven and K.O. Adams (eds.), *Life Course Transitions: An Interdisciplinary Perspective*. New York: Guilford Press.

Harrick, Edward J., Gene R. Vanek, and Joseph F. Michlitsch
1986   Alternate work schedules, productivity, leave usage and employee attitudes: A field study. *Public Personnel Management* 15(Summer/2):159-169.

Harrison, A.O.
1989   Black working women. In R.L. Jones (ed.), *Black Adult Development and Aging*. Berkeley, Calif.: Cobb and Henry.

Hartmann, Heidi I., and Diana Pearce
1989   *High Skill and Low Pay: The Economics of Child Care Work*. Washington, D.C.: Institute for Women's Policy Research.

Haskins, R.
1988   What day care crisis? *AEI Journal on Government and Society Regulation* 2:13-21.

Hayes, Cheryl D., John Palmer, and Martha Zaslow, eds.
1990   *Who Cares for America's Children? Child Care Policy for the 1990s*. Report of the Panel on Child Care Policy, Committee on Child Development Research and Public Policy, Commission on Behavioral and Social Sciences and Education, National Research Council. Washington, D.C.: National Academy Press.

Hayghe, Howard V., and Steven E. Haugen
1987   A profile of husbands in today's labor market. *Monthly Labor Review* 110(10):12-17.

Haynes, S.G., E.D. Eaker, and M. Feinleib
1984   The effect of employment, family, and job stress on coronary heart disease patterns in women. Pp. 37-48 in E.B. Gold (ed.), *The Changing Risk of Disease in Women: An Epidemiologic Approach*. Lexington, Mass.: D.C. Heath.

Heilbroner, Robert L.
1972   *The Making of Economic Society*, Fourth Edition. Englewood Cliffs, N.J.: Prentice-Hall.

Hendrickson, Susan E., and Isabel V. Sawhill
  1989   *Assisting the Working Poor.* Discussion paper from the Changing Domestic Priorities Project. Washington, D.C.: The Urban Institute (May).
Heyns, Barbara
  1982   The influence of parents' work on children's school achievement. Pp. 229-267 in Sheila B. Kamerman and Cheryl D. Hayes (eds.), *Families That Work: Children in a Changing World.* Panel on Work, Family, and Community, Committee on Child Development Research and Public Policy, Commission on Behavioral and Social Sciences and Education, National Research Council. Washington, D.C.: National Academy Press.
Hill, Martha S.
  1979   The wage effects of marital status and children. *Journal of Human Resources* 14:579-593.
Hill, Martha S., and James N. Morgan
  1990   Expanding Choices for Human Capital Expenditures: A Proposal to Enhance the Financial Security of Children. Paper prepared for the Second International Conference on Research in the Consumer Interest. Institute for Social Research, University of Michigan (August).
Hofferth, Sandra
  1987   Statement on Child Care in the U.S. before the Select Committee on Children, Youth, and Families (July 1).
  1988   The Current Child Care Debate in Context. Revised version of paper presented at the annual meeting of the American Sociological Association, Chicago (August).
Hofferth, Sandra L., and D.A. Phillips
  1987   Child care in the United States, 1970 to 1995. *Journal of Marriage and the Family* 49:554-571.
Hoffman, Lois
  1987   The effects on children of maternal and paternal employment. Pp. 362-395 in Naomi Gerstel and Harriet Engel Gross (eds.), *Families and Work.* Philadelphia: Temple University Press.
Hoffman, Lois, and F.I. Nye, eds.
  1974   *Working Mothers.* San Francisco: Jossey-Bass.
Holmes, T.S., and R.H. Rahe
  1976   The social readjustment rating scale. *Journal of Psychosomatic Research* 11:13-18.
Horvath, Francis W.
  1986   Work at home: New findings from the Current Population Survey. *Monthly Labor Review* 109 (November):31-35.
Howes, C.
  in press Current research in early day care: A review. In S. Chehrazi (ed.), *Balancing Working and Parenting: Psychological and Developmental Implications of Day Care.* New York: American Psychiatric Press.
Howes, C., and M. Olenick
  1986   Family and child influences on toddlers' compliance. *Child Development* 57:202-216.

IBM
  1988a   Friend of the family. *Think* 54(1):1-5.
  1988b   New Work Flexibility Programs Announced by IBM. News Release (October 17). IBM Corporation, Armonk, N.Y.
Institute for American Values
  1989   *Family Affairs* 2(2-3/Summer-Fall).
  1990   *Family Affairs* 3(1-/Spring).
International Bank for Reconstruction and Development
  1988   *World Development Report.*
International Labour Organisation (ILO)
  1985   *Maternity Benefits in the 80's: An ILO Survey (1964-84).* Geneva: ILO.
  1988   *Yearbook of Labour Statistics.* Geneva: ILO.
International Monetary Fund (IMF)
  1988   *Government Finance Statistical Yearbook.* Volume XII. Washington, D.C.: IMF.
  1989   *Government Finance Statistical Yearbook.* Volume XIII. Washington, D.C.: IMF.
Jackson, James, and Toni Antonucci
  1989   Work, Stress and Well-Being Among Black, Mexican American, and White Families. Paper prepared for the Panel on Employer Policies and Working Families, Committee on Women's Employment and Related Social Issues, Commission on Behavioral and Social Sciences and Education, National Research Council, Washington, D.C.
Jarman, F.C., and T.M. Kohlenberg
  1988   Health and Safety Implications of Day Care. Paper prepared for the Panel on Child Care Policy, Committee on Child Development Research and Public Policy, Commission on Behavioral and Social Sciences and Education, National Research Council, Washington, D.C.
Jennings, S., C. Mazaik, and O.S. McKinley
  1984   Women and work: An investigation of the association between health and employment status in middle-aged women. *Social Science Medicine* 19:423-431.
Johnston, William B., and Arnold E. Packer
  1987   *Workforce 2000. Work and Workers for the Twenty-First Century.* Indianapolis, Ind.: Hudson Institute.
Juster, F. Thomas, and Frank Stafford, eds.
  1985   *Time, Goods and Well-Being.* Ann Arbor, Mich.: Institute for Social Research.
Kahn, Alfred J., and Sheila Kamerman
  1987   *Child Care: Facing the Hard Choices.* Dover, Mass.: Auburn House.
Kahne, Hilda
  1988   Part-time work: A hope and a peril. In Kitty Lundy and Barbara Warme (eds.), *Part-Time Work: Opportunity or Dead End?* New York: Praeger Press.
Kamerman, Sheila B.
  1988   Child Care Policies and Programs: An International Overview. Paper prepared for the Panel on Child Care Policy, Committee on Child De-

velopment Research and Public Policy, Commission on Behavioral and Social Sciences and Education, National Research Council, Washington, D.C. (August).

Kamerman, Sheila B., and Cheryl D. Hayes, eds.
  1982   *Families That Work: Children in a Changing World.* Panel on Work, Family, and Community, Committee on Child Development Research and Public Policy, Commission on Behavioral and Social Sciences and Education, National Research Council. Washington, D.C.: National Academy Press.

Kamerman, Sheila B., and Alfred J. Kahn
  1981   *Child Care, Family Benefits, and Working Parents: A Study in Comparative Policy.* New York: Columbia University Press.
  1987   *The Responsive Workplace: Employers and a Changing Labor Force.* New York: Columbia University Press.

Kamerman, Sheila B., Alfred J. Kahn, and Paul Kingston
  1983   *Maternity Policies and Working Women.* New York: Columbia University Press.

Kanner, A.D., J.C. Coyne, C. Schaefer, and R.S. Lazarus
  1981   Comparison of two modes of stress management: Daily hassles and uplifts versus major life events. *Journal of Behavioral Medicine* 4(1):1-39.

Kanter, Rosabeth Moss
  1977a   *Men and Women of the Corporation.* New York: Basic Books.
  1977b   *Work and Family in the United States: A Critical Review and Agenda for Research and Policy.* New York: Russell Sage Foundation.
  1983   *The Change Masters: Innovation for Productivity in the American Corporation.* New York: Simon and Schuster.
  1989   *When Giants Learn to Dance: Mastering the Challenge of Strategy, Management, and Careers in the 1990's.* New York: Simon and Schuster.

Katz, Lawrence F., and Lawrence H. Summers
  1988   Can Inter-Industry Wage Differentials Justify Strategic Trade Policy? NBER Working Paper 2739. National Bureau of Economic Research, Washington, D.C.

Katz, M.H., and O.S. Piotrkowski
  1983   Correlates of family role strain among employed black women. *Family Relations* 32:331-339.

Kean, Thomas
  1988   The states' role in the implementation of infant care leave. Pp. 333-442 in Edward F. Zigler and Meryl Frank (eds.), *The Parental Leave Crisis: Toward a National Policy.* New Haven, Conn.: Yale University Press.

Keith, P.M., and R.B. Schafer
  1980   Role strain and depression in two-job families. *Family Relations* 29:483-488.

Kessler, Ronald C., and James A. McRae
  1982   The effects of wives' employment on the mental health of married men and women. *American Sociological Review* 47:216-227.

Kisker, E.E., R. Maynard, A. Gordon, and M. Shain
1989   *The Child Care Challenge: What Parents Need and What Is Available in Three Metropolitan Areas.* Princeton, N.J.: Mathematica.

Krause and Markides
1985   Gender roles, illness, and illness behavior in a Mexican-American population. *Social Sciences Quarterly* 68(1):102-121.

Krug, D.N., V.E. Palmour, and M.C. Ballassai
1972   *Evaluation of the Office of Economic Opportunity Child Development Center.* Rockville, Md.: Westat, Inc.

Kudrle, Robert T., and Theodore R. Marmor
1981   The development of welfare states in North America. In Peter Flora and Arnold J. Heidenheimer (eds.), *The Development of Welfare States in Europe and North America.* New Brunswick, N.J.: Transaction Books.

Kutscher, Ronald E.
1989   Projection summary and emerging issues. *Monthly Labor Review* 112 (11):66-74.

Kynch, Jocelyn, and Amartya Sen
1983   Indian women: Well-being and survival. *Cambridge Journal of Economics* 7(3/4):363-380.

LaCroix, D.Z., and S.G. Haynes
1987   Gender differences in the health effects of workplace roles. Pp. 96-121 in R.C. Barnett, L. Biener, and G.K. Baruch (eds.), *Gender and Stress.* New York: Free Press.

Lang, Abigail M., and Emily M. Brody
1983   Characteristics of middle-aged daughters and help to their elderly mothers. *Journal of Marriage and the Family* 45:193-202.

Leibowitz, Arlene, and Linda J. Waite
1988   The Consequences for Women of the Availability and Affordability of Child Care. Paper prepared for the Panel on Child Care Policy, Committee on Child Development Research and Public Policy, Commission on Behavioral and Social Sciences and Education, National Research Council, Washington, D.C.

Levitan, Sar A., and Elizabeth A. Conway
1988   Raising America's Children: How Should We Care? Graduate Institute for Policy Education and Research, Graduate School of Arts and Sciences, George Washington University, Washington, D.C.

Lewin/ICF, Inc.
1988   Increases in Health Insurance Coverage in Small Firms, 1986-1988. Study Conducted for the National Association for the Self-Employed (June 7).

Lewis, Susan, N.C., and Cary L. Cooper
1987   Stress in two-earner couples and stage in the life cycle. *Journal of Occupational Psychology* 60:289-303.

Linsk, N.L., Keigher, S., and Suzanne E. Osterbusch
1988   States' policies regarding paid family caregiving. *The Gerontologist* 28:204-212.

Lipsig-Mumme, Carla
1983   The renaissance of homeworking in developed economies. *Relations Industrielles* 38(3):545-566.
Liu, Korbin, Pamela Doty, and Kenneth Manton
1990   Medicaid spenddown in nursing homes and the community. *The Gerontologist* 30(1):7-15.
Liu, Korbin, Kenneth Manton, and B.M. Liu
1986   Home care expenses for the disabled. *Health Care Financing Review* 7(2):51-58.
Lodge, George C.
1987   The United States: The costs of ambivalence. Pp. 103-39 in George C. Lodge and Ezra F. Vogel (eds.), *Ideology and National Competitiveness.* Cambridge, Mass.: Harvard University Press.
Lucas, Theodore
1986   *Employer Support for Employee Caregivers.* New York: New York Business Group on Health.
Macken, Candace L.
1986   A profile of functionally impaired elderly persons living in the community. *Health Care Financing Review* 7(4):33-49.
Magid, Renee L.
1983   *Child-Care Initiatives for Working Parents: Why Employers Get Involved.* New York: American Management Association.
Makuen, Kathleen
1988   Public servants, private parents: Parental leave policies in the public sector. Pp. 195-210 in Edward F. Zigler and Meryl Frank (eds.), *The Parental Leave Crisis: Toward a National Policy.* New Haven, Conn.: Yale University Press.
Maret, Elizabeth G.
1982   How women's health affects labor force attachment. *Monthly Labor Review* 105(4):56-58.
Marr, M.
1988   *The Child Care Crisis: Are Tax Credits the Answer? An Analysis of Seven Child Care Tax Credit Bills.* Washington, D.C.: Citizens for Tax Justice.
McAuley, William J., and Rosemary Blieszner
1985   Selection of long-term care arrangements by older community residents. *The Gerontologist* 25(April):189.
McGee, Lynne F.
1988   Setting up work at home. *Personnel Administrator* (December):58-62.
McGill, Dan M.
1988   Economic and financial implications of the aging phenomenon. *Proceedings of the American Philosophical Society* 132(2).
McGuire, Jean B., and Joseph R. Liro
1987   Absenteeism and flexible work schedules. *Public Personnel Management* 16(1/Spring):47-59.
McLanahan, Sara, and Rene Monson
1989   Caring for the Elderly: Prevalence and Consequences. Paper prepared for the Panel on Employer Policies and Working Families, Committee

on Women's Employment and Related Social Issues, Commission on
Behavioral and Social Sciences and Education, National Research Council,
Washington, D.C.

Meisenheimer, Joseph R., II, and William J. Wiatrowski
1989   Flexible benefits plans: Employees who have a choice. *Monthly Labor Review* 112(12):17-23.

Mellor, Earl F.
1986   Shift work and flexitime: How prevalent are they? *Monthly Labor Review* 109(11):14-21.

Messere, K.C., and J.P. Owens
1987   International comparisons of tax levels: Pitfalls and insights. *OECD Economic Studies* 8(Spring):93-119.

Meyer, S.J.
1984   *The Five-Dollar Day.* Albany: State University of New York Press.

Meyer, Jack A., and Marilyn Moon
1988   Health care spending on children and the elderly. Pp. 171-200 in John L. Palmer, Timothy Smeeding, and Barbara Boyle Torrey (eds.), *The Vulnerable.* Washington, D.C.: The Urban Institute Press.

Michael, Robert T., Heidi I. Hartmann, and Brigid O'Farrell, eds.
1989   *Pay Equity: Empirical Inquiries.* Panel on Pay Equity Research, Committee on Women's Employment and Related Social Issues, Commission on Behavioral and Social Sciences and Education, National Research Council. Washington, D.C.: National Academy Press.

Milkovich, G.T., and L.R. Gomez
1976   Daycare and selected employee work behaviors. *Academy of Management Journal* 19:111-115.

Miller, T.I.
1984   The effects of employer-sponsored child care on employee absenteeism, turnover, productivity, recruitment, or job satisfaction: What is claimed and what is known. *Personnel Psychology* 37:277-289.

Mincer, Jacob, and Solomon W. Polachek
1974   Family investments in human capital: Earnings of women. *Journal of Political Economy* 82 (2, Part 2):S76-S108.

Mitchell, Olivia S.
1989   The effects of mandating benefits packages. Pp. 1685-1726 in *Investing in People: A Strategy to Address America's Workforce Crisis.* Commission on Workforce Quality and Labor Market Efficiency, U.S. Department of Labor. Washington, D.C.: U.S. Government Printing Office.

Moen, Phyllis
1985   Continuities and discontinuities in women's labor force activity. Pp. 113-155 in Glen H. Elder, Jr. (ed.), *Life Course Dynamics: Trajectories and Transitions, 1968-1980.* Ithaca, N.Y.: Cornell University Press,
1989   *Working Parents: Transformations in Gender Roles and Public Policies in Sweden.* Madison: University of Wisconsin Press.

Moen, Phyllis, and Donna I. Dempster-McClain
1987   Employed parents: Role strain, work time, and preferences for working less. *Journal of Marriage and the Family* 49(August):579-590.

Moen, Phyllis, and Martha Moorehouse
1983   Overtime over the life cycle: A test of the life-cycle squeeze hypothesis. In H. Lopata and J. Pleck (eds.), *Research on the Interweave of Social Roles*, Vol. 3: Families and Jobs. Greenwich, Conn.: JAI Press.

Moen, Phyllis, and Ken R. Smith
1986   Women at work: Commitment and behavior over the life course. *Sociological Forum* 1(3):450-476.

Mooney, M.
1981   Wives' permanent employment and husbands' hours of work. *Industrial Relations* 20:205-211.

Monat, Alan, and Richard S. Lazarus
1977   *Stress and Coping: An Anthology.* New York: Columbia University Press.

Moore, Joan
1989   Is there an Hispanic underclass? *Social Science Quarterly* 7(2/June):265-284.

Moore, K.A., and S.L. Hofferth
1979   Effects of women's employment on marriage: Formation, stability and roles. *Marriage and Family Review* 2:27-36.

Morgan
1984   The role of time in the measurement of transfers and well-being. Pp. 199-238 in Marilyn Moon (ed.), *Economic Transfers in the United States.* Chicago: University of Chicago Press.

Morgan, G.
1987   *The National State of Child Care Regulation, 1986.* Watertown, Mass.: Work/Family Directions.

Mortimer, J.T.
1980   Occupation-family linkages as perceived by men in the early stages of professional and managerial careers. Pp. 99-117 in *Research on the Interweave of Social Roles*, Vol. 1: Women and Men. Greenwich, Conn.: JAI Press.

Moss, Peter
1988   Consolidated Report to the European Commission on Child Care and Equality of Opportunity. London, England (February).

Mott, P.E., F.C. Mann, D. McLoughlin, and D.P. Warwick
1965   *Shift Work.* Ann Arbor: University of Michigan Press.

Moyer, N. Eugene
1989   A revised look at the number of uninsured Americans. *Health Affairs* (Summer):102-110.

Munnell, Alicia H.
1989   It's time to tax employee benefits. *New England Economic Review* (July/August):49-63.

Nelson, William J., Jr.
1989   Workers' compensation: Coverage, benefits and costs, 1986. *Social Security Bulletin* 52(3):34-41.

Nollen, Stanley D.
1979   Does flextime improve productivity? *Harvard Business Review* (September-October):12, 16-18, 22.

1982   *New Work Schedules in Practice.* New York: Van Nostrand Reinhold Company.

Norton, A.J., and P.C. Glick
1986   One parent families and a social and economic profile. *Family Relations* 35:9-17.

O'Connell, Martin
1990   Maternity leave arrangements: 1961-1985. Pp. 11-49 in *Work and Family Patterns of American Women.* Current Population Reports, Special Studies Series P-23, No. 165. (March). Washington, D.C.: U.S. Department of Commerce, Bureau of the Census.

O'Connell, Martin, and D.E. Bloom
1987   *Juggling Jobs and Babies: America's Child Care Challenge?* Population Trends and Public Policy Series, No. 12. Washington, D.C.: Population Reference Bureau, Inc.

O'Connell, Martin, and C.C. Rogers
1983   Child Care Arrangements of Working Mothers: June 1982. Current Population Reports, Series P-23, No. 129. Washington, D.C.: U.S. Department of Commerce, Bureau of the Census.

Office of Scientific and Engineering Personnel
1989   Responding to the Changing Demography: Women in Science and Engineering. Report of the Planning Group to Assess Possible OSEP Initiatives for Increasing the Participation of Women in Scientific and Engineering Careers. Office of Scientific and Engineering Personnel, National Research Council, Washington, D.C. (January).

O'Kelly, Charlotte G.
1980   *Women and Men in Society.* New York: Van Nostrand Company.

Olsen, M.
1985   The potential of remote work for professionals. Pp. 125-132 in *Office Workstations in the Home.* Board on Telecommunications and Computer Applications, Commission on Engineering and Technical Systems, National Research Council. Washington, D.C.: National Academy Press.

Olsen, M.H., and S.B. Primps
1984   Working at home with computers: Work and nonwork issues. *Journal of Social Issues* 40(3):97-112.

Organisation for Economic Cooperation and Development (OECD)
1983   *Employment Outlook.* Paris: OECD.
1986   *Living Conditions in OECD Countries.* Paris: OECD.
1987   *Employment Outlook.* Paris: OECD.
1988   *Historical Statistics, 1965-85.* Paris: OECD.
1989a   *Economic Outlook* (June). Paris: OECD.
1989b   *Economic Surveys: United States.* Paris: OECD.
1989c   *Historical Statistics, 1960-87.* Paris: OECD.

Owen, John D.
1977   Flexitime: Some problems and solutions. *Industrial and Labor Relations Review* 30(2):152-60.

Palmer, John L., Timothy Smeeding, and Barbara Boyle, eds.
1988   *The Vulnerable.* Washington, D.C.: The Urban Institute Press.

Papanek, Hanna
1973   Men, women, and work: Reflections on the two-person career. *American Journal of Sociology* 78(4):853-872.
Pechman, Joseph A., ed.
1988   *World Tax Reform: A Progress Report*. Washington, D.C.: The Brookings Institution.
Personick, Valerie A.
1989   Industry output and employment: A slower trend for the nineties. *Monthly Labor Review* 112(11):25-41.
Phillips, Deborah, ed.
1987   Quality in Child Care: What Does Research Tell Us? National Association for the Education of Young Children, Washington, D.C.
Piacentini, Joesph S.
1990   New findings on workforce trends challenge common perceptions. *Employee Benefit Notes* 11(2)3-5. Washington, D.C.: Employee Benefit Research Institute.
Piccirillo, Mary
1988   The legal background of a parental leave policy. Pp. 293-314 in Edward F. Zigler and Meryl Frank (eds.), *The Parental Leave Crisis: Toward a National Policy*. New Haven, Conn.: Yale University Press.
Piotrkowski, Chaya S.
1979   *Work and the Family System: A Naturalistic Study of Working-Class and Lower Middle-Class Families*. New York: Free Press.
Piotrkowski, Chaya S., and P. Crits-Christoph
1982   Women's jobs and family adjustment. Pp. 105-127 in J. Aldous (ed.), *Two Paychecks: Life in Dual-Earner Families*. Beverly Hills, Calif.: Sage Publications.
Piotrkowski, Chaya S., and Katz
1982   Indirect socialization of children: The effects of mothers' jobs on academic behavior. *Child Development* 53:1520-1529.
Piotrkowski, Chaya S., and R.L. Repetti
1984   Dual-earner families. In *Women and the Family: Two Decades of Change*: New York: Haworth Press.
Pleck, Joseph
1983   Husband's paid work and family roles: Current research issues. Pp. 251-326 in H.Z. Lopata and J.H. Pleck (eds.), *Research in the Interweave of Social Roles*, Vol. 2: Families and Jobs. Greenwich, Conn.: JAI Press.
1988   Fathers and infant care leave. Pp. 177-191 in Edward F Zigler and Meryl Frank (eds.), *The Parental Leave Crisis*. New Haven, Conn.: Yale University Press.
1989   Family Supportive Employer Policies and Men's Participation. Paper prepared for the Panel on Employer Policies and Working Families, Committee on Women's Employment and Related Social Issues, Commission on Behavioral and Social Sciences and Education, National Research Council, Washington, D.C.

Pleck, J.H., and L. Lang
    1978   Men's Family Role. Unpublished manuscript, Wellesley Center for
            Research on Women, Wellesley College.
Pleck, Joseph, Graham L. Staines, and Linda Lang
    1980   Conflicts between work and family life. *Monthly Labor Review* 103:29-
            32.
Polachek, Solomon W.
    1979   Occupational segregation: Theory, evidence and prognosis. In Cynthia
            Lloyd, Emily Andrews, and Curtis Gilroy (eds.), *Women in the Labor
            Market*. New York: Columbia University Press.
    1981   Occupational self-selection: A human capital approach to sex differ-
            ences in occupational structure. *The Review of Economics and Statis-
            tics* 63(1):60-69.
    1987   Occupational segregation and the gender wage gap. *Population Re-
            search and Policy Review* 6:47-67.
Presser, Harriet B.
    1988   Shift work and child care among young dual-earner American parents.
            Journal of Marriage and the Family 50:133-148.
    1989   Can we make time for children? The economy, work schedules, and
            child care. *Demography* 26(4):523-543.
Presser, Harriett, and Wendy Baldwin
    1980   Child care as a constraint on employment: Prevalence, correlates, and
            bearing on the work and fertility nexus. *American Journal of Sociology*
            85:1202-1203.
Presser, Harriet B., and Virginia S. Cain
    1983   Shift work among dual-earner couples with children. *Science* 219(Feb-
            ruary 18):876-879.
Preston, Samuel H.
    1984   Children and the elderly: Divergent paths for America's dependents.
            Demography 21(4):435-457.
Price, Richard J., and Carol O'Shaughnessy
    1988   Long-Term Care for the Elderly. Issue Brief IB88098. Education and
            Public Welfare Division, Congressional Research Service, Washington,
            D.C.
Quadagno, Jill
    1988   *The Transformation of Old Age Security*. Chicago: University of Chi-
            cago Press.
Quinn, Robert P., and Graham L. Staines
    1979   *The 1977 Quality of Employment Survey*. Ann Arbor: University of
            Michigan.
Racki, Georg H.E.M.
    1975   The Effects of Flexible Working Hours. Ph.D. dissertation, University
            of Lausanne. (Cited in Kanter, 1977b.)
Rallings, E.M., and F.I. Nye
    1979   Wife-mother employment, family and society. In W.R. Burr et al. (eds.),
            Contemporary Theories About the Family, Vol. 1. New York: Free
            Press.

Ramey, C.T., D.M. Bryant, and T.M. Suarez
1985   Preschool compensatory education and the modifiability of intelligence: A critical review. *Current Topics in Human Intelligence* 1:247-296.
Ransom, Cynthia, and Sandra Burud
1986   Productivity Impact Study. Conducted for Union Bank Child Care Center, Monterey, Calif.
Ratner, R.S.
1986   The paradox of protection: Maximum hours legislation in the United States. *International Labour Review* 119:187-188.
Reich, Robert B.
1987   *Tales of a New America.* New York: Times Books.
Rein, Martin
1989   The Social Policy of the Firm and the State. Paper prepared for the Panel on Employer Policies and Working Families, Committee on Women's Employment and Related Social Issues, Commission on Behavioral and Social Sciences and Education, National Research Council, Washington, D.C.
Reisman, B., A. Moore, and K. Fitzgerald
1988   *Child Care: The Bottom Line—An Economic and Child Care Policy Paper.* New York: The Child Care Action Campaign.
Repetti, Rena L.
1987   Linkages between work and family roles. Pp. 98-127 in Stuart Oskamp (ed.), *Applied Social Psychology Annual*, Vol. 7: Family Processes and Problems. Beverly Hills, Calif.: Sage Publications.
Repetti, Rena L., Karen A. Matthews, and Ingrid Waldron
1989   Employment and women's health: Effects of paid employment on women's mental and physical health. *American Psychologist* 44(11):1394-1401.
Ridley, Carl A.
1973   Exploring the impact of work satisfaction and involvement on marital interaction when both partners are employed. *Journal of Marriage and the Family* 35(2):229-237.
Rivlin, Alice M., and Joshua M. Wiener, with Raymond J. Hanley and Denise A. Spence
1988   *Caring for the Disabled Elderly: Who Will Pay?* Washington, D.C.: The Brookings Institution.
Rix, Sara E.
1984   Older Women: The Economics of Aging. Women's Research and Education Institute of the Congressional Caucus for Women's Issues, Washington, D.C.
Robins, P.
1988   Federal support for child care: Current policies and a proposed new system. *Focus* 11(2):1-9. Madison: Institute for Research on Poverty, University of Wisconsin.
Robinson, John
1977a   *Change in Americans' Use of Time: 1965-1975.* Cleveland: Communications Research Center, Cleveland State University.
1977b   *How Americans Use Time: A Social-Psychological Analysis.* New York: Praeger.

Robinson, Olive
    1979   Part-time employment in the European Community. *International Labour Review* 118(3):299-314.
Rodman, H.
    1971   *Lower-Class Families.* New York: Oxford University Press.
Roman, Paul
    1988   Growth and transformation in workplace alcoholism programming. Pp. 131-158 in M. Galanter (ed.), *Recent Developments in Alcoholism*, Volume 6. New York: Plenum.
Rosenfield, S.
    1989   The effects of wives' employment: Personal control and sex differences in mental health. *Journal of Health and Social Behavior* 30:77-91.
Ross, Catherine E., John Mirowsky, and Joan Huber
    1983   Dividing work, sharing work, and in-between: Marriage patterns and depression. *American Sociological Review* 48:809-823.
Ross, Susan Deller
    1990   Parental leave: At the crossroads. In J.S. Hyde and M.J. Essex (eds.), *Parental Leave and Child Care: Setting a Research and Policy Agenda.* Philadelphia: Temple University Press.
Ruben, George
    1989   Collective bargaining in 1989: Old problems, new issues. *Monthly Labor Review* 113(1):19-29.
Ruopp, R., J. Travers, F. Glantz, and C. Coelen
    1979   *Children at the Center: Final Results of the National Day Care Study.* Boston: Abt Associates.
Saltford, Nancy, and Ramona Heck
    1989   An Overview of Employee Benefits Supportive of Families. Paper prepared for the Panel on Employer Policies and Working Families, Committee on Women's Employment and Related Social Issues, Commission on Behavioral and Social Sciences and Education, National Research Council, Washington, D.C.
Sandefur, G.D.
    1985   Variations in interstate migration of men across the early stages of the life cycle. *Demography* 22:353-366.
Schatz, Ronald W.
    1983   *The Electrical Workers: A History of Labor at General Electric and Westinghouse, 1923-1960.* Urbana: University of Illinois Press.
Schnitzer, Martin C., and James W. Nordyke
    1983   *Comparative Economic Systems.* Cincinnati: South-Western Publishing Co.
Schwartz, Felize N.
    1989   Management women and the new facts of life. *Harvard Business Review* 67(1):65-76.
Scott, J.A.
    1987   The coalminers' fight for parental leave: Part II. *ILF Report* 25(1):24-27.

Service Employees International Union
1989   Employer-Paid Health Insurance Is Disappearing: A Survey of Benefit Takeaways in Contract Bargaining. SEIU Department of Public Policy (July).

Sexton, Patricia Cayo
1982   *The New Nightingales: Hospital Workers, Unions and New Women's Issues.* New York: Enquiry Press.

Shamin, Teodor, ed.
1987   *Peasants and Peasant Societies*, Second Edition. New York: Blackwell.

Shinn, M., B. Ortiz-Torres, A. Morris, P. Simko, and N. Wong
1987   Child Care Patterns, Stress, and Job Behaviors Among Working Parents. Paper presented at the annual convention of the American Psychological Association, New York (August).

Short, P., and J. Leon
1990   *Use of Home and Community Services by Persons Age 65 and Older with Functional Difficulties.* DHHS Publication No. PHS 90-3466. National Medical Expenditure Survey Research Findings 5, Agency for Health Care Policy and Research. Rockville, Md.: Public Health Service.

Silver, Hilary
1989   The demand for homework: Evidence from the U.S. Census. Pp. 103-129 in Eileen Boris and Cynthia R. Daniels (eds.), *Homework: Historical and Contemporary Perspectives on Paid Labor at Home.* Urbana: University of Illinois Press.

Silvestri, George, and John Lukasiewicz
1989   Projections of occupational employment, 1988-2000. *Monthly Labor Review* 112(11):42-65.

Simpson, I.H., and Paula England
1982   Conjugal work roles and marital solidarity. Pp. 147-172 in J. Aldous (ed.), *Two Paychecks: Life in Dual-Earner Families.* Beverly Hills, Calif.: Sage Publications.

Slaughter, D.T.
1983   Early intervention and its effects on maternal and child development. *Monographs of the Society for Research in Child Development* 48(4, Serial No. 202).

Smith, S.J.
1983   Estimating annual hours of labor force activity. *Monthly Labor Review* 106(February):13-22.

Smyer, M.
1980   *The Elderly Home Care Population: National Prevalence Rates, Selected Characteristics, and Alternative Sources of Assistance.* Working Paper 1466-29. Washington, D.C.: The Urban Institute.

Soldo, Beth J., and Kenneth G. Manton
1985   Health status and service needs of the oldest old: Current patterns and future trends. *Health and Society* 63(2):286-319.

Sonenstein, F.L., and D.A. Wolf
1988   Caring for the Children of Welfare Mothers. Paper presented at the annual meeting of the Population Association of America (April).

Spalter-Roth, Roberta M., and Heidi I. Hartmann
  1990   Unnecessary Losses: Costs to Americans of the Lack of Family and
          Medical Leave. Washington, D.C.: Institute for Women's Policy Re-
          search.
Spalter-Roth, Roberta M., Heidi I. Hartmann, and Linda Andrews
  1989   Who Needs a Family Wage? The Implications of Low-Wage Work for
          Family Well-Being. Paper prepared for the Panel on Employer Policies
          and Working Families, Committee on Women's Employment and Re-
          lated Social Issues, Commission on Behavioral and Social Sciences
          and Education, National Research Council, Washington, D.C.
Spitze, Glenna
  1988   Women's employment and family relations: A review. *Journal of
          Marriage and the Family* 50(3):595-618.
Spitze, Glenna, and Scott J. South
  1985   Women's employment, time expenditure, and divorce. *Journal of Fam-
          ily Issues* 6:307-29.
Staines, Graham L.
  1989   Working hours flexibility. Pp. 1609-1644 in *Investing in People: A
          Strategy to Addressing America's Workforce Crisis.* Commission on
          Workforce Quality and Labor Market Efficiency, U.S. Department of
          Labor. Washington, D.C.: U.S. Goverment Printing Office.
Staines, Graham L., and Joseph L. Pleck
  1983   The Impact of Work Schedules on the Family. Ann Arbor: University
          of Michigan Survey Research Center, Institute for Social Research.
State of New York Workers' Compensation Board
  1986   Disability Benefits Program: Claim Statistics, 1967-1986. Prepared
          by Office of Research and Statistics, Workers' Compensation Board,
          State of New York.
Stephen, Sharon, and Anne Stewart
  1989   Side-by-Side Comparison of H.R. 3 as reported by the Education and
          Labor Committee and Ordered Reported by the Ways and Means Com-
          mittee, Congressional Research Service, Washington, D.C. (September
          15).
Stewart, Anne C.
  1990   Child Day Care. CRS Issues Brief IB89011 (January 18). Congres-
          sional Research Service, Washington, D.C.
Stoiber, Susanne A.
  1989   *Parental Leave and Woman's Place: The Implications and Impact of
          Three European Approaches to Family Leave Policy.* Washington, D.C.:
          Women's Research and Education Institute.
Stoller, Eleanor Palo
  1983   Parental caregiving by adult children. *Journal of Marriage and the
          Family* 45:851-858.
Stone and Kemper
  1989a   Spouses and children of disabled elders: How large a constituency for
          long-term care reform? *The Milbank Quarterly* 67(3-4):485-507.
  1989b   Spouses and Children of Disabled Elders: Potential and Active Caregivers.

Paper prepared for the National Center for Health Services Research and Health Care Technology Assessment, Public Health Service, U.S. Department of Health and Human Services. Washington, D.C.: U.S. Government Printing Office (January).

Stone, Robyn I., Gail Lee Cafferata, and Judith Sangl
1987   Caregivers of the Frail Elderly: A National Profile. National Center for Health Services Research and Health Care Technology Assessment, Public Health Service, U.S. Department of Health and Human Services. Report No. 181-345:60026. Washington, D.C.: U.S. Government Printing Office.

Summers, Lawrence R.
1989   Some simple economics of mandated benefits. *American Economic Review* 19(2/May):177-183.

Swain, Frank S.
1988   Statement before the Panel on Employer Policies and Working Families, Committee on Women's Employment and Related Social Issues, Commission on Behavioral and Social Sciences and Education, National Research Council, Washington, D.C. (November 11.)

Swartz, Katherine
1989   *The Medically Uninsured: Special Focus on Workers.* Washington, D.C.: The Urban Institute.

Taeuber, Cynthia
1983   *America in Transition: An Aging Society.* Current Population Reports, Special Studies Series P-23, No. 128. Washington, D.C.: U.S. Department of Commerce, Bureau of the Census.

Thomas, Sandra, Kay Albrecht, and Priscilla White
1984   Determinants of marital quality in dual-career couples. *Family Relations* 33(4):513-521.

Thornton, Arnold, and Deborah Freedman
1983   *The Changing American Family.* Washington, D.C.: Population Reference Bureau.

Thurow, Lester
1989   *Toward a High-Wage, High-Productivity Service Sector.* Washington, D.C.: The Economic Policy Institute.

The Travelers' Companies
1985   The Travelers' Employee Caregiver Survey: A Survey on Caregiving Responsibilities of Travelers' Employees for Older Americans (June).

Treiman, Donald, and Heidi W. Hartmann, eds.
1981   *Women, Work, and Wages: Equal Pay for Jobs of Equal Value.* Committee on Occupational Classification and Analysis, Assembly of Behavioral and Social Sciences, National Research Council. Washington, D.C.: National Academy Press.

Trzcinski, Eileen
1988a   Incidence and Determinants of Maternity Leave Coverage. Unpublished paper, April.
1988b   Wage and Employment Effects of Mandated Leave Policies. Unpublished paper, April.

1989   Parental Leave: Issues and Findings from a Connecticut Survey of Employees. Paper prepared for the Panel on Employer Policies and Working Families, Committee on Women's Employment and Related Social Issues, Commission on Behavioral and Social Sciences and Education, National Research Council, Washington, D.C.

United Nations
1986   *Demographic Yearbook, 1985.* New York: United Nations.

U.S. Chamber of Commerce
1987   Testimony of Frances Shaine on Behalf of the Chamber of Commerce of the United States on S.249, Parental and Medical Leave Act of 1987. Presented to the Subcommittee on Children, Family, Drugs and Alcoholism of the Senate Committee on Labor and Human Resources (February 19).

1988   Employee Benefits: Survey Data from Benefit Years, 1987. Washington, D.C.: U.S. Chamber Research Center, Economic Policy Division.

1989   Statement by Earl Hess before the U.S. House Committee on Education and Labor, Subcommittee on Labor-Management Relations on Parental Leave (February 7).

U.S. Congress, House
1987   *Exploding the Myths: Caregiving in America.* Subcommittee on Human Services, Select Committee on Aging. 100th Congress, 1st Session. Committee Publication No. 99-611. Washington, D.C.: U.S. Government Printing Office.

1988   *1987 Omnibus Budget Reconciliation Act.* Washington, D.C.: U.S. Government Printing Office.

1989   *U.S. Children and Their Families, Current Conditions and Recent Trends, 1989.* Report to the U.S. House of Representatives, 100th Congress. Washington, D.C.: U.S. Government Printing Office.

U.S. Department of Health and Human Services, Social Security Administration
1985   *Social Security Programs Throughout the World.* Washington, D.C.: U.S. Government Printing Office.

U.S. Department of Labor
1988   *Childcare: A Workforce Issue.* Report of the Secretary's Task Force, April 1988.

U.S. National Center for Health Statistics
1984   *Vital Statistics of the United States, Annual.*

U.S. Small Business Administration
1987   *The State of Small Business: A Report of the President.* Washington, D.C.: U.S. Government Printing Office.

Verbrugge, Lois M.
1987   Role responsibilities, role burdens and physical health. In Faye J. Crosby (ed.), *Spouse, Parent, Worker: On Gender and Multiple Roles.* New Haven, Conn.: Yale University Press.

Vickery, Clair
1977   The time-poor: A new look at poverty. *Journal of Human Resources* 12(1):27-48.

Voydanoff, Patricia
1984   Work Role Characteristics, Family Structure Demands and Quality of

Family Life. Paper presented at the annual meeting of the National Council on Family Relations.
1987   *Work and Family Life. Family Studies Text Series No. 6.* Newbury Park, Calif.: Sage Publications.
1988   Work role characteristics, family structure demands, and work/family conflict. *Journal of Marriage and the Family* 50(August):749-761.

Voydanoff, Patricia, and R.F. Kelly
1984   Determinants of work-related family problems among employed parents. *Journal of Marriage and the Family* 46:881-892.

Wade, Michael
1973   *Flexible Working Hours in Practice.* New York: John Wiley and Sons.

Waite, Linda J., Arleen Leibowitz, and Christina Witsberger
1988   What Parents Pay For: Quality of Child Care and Child Care Costs. Santa Monica, Calif.: Rand Corporation (March).

Waldstein, Louisa
1989   Service sector wages, productivity and job creation in the U.S. and other countries. Pp. 15-57 in Lester Thurow (ed.), *Toward a High Wage, High Productivity Service Sector.* Washington D.C.: Economic Policy Institute.

Walker, Deborah
1988   *Mandating Family-Leave Legislation: The Hidden Costs.* Washington, D.C.: Cato Institute.

Walker, Katherine, and William Gaugere
1973   The Dollar Value of Household Work. Information Bulletin No. 60. New York State College of Human Ecology, Cornell University.

Walker, Katherine E., and Margaret E. Woods
1976   *Time Use: A Measure of Household Production of Family Goods and Services.* Washington, D.C.: American Home Economics Association.

Watkins, Susan C., and Jane Menken
1987   Demographic foundations of family change. *American Sociological Review* 52(June):346-358.

Weiner, Steve
1989   We decided to show how things can work. *Forbes* (September 18):180-188.

Welter, Barbara
1978   The cult of true womanhood, 1820-1860. Pp. 313-333 in Michael Gordon (ed.), *The American Family in Social-Historical Perspective.* New York: St. Martin's Press.

Whitebook, Mary, Deborah Phillips, and Carollee Howes
1989   *Who Cares? Child Care Teachers and the Quality of Care in America.* Oakland, Calif.: Child Care Employee Project (October).

Whyte, William H., Jr.
1951   The wives of management. *Fortune* (October):86-88, 204-213 and (November):109-111, 150-158.

Wiatrowski, William J.
1988   Comparing employee benefits in the public and private sectors. *Monthly Labor Review* 111(12):3-8.

Wilensky, Harold L.
1976   The New Corporation: Centralization and the Welfare State. London: Sage Publications.
1983   Political legitimacy and concerns: Missing variables in the assessment of social policy. In S.E. Spuro and E. Yuchtman-Yaar (eds.), Evaluating the Welfare State: Social and Political Perspectives. New York: Academic Press.

Wilensky, Harold, Gregory M. Luebbert, Susan Reed Hahn, and Adrienne M. Jamieson
1985   Comparative Social Policy. Berkely, Calif.: University of California, Institute of International Studies.

Will, George
1989   A school for families. Newsweek October 9:118.

Williams, Wendy
1985   Equality's riddle: Pregnancy and the equal treatment/special treatment debate. New York University Review of Law and Social Change 13(2):325-380.

Wilson, William Julius
1987   The Truly Disadvantaged: The Inner City, the Underclass, and Public Policy. Chicago: University of Chicago Press.

Wohl, Faith A.
1989   Management women: Debating the facts of life. Harvard Business Review 67(3):183.

Woodbury, Stephan A.
1989   Current economic issues in employee benefits. In Investing in People: A Strategy to Address America's Workplace Crisis. Commission on Workforce Quality and Labor Market Efficiency, U.S. Department of Labor. Washington, D.C.: U.S. Government Printing Office.

Wyatt Company
1988   A Survey of Health and Welfare Plans Covering Salaried Employees of U.S. Employers.

Young, M., and P. Wilmott
1973   The Symmetrical Family. New York: Penguin Books.

Youngblood, Stewart A., and Kimberly Chambers-Cook
1984   Child care assistance can improve employee attitudes and behavior. Personnel Administrator (February):45-46, 93-95.

Zigler, Edward F., and Meryl Frank, eds.
1988   The Parental Leave Crisis: Toward a National Policy. New Haven, Conn.: Yale University Press.

Zitter, M.
1989   Summary of Workshop on Disability Statistics, Committee on National Statistics, Commission on Behavioral and Social Sciences and Education, National Research Council, Washington, D.C. (August 17).

Zuckerman, Harriett
1987   Persistence and change in the careers of men and women scientists and engineers: A review of current research. In Linda S. Dix (ed.), Women: Their Underrepresentation and Career Differentials in Science and Engineering. Washington, D.C.: National Academy Press.

APPENDIX

A

Background Materials

PAPERS

In the course of its study, the panel commissioned papers on a number of topics: the prevalence and consequences of caring for elderly people; work, stress, and well-being among black, Mexican American, and white families; the implications of low-wage work for family well-being; an overview of employee benefits supportive of families; a state survey of employers on parental leave; the role of collective bargaining for work and family issues; the role of men's participation in family-supportive policies; an international comparison of the social welfare policy of the firm and the state; and case studies on the implementation of flexible time and leave policies in Sweden and Germany.

The papers listed below are available from the Women's Bureau, U.S. Department of Labor.

Family Perspectives

Work, Stress, and Well-Being Among Black, Mexican American, and White Families
    James S. Jackson and Toni C. Antonucci
    Institute for Social Research, University of Michigan

Caring for the Elderly: Prevalence and Consequences
    Sara A. McLanahan and Renee Monson
    Department of Sociology, University of Wisconsin

234

Who Needs a Family Wage? The Implications of Low-Wage Work for Family Well-Being
  Roberta M. Spalter-Roth, Heidi I. Hartmann, and Linda Andrews
  Institute for Women's Policy Research, Washington, D.C.

Employer and Union Initiatives

Work, Family, and Collective Bargaining
  Alice H. Cook
  School of Industrial and Labor Relations, Cornell University

An Overview of Employee Benefits Supportive of Families
  Nancy C. Saltford
  Employee Benefit Research Institute, Washington, D.C.
  Ramona K. Z. Heck
  Department of Consumer Economics, Cornell University

Family-Supportive Employer Policies and Men's Participation
  Joseph H. Pleck
  Department of Psychology, Wheaton College

Parental Leave: Issues and Findings from a Connecticut Survey of Employers
  Eileen Trczinski
  Bush Center, Yale University, and Department of Consumer Economics, Cornell University

International Comparisons

The Implementation of Flexible Time and Leave Policies: Observations from European Employers
  Ellen Galinsky
  Bank Street College

The Social Policy of the Firm and the State
  Martin Rein
  Department of Urban Studies and Planning, Massachusetts Institute of Technology

EXPERTS IN RELATED AREAS

The panel met with the following experts in the course of its five meetings and at a 2-day workshop on March 20-21, 1989.

Emily Andrews, Research Director, Employee Benefit Research Institute, Washington, D.C.

Helen Axel, Director, Work and Family Information Center, The Conference Board, New York

Doug Besharov, American Enterprise Institute, Washington, D.C.

Joanne Browne, Service Employees International Union, Washington, D.C.

May Chen, International Ladies Garment Workers Union, New York

Michael Creedon, Director of Corporate Programs, National Council on Aging

Margaret Doolin, Governor's Office of Employee Relations, New York State

Jeri Eckhart, Associate Deputy Secretary, U.S. Department of Labor

Jill Emery, Deputy Director, Women's Bureau, U.S. Department of Labor

Lela Foreman, Communications Workers of America, Washington, D.C.

Dana Friedman, Work and Family Information Center, The Conference Board, New York

Nancy Gordon, Assistant Director, Human Resources and Community Development, Congressional Budget Office

Sandra Hofferth, Demographic and Behavioral Science Branch, National Institute of Child Health and Human Development

Karen Ignoni, Associate Director, Department of Occupational Health, Safety and Security, AFL-CIO, Washington, D.C.

Sheila Kamerman, School of Social Work, Columbia University

Richard Kleinert, Mercer, Meidinger, Hansen, Cleveland, Ohio

Alan Kraut, Department of Personnel Research, IBM Corporation

Barbara Leonard, Director of Children's Programs, General Services Administration, Washington, D.C.

Michelle Lord, Director, Congressional Caucus for Women's Issues

Georgina Lucas, Vice President, The Traveler's Companies, Hartford, Connecticut

Janet Norwood, Director, Bureau of Labor Statistics, U.S. Department of Labor

Harriett Presser, Department of Sociology, University of Maryland

Rhona Rapaport, Institute of Family and Environmental Research, London

Peter Reinecke, Research Director, Subcommittee on Health and Long-Term Care, Committee on Aging, U.S. Congress

Fran Rodgers, Co-president, Work/Family Directions, Watertown, Massachusetts

Ann Rosewater, Select Committee on Children, Youth, and Families, U.S. Congress

Christine Russell, U.S. Chamber of Commerce, Washington, D.C.

Isabel Sawhill, The Urban Institute, Washington, D.C.

Howard Shafer, Vice President, Public Employees Federation, New York State

Margaret Simms, Joint Center for Political Studies, Washington, D.C.

Joy Simonsen, Employment and Housing Subcommittee, House Government Operations Committee, U.S. Congress

Frank Swain, Chief Counsel for Advocacy, U.S. Small Business Administration

Robyn Stone, Research Fellow, National Center for Health Services Research

Virginia Thomas, Manager, Employee Relations, U.S. Chamber of Commerce, Washington, D.C.

Martha Zaslow, Research Associate, Panel on Child Care Policy, Committee on Child Development Research and Public Policy, National Research Council

B

Data Needs and Research Agenda

DATA NEEDS

Adequate data and sound research are indispensable foundations for policy making. Throughout this report we mainly used data collected by government agencies, supplemented by surveys done by nonprofit institutions and, to a much lesser extent, surveys by businesses and business associations. It is to be hoped that, despite tight budgets, government data collection will not only be continued, but will also be expanded to include more data on individuals, families, and firms, which are now all too scarce. Such efforts need to be on a substantial scale in order to avoid problems of selection bias. Nonprofit institutions also need adequate funds to pioneer new ideas and innovative methods. To the extent that rules of confidentiality permit, data collected from employers and unions should be made available to the public in a timely fashion. It would also be useful if private firms could find ways to share the information they gather with each other and make that information available to researchers.

Because most of our suggestions are for additions to work that has already proven to be fruitful, the payoff can be expected to be large in relation to relatively modest costs. Thus, the data collection efforts we propose should be attractive even in this era of budget cutting. Skimping on data collection is a false economy, because the costs of shaping policies without adequate information are likely to greatly exceed any short-term savings.

Data on Individuals and Families

As discussed in this report, understanding of work and family relationships has been substantially enhanced by the availability of the relatively recent longitudinal data sets, which are particularly well suited to studying the impact of changes. They include the widely used Michigan Panel Study of Income Dynamics, the Ohio State University National Longitudinal Surveys, the Census Bureau's Survey of Income and Program Participation, and the University of Wisconsin's new National Survey of Families and Households. Important contributions have also been made by one-time surveys that focused on particular issues, such as the Long-Term Care Survey, and particular populations, such as the National Survey of Black Americans and the National Survey of Americans of Mexican Descent. Because the federal government is best equipped to carry out large-scale, long-term data collection, it should consider institutionalizing some of these projects initiated by research organizations. All of these surveys cover basic income data and some household characteristics. In addition, new initiatives are needed in the areas described below.

One subject on which there is very little information is people's use of time. Far less is known about how people spend their time than about how they spend their money, although awareness is growing that in American society there are many individuals and families who are "time poor" (Vickery, 1977). Some researchers, notably Walker and Gauger (1973), Walker and Woods (1976), Robinson (1977a, 1977b), and Juster and Stafford (1985) have done pioneering work in this area. Such information aids in evaluating the usefulness of various approaches to helping people manage the competing claims of work and family. Large-scale samples would provide information about the differences in use of time among individuals by gender, race, ethnicity, and class, as well as work and family status.

Better data on time use would also help to develop more reliable estimates of the value of nonmarket time and, more particularly, nonmarket work. Such data are crucial for the development of a useful measure of real income, a far better proxy for well-being than money income alone. Ignoring nonmarket time and work leads to such unrealistic conclusions as considering as equal two families with the same number of persons and the same earnings, whether or not there is a full-time homemaker.

Just as a great deal of data is collected on expenditures of money but not on expenditures of time, so are large amounts of information gathered about earnings but not about the rewards workers receive in the form of benefits. Asking questions about benefits, and perhaps also about working conditions, in addition to the usual ones about wages, will give a fuller picture of the total compensation employees receive. Such data would reveal whether differences in earnings overstate or understate differences in compensation. This is particularly important for a better understanding of the situation of low-wage workers, and hence of the situation of minorities and women, who are heavily represented among them. It would be particularly helpful for accurate estimates and fruitful analysis to have matched data from employers and employees.

One issue involved in using money income as an indicator of value received that has been generally recognized is the importance of adjustments for the cost of living. Adjustments are not entirely satisfactory, however, when a single index is used, because it does not take into account that expenditure patterns vary considerably among individuals and groups. Thus, for instance, using the same index for the elderly as for the rest of the population does not reflect the fact that costs for health care and prescription drugs—a much larger proportion of expenditures for older people than for the general population—have been increasing much more rapidly than prices of most other goods and services. Use of separate cost-of-living indices for some population segments would significantly improve understanding of real cost-of-living trends.

Finally, most data are collected only for individuals, not families, yet for many purposes the former are not adequate. A good illustration of this lack is when there is information on the number of persons who earn the minimum wage, but not on the total income of the families in which they live. Similarly, there are data on how many workers are covered by their own health insurance, but little about how many of them are or could also be covered as family members of another worker.

Establishment-Level Data

As detailed in Chapters 5 and 6, a fair amount of information has been collected on the extent to which public employees and workers in large- and medium-sized firms have access to various types of benefits. However, data for smaller firms, which employ a large and growing part of the labor force, are generally inadequate.

For all types of establishments, little is known about utilization (as opposed to availability) of programs. Government and research organizations are most likely to play a major role in collecting the needed data, but businesses need to cooperate, at least, and might even take the initiative. In some cases, employers are already collecting such data for their own use. The value of the knowledge gained should more than outweigh the costs for businesses so long as proper care is exercised with regard to issues of confidentiality. Such data would make it possible to relate the availability and use of programs to characteristics of both employers and employees, as well as to the laws governing that establishment. Surveys of employers, such as that by Trzcinski (1989), are a promising beginning. In-depth case studies of individual companies also can be a rich source of useful information for initiating and evaluating policies and programs. Finally, more information on the presence and role of labor unions would add to our understanding of establishment-level data.

A RESEARCH AGENDA

Data, of course, are useful only to the extent that they are used in relevant research. Our suggestions for topics on which additional investigations would be especially useful cover three broad categories: the impact of employment on families, the impact of families on work performance, and the costs of employer benefit programs.

Impact of Employment on Families

The great increase in the proportion of women who are employed—particularly, the influx of mothers of young children into the labor force—as well as the growth in the number of female-headed families have led to a great deal of work examining the effects of these trends on women, men, and, especially, children. Nonetheless, there is much still to be learned. For the most part, only short-term outcomes have been examined, although, particularly for children, long-term outcomes are of great interest. Little work has been done on issues relating to the care of elderly and handicapped family members. Relatively scant attention has been given to the changing role of men in the family and the effects of this development. Much of the research on the well-being of families has relied on subjective perceptions, rather than on objective measures that might be expected to be more reliable. Another question that has been neglected is the preferences of workers and their families when given choices of different types and different amounts of benefits, as well as the effect of their choices on levels of stress and satisfaction.

Among the main lessons learned from existing research are that well-being is not unidimensional, that outcomes are therefore often mixed, and that outcomes are generally not the same for all family members. These insights make clear that it is far too simplistic to ask, for example, if the effect of mothers' working is good or bad for children, let alone whether it is good or bad for families. In view of these complexities, it is not surprising that much remains to be learned about policy interventions that are most likely to be successful in mitigating the problems of the growing number of women and men with dual roles.

At the employer level, further research on both barriers to the adoption of family-related policies and ways to facilitate their adoption and implementation is also strongly recommended. Such research would require the use of carefully selected samples of the labor force in private- and public-sector workplaces, both unionized and nonunionized, with information from management as well as employees. Such work would help to understand why some employers adopt new policies and others do not and would provide insights on the dynamics of their successful implementation. For example, additional investigation of the effectiveness of employee assistance programs in addressing family issues would be very helpful.

Among the most promising ways of pursuing such further research is systematic evaluation of programs that have already been implemented, whether voluntarily by individual enterprises, as a result of negotiations with unions, or because of government requirements in particular states or other countries. Studies of individual companies in the United States, such as that by Burden and Googins (1987), and in other countries, such as that by Galinsky (1989a), begin to provide this kind of information, although problems of confidentiality have been a barrier to more such work.

In addition, demonstration projects, or social experiments, would be very useful in some instances. A thorough discussion of their advantages and limitations is found in Ferber and Hirsch (1982). Such projects are likely to be very expensive; even so, labor unions, business associations, and governments may find them worthwhile because instituting full-fledged programs without adequate knowledge may be far more costly.

Impact of Families on Work Performance

Although much remains to be learned about the effects of work on families, even more research is needed about the effects of the family on work. To the extent that research has been done on this subject, it has focused on the relation of various characteristics of the worker to particular types of behavior, including tardiness, absenteeism, work interruptions, and turnover and how such behavior can be influenced by various policies. While these variables have some interest in themselves, they are often used as proxies for the "bottom-line" issue of productivity, or how much a worker contributes to output and hence to revenue. As discussed in Chapter 6, this question has so far proven to be rather intractable, although there is a body of research concerned with productivity primarily among production workers. Work on this important subject would necessarily involve studies of individual enterprises with a focus on the effects of implementing innovations. Just as demonstration projects can be expected to be useful for learning about the effects of workplace conditions and policies on families, so can they be useful for learning about the impact of family situations and family-oriented policies on work performance.

Costs of Employer Programs

As discussed in Chapter 1, estimates of direct costs to employers do not show who really bears the costs, which may be shifted, to a greater or lesser extent, to workers, consumers, or the public. How much of this can be done will vary from one business to another and is likely to vary over time even for the same enterprise. Unfortunately, there is little work to date that offers promise on this topic. Observations from existing programs, let alone demonstration projects, are not very helpful because so much depends on the context of the economy and the society. The record of public finance specialists in demonstrating how much shifting of tax burdens takes place has not been convincing; nevertheless, the topic is important and should be studied. At the very least, experts can make it clear that one cannot simply assume that no shifting takes place.

SUMMARY

Our proposals for data and research are based on the assumption that it is possible to make significant progress in gaining more knowledge about, as well as understanding of, family-workplace interrelations at an expense that would be justified by the possibilities for improved policy making. Learning from programs that have been adopted by some companies, by individual states, or by other countries is often particularly expeditious. Even so, it is impossible to learn everything about the consequences of proposed programs. It is to be hoped that recognition of the limits of possible knowledge will act as a safeguard against large-scale implementation when small-scale experiments and model programs are feasible. At the same time, businesses and governments should not fail to implement useful programs while waiting for perfect solutions. It is as important to count the price of inaction in the face of serious challenges as it is to avoid costly mistakes.

Biographical Sketches

LA RUE ALLEN is associate professor in the University of Maryland's clinical/community psychology program. She is on the editorial boards of the *American Journal of Community Psychology* and the *Journal of Child Clinical Psychology*. Her main research foci are on risk factors in adolescent development, the influence of gender and ethnicity on socioemotional development in children and youth, and humor responsiveness as a measure of adaptive behavior. She received a B.A. from Harvard University and a Ph.D. in 1980 from Yale University.

MAXINE BACA-ZINN is professor and senior associate in the Department of Sociology at Michigan State University. She is a former president of the Western Social Science Association; currently, she serves on the Committee for Public Policy Research on Contemporary Hispanic Issues of the Inter-University Program for Latino Research and the Social Science Research Council and on the board of directors of the Society for the Study of Social Problems. Her research has centered on family life among racial ethnics and on gender within minority communities. She has a B.A. from California State University at Long Beach, an M.A. from the University of New Mexico, and a Ph.D. from the University of Oregon, all in sociology.

LOTTE BAILYN is professor of organizational psychology and management at Sloan School of Management, Massachusetts Institute of Technology, where she has taught for more than 20 years. Her work has emphasized the intersection of people's lives and careers with the policies and practices of the organizations in which they are employed: one focus has concerned the lives of technically trained people; and the management of careers in research and development laboratories. Others are on male and female engineers, telecommuting, and organizational responses to employees' family concerns. She is the author of *Living with Technology: Issues at Mid-Career* and numerous journal articles. She has a Ph.D. in social psychology from Harvard University.

SUSAN BIANCHI-SAND is president of the Association of Flight Attendants (AFA), AFL-CIO, the largest flight attendant union in the world, representing 30,000 flight attendants on 18 airlines. She was elected to a variety of local union positions and as national vice president of AFA before being elected president in 1986. She is one of two women international union presidents and is one of three women on the 33-member AFL-CIO Executive Council, the highest governing body of the labor federation. She currently serves on the board of directors of the A. Philip Randolph Institute. She received a B.A. from the University of Maryland.

JUNE H. BROWN is associate professor and associate dean at the School of Social Work, University of Southern California (USC). Her scholarly interests are the history and evolution of American social welfare, with specializations in twentieth century reform and contemporary issues in family and child welfare. She served as chair of the faculty group that developed USC's curriculum for the specialization in social work practice with families and children. In addition to membership in the National Association of Black Social Workers, the National Association of Social Workers, and the Council on Social Work Education, she currently serves as a member of the editorial board of *Child Welfare*, the journal of the Child Welfare League of America. She has a B.A. from the University of California at Los Angeles and master's and doctorate degrees in social work from USC.

RICHARD V. BURKHAUSER is professor of economics and senior research associate at the Maxwell School of Citizenship and Public Affairs, Syracuse University. He is coeditor of the *Journal of Human Resources* and is on the editorial boards of *The Gerontologist, The Journal of Gerontology*, and *The Review of Income and Wealth*. He has published widely on the behavioral and income distribution effects of government policy toward older workers and is coauthor of *Passing the Torch: The Influence of Economic Incentives on Work and Retirement*. He received a Ph.D. in economics from the University of Chicago.

THOMAS G. CODY is a partner in the career transition firm of Jannotta/ Bray, deRecat & Maguire Associates, Inc. Prior to that he was a corporate officer and director of corporate human resources of Baxter International,

Inc., a $7.5 billion health care company; executive director of the Equal Employment Opportunity Commission; and assistant secretary for administration at the U.S. Department of Housing and Urban Development. He currently serves on a number of corporate and nonprofit boards, has published two books, and is preparing a manuscript on the history of the U.S. health care industry. He received an M.B.A. from Harvard University.

PAULA S. ENGLAND is professor of sociology at the University of Arizona. Her research and teaching are concerned with occupational sex segregation, the sex gap in pay, and the changing roles of women and men. She is coauthor (with George Farkas) of *Households, Employment, and Gender* and author of numerous journal articles in the fields of sociology, women's studies, and economics. She received an M.A. and a Ph.D. in sociology from the University of Chicago.

MARIANNE A. FERBER is professor of economics at the University of Illinois at Urbana-Champaign and was previously director of women's studies. She is former president of the Midwest Economic Association, was chair of the American Statistical Association's Committee on Women in Statistics, and is a member of the American Economic Association's Committee on Economic Education and Committee on the Status of Women in the Economics Profession. Within the broad field of the economic status of women, she has focused particularly on the standing of women in academia, the family as an economic unit, and international comparisons in the position of women. Born in Czechoslovakia, she obtained a B.A. degree from McMaster University in Canada and an M.A. and a Ph.D. from the University of Chicago.

JAMES N. MORGAN is an emeritus research scientist at the Institute for Social Research and emeritus professor of economics at the University of Michigan. He has conducted national survey research studies on the affluent, the poor, retirement, and productive activities. He was the first director of the Panel Study of Income Dynamics, a national longitudal study that is still continuing. He is a member of the National Academy of Sciences and a fellow of the American Statistical Association, the American Academy for the Advancement of Science, and the Gerontological Society of America. He has served on advisory boards to the U.S. census, the Social Security Administration, the Social Science Research Council, and the Consumers Union. He received a Ph.D. in economics from Harvard University.

BRIGID O'FARRELL is study director of the Committee on Women's Employment and Related Social Issues and the Panel on Employer Policies and Working Families, at the National Research Council. Her research has focused on the implementation of child care, educational equity, and equal employment opportunity policy, particularly for women in blue-collar and clerical occupations. She holds an Ed.M. in social policy from Harvard University.

PAUL M. ROMAN is professor of sociology and director of the Center for Research on Deviance and Behavioral Health in the Institute for Behavioral Research at the University of Georgia. Previously he served on the faculties of the departments of sociology and epidemiology at Tulane University. He has played a central role with government, professional associations, and private sector organizations in the design and international diffusion of employee assistance programs (EAPs). His research program has most recently focused on social interactions in the workplace that precede EAP referrals, the organizational design of privately based substance abuse treatment, and the design of human resource interventions to deal with emergent social problems that impact the workplace. He received a B.S. in rural sociology and a Ph.D. in organizational behavior, both from Cornell University.

WENDY W. WILLIAMS is associate dean of the Georgetown University Law Center. Previously she was a visiting professor at the law schools of the University of California at Berkeley and Harvard University; an attorney with Equal Rights Advocates, Inc., a nonprofit, public interest law firm in San Francisco that she cofounded in 1974; clinical instructor at Stanford Law School; and a partner at Davis, Dunlap & Williams, a San Francisco law firm specializing in sex discrimination litigation. She has published numerous works focusing on sex discrimination in the workplace and is presently working on a casebook entitled *Sex Discrimination: Causes and Remedies*. She received an A.B., an M.A. in English literature, and a J.D. from the University of California at Berkeley.

Index

A

Absenteeism from work
  causes, 58–59, 62
  child care and, 58, 59, 62, 74, 133, 145
  effects of families on, 3, 10, 54, 62
  flexible schedules and, 127
Adoption benefits, 115, 119
Adult day care, 69
Age, and employment, 39
Aid to Families With Dependent Children,
    56, 84, 145, 147, 150
Amalgamated Clothing and Textile Workers
    Union, 131, 141
Amalgamated Transit Workers, 142
American Express Company, 87
American Federation of Government
    Employees, 141
American Federation of State, County, and
    Municipal Employees, 130, 141
American Society of Personnel Administra-
    tors survey, 136
Antinepotism rules, 136
Association of Flight Attendants, 142
AT&T
  child care program, 134, 135
  parental leave policy, 144

B

Baby boomers, 23
Bank of America, child care initiative,
    134

Belgium
  child care programs, 168
  economic performance, 171, 173
  holiday and vacation leave, 160
  income distribution, 175
  part-time work, 165
  quality of life, 174, 176
  social welfare expenditures, 157, 159
Benefits (nonwage), 9
  evolution, 23, 40
  government role in shaping, 12
  levels of compensation, 23
  payment, 13–14
  providers, 12–13
  union role in obtaining, 11-12
  see also Family-related benefits;
      Standard employee benefits;
      Voluntary benefits and programs
Blacks
  disabled, 84–85
  educational attainment, 40
  family structure, 49
  family-work conflicts, 50
  health insurance status, 109
  income, 28, 33–34
  labor force participation, 24, 25
  life satisfaction, 50
  poverty rates, 30, 65–66, 76
  single-adult households, 28, 30
  unemployment, 40
  in unions, 36

C

Cafeteria plans, *see* Flexible benefit
    programs
California
    Child Care Initiative, 134
    disability laws, 93, 148
Canada
    child allowance programs, 147, 151
    economic performance, 171, 173
    income distribution, 175
    part-time work, 164, 165, 166
    quality of life, 174, 176
    social welfare programs, 156, 157, 159
Caregivers
    depression, 46
    for disabled adults, 85
    earnings, 79
    for elderly people, 73–74
    family day care providers, 129
Center care, 22, 79–80
Chicago Five Hospital Home-Bound Elderly
    Program, 71
Child care
    and absenteeism, 58, 59, 62, 74
    availability and need, 3, 56, 59, 64, 81
    by babysitters (in-house), 77, 79
    benefits to employers, 74–75, 145
    in Canada and Western Europe, 168–170
    center-based, 77, 78, 79–80, 86
    and child development, 47, 62, 83
    costs of, 56, 64, 81–82, 83
    development block grant program, 152
    and elder care by women, 73–74
    employee participation, 102, 134
    employers' concerns about education
        and, 77
    employer-sponsored, 2, 4, 22, 84, 115,
        119, 128, 132, 145
    family day care, 77, 79, 86
    finding, 59
    firm size and, 102, 137–138
    government programs, 81–82, 84, 146,
        147, 151–152
    health and safety concerns, 48
    insurance liability issues, 134
    legislative initiatives, 146–147, 152
    by nannies, 77, 78–79
    occupational status and, 61–62
    by parents, 43, 52, 77–78, 80
    patterns and trends, 75–76
    problems of parents, 16, 56
    and productivity at work, 60
    quality, 47–48, 59, 64, 83–84

    regulation, 79, 80, 83
    by relatives, 56, 77, 78–79
    resource and referral services, 134–135,
        146, 153
    for school-age children, 59, 133
    school-based, 77, 78, 79–80
    self-care, 78
    for sick children, 133
    in single-parent families, 76
    summer camp programs, 133
    types, 77–80, 115
    union negotiations for, 131, 141–142
    vouchers, discounts, 115, 133, 146
    and work schedule, 56, 77, 86, 128, 133
    work-site centers, 131–133, 147
Child development
    child care and, 47, 62, 83
    mother's work status and, 46, 127
    in single-parent families, 3
    work and, 3, 47–48
Child labor laws, 131
Childbearing
    costs in wages losts, 123
    women's employment and, 24, 56
Children
    demands on parents, 31
    effects of job-related travels on, 52
    gender stereotypes, 47
    health insurance coverage, 110, 112,
        148
    homeless, 76
    latchkey, 78, 81
    in poverty, 28, 76
    responsibilities of in families, 20
    well-being, 62
Children's age
    and care arrangements, 79–80
    and changes in work locations, 61
    and child care availability, 47, 59
    and labor force participation by mothers,
        26–27, 57, 75
    and parental absenteeism from work, 58
Civil Rights Act of 1964, 88, 118
Civil Service Employee Association, 141
Civil Service Retirement System, 98
Collective bargaining, 11–12
    family care initiatives, 140–145
    goals, 20, 22, 36, 41
    in Western Europe, 161
Communication Workers of America,
        141, 144
Community care, 69–72
Consolidated Omnibus Budget Reconcilia-
    tion Act of 1985, 99

Counseling, 115–116, 128, 135
Cross-national comparisons
    alternative schedules and locations, 166–168
    evolution of social welfare provisions, 155–156
    government-supported child care programs, 168–170
    holidays and vacations, 160–161
    maternity and family leaves, 161–164
    part-time work, 164–166
    quality of life, 170–177
    social welfare expenditures, 157–160
    see also individual countries
Cuban Americans, 49
Current Population Survey, 35, 57, 84, 101, 105, 109, 128

D

Data collection, 197–198
    constraints, 9–10
    establishment-level, 239–240
    on individuals and families, 237–239
    needs, 5, 237–240
Day care centers, employer-supported, 11
Death benefits, 88, 116
Demonstration projects, 5, 71
Denmark
    child care programs, 168, 169
    economic performance, 171, 173
    holiday and vacation leave, 160, 161
    income distribution, 175
    maternity leave, 161, 162
    part-time work, 165
    quality of life, 174, 176
    social welfare expenditures, 157, 159
Department of Veterans Affairs, 70, 71
Dependent care, 4
    approaches, 16
    availability, 3
    costs, 86
    counseling programs, 135
    for disabled adults, 84–85
    employer-supported, 2, 85–86, 131–134
    firm size and, 138
    flextime and, 127–128
    government-supported, 16
    and health of caregiver, 46, 49, 54
    and labor force participation, 57
    life cycle and responsibilities, 86
    regulation, 86
    by relatives, 19, 57
    tax credits, 12, 16, 72, 82, 146, 147

    work schedule and, 52
    see also Child care; Elder care; Quality of dependent care
Dependent Care Assistance Plans, 115, 137, 141–142, 146
Dependents (other than children)
    effects of work on, 48–49
Depression
    in caregivers, 46, 54
    in employed wives, 46
    in husbands of employed women, 46
Direct services
    providers, 13
    see also Child care; Counseling; Elder care; Health insurance
Disabled adults/disability
    care for, 19, 49, 54, 57, 84–85
    definition, 84
    earnings, 85
    employer programs, 4
    funding for programs, 85
    in nursing homes, 84
    participation in programs, 85
    prevalence and severity, 84
    race/ethnicity, 84–85
    rehabilitation programs, 85
    spouses, 49, 85
    work losses, 84
Disability insurance/programs, 4, 23, 85, 88, 100
    availability, 118
    costs, 92–96
    employee participation, 102, 107
    employer costs, 104
    firm size and, 102
    life-cycle stage and, 115–116
    long-term, 96, 97, 100, 102, 107
    pregnancy-related claims, 124
    short-term programs, 92, 100, 112, 117, 121
    state laws, 93–95, 117
Disability leave, 111, 115
Discounts on goods and services, 96, 102
Discrimination
    effects on workers, 15–16
    maternity-related, 121–122
Divorce
    and health coverage, 115
    hours worked and, 51
    and labor force participation by women, 20–21, 24, 29, 46
Dual-earner families
    careers of both parents, 61–62
    child care as percentage of income, 82

earnings, 30–31
employment, 30–31
evolution of, 20–21
family performance, 44, 62
flexible benefit plans, 137
growth, 1, 7, 23, 41
household responsibilities, 31, 52
job performance, 44, 62
marital satisfaction, 46, 62
social acceptability, 23–24

E

Earned time off policies, 115
Earnings
    of disabled adults, 85
    and employment, 24–39; see also Family
        income; Income
    and health insurance status, 109
    marital status and, 55
    race/ethnicity and, 37–38
Economic conditions
    and family structure, 49
    and labor force participation rates, 40
Economic performance
    and quality of life, 170–177
    and wages, 24
Economic Recovery Act of 1981, 137
Economic security, 15, 46
Economies
    industrial, 19–21
    preindustrial, 18–19
Education
    on benefit programs, 5
    and earnings, 25–26
    employers' concerns, 77
    and employment, 25–26, 39, 76–77
    and labor force composition, 24
    and labor force participation by women,
        25–26
    and labor shortages, 40
    public, 20, 76
    quality, 76–77
    and race segregation, 38
    sex differences, 25
    subsidized, 96, 102
    union bargaining initiatives, 141–142
Elder care
    and absenteeism, 58
    availability, 70
    and child care by women, 73–74
    by children, 57
    community-based programs, 70–72
    costs, 64, 66, 73

elements, 73
employer-based programs, 4, 116, 119
    and family responsibilities, 66, 73
    federal support, 70–72
    geographic mobility and, 72
    home, 66–70, 86
    long-term, use, 67
    need for, 48
    noninstitutional services, 69
    in nursing homes, 66–69, 71, 86
    paid, 66, 68, 69–72, 86
    payment, 70–71
    predictor of institutionalization, 72
    problems in obtaining, 16
    projections, 67
    providers, 73
    by relatives, 2, 19, 46, 57, 66, 68, 71–74
    time expenditures, 74
    types, 66–68
    unpaid, 72–74
    women's employment and, 31, 49, 72,
        73–74
Elderly people
    economic status and health, 86
    frail, 66, 70, 71, 72
    geographic distribution, 65, 72
    income, 65, 66
    living arrangements, 65, 70
    population growth, 31, 48, 64–65, 72
    in poverty, 65–66
    use of long-term care, 67
    use of paid home and community
        services, 70–71
Empire State Child Care system, 132, 140
Employee Assistance Programs, 115, 119,
    135
Employee Retirement Income Security Act,
    96, 98
Employer-supported policies and programs
    alternative schedules and locations, 124–
        130
    bases for changes, 10–11
    business conditions and, 143–145
    costs, 12, 104, 144, 242
    counseling, 135, 191–192
    dependent care, 4, 22, 131–134, 192–193
    development, implementation, and
        dissemination, 5, 195–197
    direct provision of services, 4–5, 13,
        190–191
    effects on employers, 4–5, 123–124,
        133–134, 145, 153
    effects on families, 4–5, 53–54
    employee participation, 97, 102

flexible benefits, 4, 194–195
government support, 5
health insurance, 2, 5, 16–17, 193–194
industry and occupational differences, 139
legal constraints, 130–131
by life-cycle stages, 115–116
research needs, 242
resource and referral services, 4, 84, 134–135
size of firm and, 2, 12, 97, 101, 102, 112, 138–139
types, 2
unionization and, 11, 140
women employees and, 139
workplace culture and, 140, 143
see also Benefits; Insurance; Leave
Employment
definition, 9
and earnings, 24–39
and health insurance status, 109
interdependence between families and, 43
projected trends, 39–40, 41
by sector, 34–35
status by working status of spouse, 28
see also Self-employment; Work
Equal employment opportunity, 8, 15–16
government programs, 148–150, 131
Equal Employment Opportunity Commission, 121–122
Europe, see Western Europe; and specific countries
European Economic Community, parental leave legislation, 163–164
Extended family constellations, 19

F

Fair Labor Standards Act, 130
Families
changes in composition, 1, 7, 18–21, 40
definition, 9, 26
economic well-being, 41
effects of work, 2–3, 44–54, 181, 240–241
effects on work, 3, 23, 54–62, 181–183, 241
in industrial economies, 19–20
interdependence between employment and, 43
in preindustrial economies, 18–19
size trends, 30–31
traditional, 20, 22

see also Dual-earner families; Extended family constellations; Household responsibilities; Low-income families; Minority families; Single-adult households; Single-earner families
Family and Medical Leave Act of 1990, 150
Family Assistance Act of 1988, 150
Family assistance programs, 40, 151
Family day care, 79
Family income
distribution trends, 29
household composition and location, 33
race/ethnicity and, 33–34
Family leave
Canada and Western Europe, 161–164
costs of implementing policies, 149–150
effects on families, 4, 154
employer contributions, 105–106
legislation, 120–121
by occupation, 119
types and definition, 117
union bargaining initiatives, 141–142
in United States, 148–150
Family-related benefits
alternative schedules and locations, 124–131
employer-sponsored programs, 114–138
family support services, 131–136
flexible benefit programs, 136–138
and health insurance, 2
legal constraints, 130–131
see also Child care; Employer-supported policies and programs
Family status
and effects of terms of employment, 43
and employment and earnings, 26–27, 40, 41
Fathers
child care by, 52, 77, 80
responsibilities, 20
use of leave, 122–123, 163
Federal Employees Health Insurance System, 137
Federal Unemployment Tax Act of 1939, 92
Female-headed families
benefit coverage, 102
earnings, 41
labor force participation by mothers, 76
minorities, 49
poverty rates, 76
prevalence, 28, 41
Fertility, and labor force composition, 24

Financial assistance programs, by life-cycle
    stages of employees, 115–116
Finland
    child care programs, 169
    economic performance, 171, 173
    expenditures on social welfare, 159
    maternity leave, 161
    income distribution, 175
    part-time work, 164, 165
    quality of life, 174, 176
Flexible benefit programs, 4, 114, 153
    disadvantages, 144
    employee satisfaction, 137
    firm size and, 138–139
    health insurance, 136–137
    by occupation, 119
Flexible spending accounts, 13, 137, 138
Flexibile work schedules, 114
    advantages to employees, 167
    benefits to employers, 145
    compressed work week, 125, 127, 131,
        167
    effects, 2, 3, 4, 127, 188–189
    employee abuses, 127
    firm size and, 138
    flextime, 125, 127, 128, 131, 138, 145,
        167
    home-based work, 125, 128–129, 153
    job sharing, 125, 128, 167
    legal constraints, 130–131
    life-cycle stages and, 115
    maxiflex, 127
    occupation and, 167
    and overtime, 131
    phased retirement, 125
    regulation, 129
    union bargaining initiatives, 141–142
    in Western Europe, 167
Food stamps, 65
Ford, Henry, 22
Ford Foundation, 133
Ford Motor Company, welfare capitalism in,
    21–22
Framingham Heart Study, 53
France
    child care programs, 168–169
    economic performance, 171, 173
    holiday and vacation leave, 160
    income distribution, 175
    maternity leave, 161
    part-time work, 165, 166
    quality of life, 174, 176
    social welfare expenditures, 157, 159
Funeral leave, 97, 101, 107

G

Gender stereotypes, 47
Geographic mobility of workers
    effects of family on, 54, 62
    and elder care, 72
Germany
    economic performance, 171, 173
    health insurance, 162
    holiday and vacation leave, 160, 161
    income distribution, 175
    maternity leave, 161, 162
    part-time work, 165, 166
    quality of life, 174, 176
    social insurance, 156, 166
    social welfare expenditures, 157, 159
Government programs and policies, 8
    alternative policies, 198–201
    benefit programs in United States, 90–91;
        see also specific programs
    Canada and Western Europe, 168–170
    for child care, 132
    exemptions from benefit coverage, 12
    for elder care, 70
    employee participation, 97
    equal employment opportunity, 148–150
    family leave, 148–150
    tax credits and incentives, 12, 14, 23,
        146–148
    for working poor, 150–152
    see also Public sector
Great Depression, 22, 88
Greece
    maternity leave, 162

H

Hawaii, disability laws, 93, 148
Head Start, 77, 83, 84
Health
    caregivers, 54
    children in care settings, 48
    job satisfaction and, 52
    multiple roles and, 52–53
    outcomes in Western Europe, 176
    social support at work and, 53
    work and, 45–46, 62
Health care
    costs and coverage, 16, 99
    government role, 16–17
    long-term, 16
    physician visits by uninsured people,
        110–111
    uncompensated care costs, 111

Health insurance, 5, 8, 11, 96, 98–99
    for children, 110, 112, 148
    cost, availability, and participation, 15,
        98–99, 105–109, 112, 152
    coverage, 105–109, 143–144
    employee participation, 97, 102, 107
    employer costs, 96, 99, 104, 112, 143–
        144
    family coverage, 107, 108, 109, 115
    family-oriented benefits and, 2
    flexible coverage plans, 136–137
    firm size and, 12, 99, 102, 106, 109
    government initiatives, 152
    life-cycle stage and, 115–116
    long-term care, 119
    mandatory employer-provided, 16–17, 152
    maternity leave and, 123
    nonparticipants, characteristics of, 108
    occupation and, 119
    regulation, 99
    as a standard benefit, 89
    union negotiations for, 89
    see also Uninsured Americans
Health Interview Survey, 110
Health promotion plans, 115, 119
High school dropouts, 39, 56
Hispanics
    economic conditions within communities,
        49
    educational attainment, 40
    health insurance status, 109
    income, 28, 33–34
    labor force participation, 24, 25–26
    poverty rates, 30, 66, 76, 109
    single-adult households, 28, 30
    unemployment, 40
    in unions, 36
Holiday leave, 96, 97, 101, 107, 115, 160–161
Home care for elderly people
    benefits, 71
    demonstration projects, 71
    and nursing home and hospital use, 71
    paid, 69–72
    tax incentives, 72
    unpaid, 72–74
    see also Elder care
Home health aides, 69
Home-based work, 125, 128–131
Homemakers
    full-time, 2, 7, 22, 145
    help for elderly people, 69
    men as, 30
Household responsibilities
    discrimination, 15–16

    in dual-earner families, 31
    and health, 46
    housework, 43
    and job-related travel, 52
    lack of time for, 3
    of men, 25, 31, 43
    and productivity at work, 60
    specialization in, 19
    and stress, 43
    technology and, 20
    of women, 31, 43, 60
    see also Child care; Elder care
Households, definition of, 25
Housing subsidies, 65

I

IBM, 74, 135, 144
Income, 44–45
    and availability of benefits, 112, 158
    child care costs as percentage of, 82
    of elderly people, 65
    household, 33
    and men and women by occupation, 32–
        33
    minimum, 15, 20
    race/ethnicity and, 28, 33–34, 37
    real, and benefits, 3
    and stress, 60
    supplements, 15
    tax rates, 3
    in Western Europe, 175
    and work-family interference, 62
    see also Family income; Wages
Identity, work and, 44–45
Industrialization, and labor force composi-
        tion, 24
Industry
    benefit differences by, 103
    and earnings variation, 34–35
    and employer costs for benefits, 104
    and employer-sponsored programs, 2,
        101, 139
    private-public partnerships in education,
        77
    and unionization, 34–36
Infants
    attachment to mothers, 48
    leave for care, 122, 149
    out-of-home care, 47, 59, 79, 81, 86
Insurance, see Health insurance; Life
        insurance
Internal Revenue Service, on-site child care
        for employees, 132

International Brotherhood of Electrical
    Workers, 142, 144
International comparisons, see Cross-
    national comparisons
International Ladies Garment Workers, 142
International Union of Electrical Workers,
    142
Italy
    economic performance, 171, 173
    holiday and vacation leave, 160
    income distribution, 175
    maternity leave, 162
    part-time work, 164, 165
    quality of life, 174, 176
    social welfare expenditures, 157, 159

J

Job demands, *see* Terms of employment
Job performance
    in dual-earner families, 44
    effects of families, 54, 62
Job satisfaction, 52, 74, 127, 130, 133
Job sharing, 125, 127, 128, 167
Jobs
    availability of, and labor force participa-
      tion, 56–57
    opportunities for women, 24, 26
    sectoral shift in availability, 24
Jury duty leave, 97, 101, 107

L

Labor demand
    and benefits, 88
    and women's employment, 24
Labor force
    composition of, 41
    turnover, 62
Labor force participation
    availability of jobs and, 56–57
    effects of families, 55–57
    family status and, 41, 55
    and health, 45, 62
    marital status and, 42
    by men, 25, 28, 42
    motivation, 57
    race/ethnicity and, 25–26, 28, 41
    sex differences, 36, 41
    and work status of spouse, 28
Labor force participation by women
    age of children and, 26, 57
    causes of increase, 20–21, 23, 24
    and childbearing, 24

    and child development, 47
    education and, 25–26
    effects on families, 2–3, 7
    and elder care, 31, 49
    as heads of households, 76
    and husbands' attitudes toward wives,
      45, 46, 62
    husband's occupation and, 30
    family status and, 26–27
    importance, 45
    marital status and, 24, 29, 56
    "Mommy track," 61
    in nontraditional occupations, 47
    projections, 25, 39–40
    race/ethnicity and, 25–26
    social acceptability, 23–24
    trends, 1, 23, 25, 56
    and work schedules, 56–57
    and work status of spouse, 28
Labor movement, weakening of, 11; *see also*
    Collective bargaining; Unions/
    unionization
Labor supply
    and benefits, 11
    shortages, 40
Leave
    availability of, 117–123, 185
    costs of, 124
    effect on employers, 123–124
    effects on families, 122, 185–187
    employer attitudes on, 54, 122–123, 140,
      143
    flexible, 128
    government programs, 148–150
    by life-cycle stages, 115–116
    mandatory entitlement, 119–120
    scope of the problem, 117–123
    unpaid, 101, 144, 154
    see also specific kinds of leave
Legal constraints on benefit programs, 130–131
Leisure time, 43
Life expectancy, and labor force composi-
    tion, 24
Life insurance, 96, 97, 100, 104, 107, 115–116
    for dependents, 115
Life satisfaction, in minority families, 50
Location of work
    alternatives, 4, 128–130, 167–168
    effects of families, 3, 4
    flexible, 127, 128–129, 167, 189–190
    home-based, 127, 128–129, 167–168
    relocation policies, 136
    sex differences in willingness to move,
      61

Western Eurpoean policies, 167–168
Low-income families
    benefit coverage, 103, 106, 112
    child care arrangements, 78–79, 81
    corporate community school for children,
        77
    effects of child care on children, 48
    effects of work, 3
    labor force participation by mothers, 20
    quality of dependent care, 83
    work-family interference, 62
Low-wage workers
    benefit coverage, 12, 15
    economic security for, 15

M

Marital satisfaction
    hours worked and, 51
    work and, 46
Marital status
    and earnings, 55
    and elder care by children, 57
    and labor force participation, 42, 46, 55–
        56
    and schedule, 55
Marriage
    leave for, 115
    women's employment and, 24
Married women
    labor force participation, 2, 20, 26, 75–76
    part-time work, 125–126, 166
    unpaid work, 22
Maternity leave, 2, 4
    availability, 113, 117, 153
    definition, 117
    employer-sponsored programs, 115
    and employment during pregnancy, 56
    legislative initiatives, 148
    occupation and, 119
    and public assistance costs due to lack,
        123
    use, 123
    in Western Europe, 161–164
Meals on wheels, 69
Medicaid, 65, 70, 152, 152
    coverage of in-home services, 71
    expenditures for benefits, 71, 91
    payment of family members for elder
        care, 71–72
    "spend down" for nursing home care, 68
Medicare, 65, 70, 86, 99, 112, 152
    expenditures on home care for elderly
        people, 71

Part A, 91
Part B, 91
Men
    effects of shift work, 51
    employment as a part of identity, 44–45
    labor force status, 27
    see also Fathers; Paternity leave
Mexican Americans, 49, 50
Military leave, 97, 101, 107
Minimum Health Benefits for All Workers
    Act, 152
Minority families
    earnings, 41
    effects of work, 3, 48–49
    labor force participation, 25, 40, 41, 56
    life satisfaction, 50
    perspectives on work and family, 49–50
    in poverty, 76
    structural changes, 49
"Mommy track," 61
Mothers, responsibilities of, 20

N

Nanny care, 78–79
National Federation of Independent
    Businesses, 103
National Health Interview Survey, 58–59
National Informal Survey of Caregivers, 73
National Institute on Alcohol Abuse and
    Alcoholism, 135
National Long-Term Care Survey, 66, 68,
    73
National Longitudinal Survey of Youth, 82
National Nursing Home Survey, 68
National Research Council Panel on Child
    Care Policy, 149
National Survey of Caregivers, 57
National Survey of Families and House-
    holds, 85
National Treasury Employees Association, 141
Netherlands, 157
    child care programs, 168–169
    economic performance, 171, 173
    holiday and vacation leave, 160, 161
    income distribution, 175
    maternity leave, 162
    part-time work, 165, 166
    quality of life, 174, 176
    social welfare expenditures, 157, 159
New Deal, 88
New Jersey, disability laws, 94, 148, 149
New York, disability laws, 94, 148, 149
Newspaper Guild, 142

Norway
  economic performance, 171, 173
  expenditures for public assistance
    programs, 159
  holiday and vacation leave, 160
  income distribution, 175
  part-time work, 165
  quality of life, 174, 176
Nursing home care
  avoidance by elderly people, 72–73
  bed supply, 66, 69, 72
  costs, 66, 68, 69, 86
  for disabled adults, 84
  and family responsibilities, 66
  Medicaid payment, 68–69
  profit status of institutions, 68
  quality, 68, 69
  quality of life, 69
  regulation, 69
  staff, 69

O

Occupational safety and health rules, 8, 131
Occupational segregation, 36, 38, 60
Occupational stressors, 53
Occupations
  and demand for women's labor, 21
  and earnings, 32–34
  and employer-sponsored programs, 2,
    112, 139
  family-related benefit programs by, 119
  fastest growing, 40
  and household responsibilities, 32
  husband's, and labor force participation
    by wives, 30
  and paid leave coverage, 111, 112
  and participation in benefit programs,
    107
  status of, and dependent care, 61–62
  and terms of employment, 22, 32–34
  and work schedule, 125
  see also Jobs
Oil, Chemical and Atomic Workers, 142
Old Age, Survivors, Disability, and Health
  Insurance, 91
Older Americans Act, 70, 71
Omnibus Budget Reconciliation Act of 1981,
  71
Omnibus Budget Reconciliation Act of 1990,
  151
Organisation for Economic Cooperation and
  Development Countries, holiday and
  vacation leave, 160–161

P

Paid leave, 4
  amount, 111
  Canada and Western Europe, 160–164
  coverage, 111, 112–113
  definition, 117
  employee participation, 97, 107
  employer costs, 96, 104
  firm size and, 111
  occupation and, 111
  voluntary benefits, 100–101
  see also specific types of leave
Panel Study of Income Dynamics, 57, 58,
  59, 101, 123
Parental leave, 115, 117, 122, 140, 141–142,
  144, 148–149, 163
Part-time work/workers
  advantages, 126
  benefits, 2, 27, 101, 105, 126, 166
  Canada and Western Europe, 164–166
  commitment to work, 57
  defined, 125
  disadvantages, 27, 51, 127
  effects on families, 4, 187–188
  and elder care, 68
  employer motivation, 127
  growth, 35–36
  and health insurance, 17, 126
  job sharing, 127–128
  and marital satisfaction, 51
  marital status and, 56
  permanent, 127
  phased retirement, 127
  policies encouraging, 165–166
  sectoral trends, 34, 35–36
  sex differences, 27, 50, 56
  voluntary, 128
  wages, 105, 126
  in Western Europe, 164–166
  by women, 165
  work sharing, 127–128
  see also Flexible work schedules
Paternalism, 21, 134
Paternity leave, 53–54
  availability, 122, 153
  definition, 117
  occupation and, 119
  use, 143
  Western Europe, 162
Pension Benefit Guarantee Corporation, 98
Pension/retirement benefits, 2, 8, 11, 20, 23,
  88, 96, 98
  child-care-related losses, 81
  defined benefit, 97, 98, 107

defined contribution, 97, 98, 107
employee participation, 97, 101, 107
employer costs, 96, 104
evolution, 88
firm size and, 102
life-cycle stage and, 115–116
maternity leave and, 123
regulation, 98
union negotiations, 89
see also Social Security
Personal care for elderly people, 69
Personal leave, 97, 101, 107, 115, 119
Polaroid, 133
Poor, working
child care as percentage of income, 82
effects of tax credits, 146
and health insurance coverage, 110
public programs, 150–152
Postal Workers/Letter Carriers, 142
Poverty
children, 28, 76
and dependent care, 19, 69, 81
elderly people, 65–66, 69
and health insurance coverage, 109
level, for family of four, 33
race/ethnicity and, 65–66
rates, 28–29
and work-family stress, 76
Pregnancy
disability, 117, 140
employment during, 56
Pregnancy Discrimination Act, 118, 121–122, 148, 153–154
Productivity at work
child care arrangements and, 60, 145
flextime and, 145
Public sector
family-oriented programs offered, 139
growth of jobs, 36
Puerto Ricans, 49
Puerto Rico, disability laws, 94, 148

Q

Quality of dependent care
child care, 47–48, 59, 64, 83–84
and costs, 83
employer programs, 132
evaluation, 16
factors affecting, 86
job status and, 62
measures, 83
nursing homes, 68, 69
stress in caregiver and, 49

terms of employment and, 42
Quality of Employment Survey, 50–51, 54, 57, 61, 103
Quality of life
economic performance and, 170–177
in nursing homes, 69
work schedule and, 51–52

R

Race/ethnicity
and disability, 84–85
of elderly people in poverty, 65–66
and employment and earnings, 36–38
and income, 28, 33–34, 37
and labor force participation, 24, 25–26, 41
and poverty rates, 76
segregation by, 38
and union membership, 36
see also Blacks; Hispanics; Minority families
Recruitment of workers
and benefit packages, 114, 133, 143
effects of family, 54
Research approaches
case studies, 43
surveys, 44; *see also specific surveys*
Research needs, 197–198
costs of employer programs, 10, 242
on dependent care, 6, 16
effects of employment on families, 6, 240–241
effects of families on work performance, 241
effects of occupational status, 61
productivity of workers, 9–10
Resource and referral services, 4, 84, 128, 134–135, 141–142
Respite care, 69
Retention of workers
benefits and, 144
effects of family, 3, 54
Retired people, 20
health benefits, 99
Retirement
age of, 25; *see also* Pension/retirement benefits
phased, 125, 127
Retirement Equity Act, 96
Rhode Island, disability laws, 94, 148
Role conflict and overload
and child development, 48
and mothers with infants, 48

social support at work and, 53
in women, 45–46, 48
Rural-to-urban migration, 24

S

Satisfaction, *see* Job satisfaction; Marital
satisfaction
Schedules, work
afternoon shifts, 51
alternative, in Canada and Western
Europe, 164–166
and child care, 56, 77, 86
effects of families, 54
effects on families, 4, 32, 42, 43, 50–52, 54
hours and weeks worked, 3, 22, 32, 34,
38, 51, 54, 55, 89, 124–125
and interaction of family, 77
legal constraints, 88, 130–131
marital status and, 55
negotiation, 89
night shifts, 51
occupation and, 125
racial/ethnic differences in, 38
traditional, 124–125
see also Flexible work schedules; Part-
time work/workers
Scientists and engineers, women, 60–61
Self-employment, 9, 129
Service Employees International Union, 105,
108, 141
Services sector
demand for women, 24, 34
employment shift, 40
growth, 35, 41
Sex
and earnings, 32–33, 36–38
and home-to-work spillover, 55
and household responsibilities, 19
and labor force participation, 24–26, 41
and location of work, 61
nonday shifts, 50
rotating shifts, 50
segregation, 32
and union membership, 36
and work schedules, 50
Sick child/family member leave, 2, 101, 119,
121, 141–142, 170
Sick leave, 2, 4, 23, 89, 96, 97, 101, 102,
107, 112, 115, 119
Single-adult households
child care problems, 76, 81, 82
effects of work, 3, 55
growth, 1

income, 28
male-headed, 55
part-time work, 27
in poverty, 76
prevalence, 27–28
problems, 28
work-family interference, 62
see also Female-headed families
Single-earner families
earnings, 27–30
terms of employment, 22
Single mothers
absenteeism from work, 58
labor force participation, 26, 56
poverty rates, 29–30
prevalence, 49
see also Female-headed families; Single-
adult households
Small businesses
benefits provided, 89
effects of leave policies, 124
growth, 35, 41
health insurance, 12, 99, 106, 109
Social insurance
evolution, 40, 91
provisions in other countries, 155–157,
166, 170
Social policy in Canada and Western
Europe, 155–160
Social Security, 8, 12, 65, 86, 89, 112
compliance problems of small firms,
122
disability benefits, 100
exemption, 137
funding, 91, 98
initiation, 20, 22, 88, 90–91
retirement benefits, 91, 98
Social Security Act of 1935, 90–91
Social support at work, 53–54
Social welfare
expenditures in other countries, 157–160
in United States and Canada, 156
Spouse benefits, life-cycle stage and, 115–116
Standard employee benefits
aggregate value, 89–90
coverage among workers, 101–111
employee costs, 106
employer costs, 23, 90, 92, 104
evolution, 87–90, 112
federal programs, 90–91
legally required, 23, 90–96, 104, 112
state programs, 91–96
tax exemptions, 92
State benefit programs, 91–96

Stress
  counseling programs for, 135
  defined, 54
  income level and, 60, 76
  and job performance, 62
  job satisfaction and, 61–62
  level of job and, 60, 61–62
  role conflict and, 54, 127
Stride-Rite Intergenerational Center, 131
Supplemental Security Income program, 85
Supplementary Medical Insurance, 91
Survey of Income and Program Participation,
  56, 82, 101, 117, 122, 123
Surveys, about employee benefits, 87; *see
  also specific surveys*
Sweden
  child care programs, 168, 169, 170
  economic performance, 171, 173
  holiday and vacation leave, 160
  income distribution, 175
  maternity leave, 161–162
  part-time work, 165, 166
  quality of life, 174, 176
  social welfare expenditures, 159
Switzerland
  economic performance, 171, 173
  income distribution, 175
  quality of life, 174, 176
  social welfare expenditures, 158, 159

T

Tardiness at work
  child care and, 74
  effects of families, 3, 10, 54, 62
  flexible schedules and, 127
  sources, 58–59
Tax credits and incentives, 14
  changes in, 3
  costs to government, 90, 147, 151, 152
  for dependent care, 12, 16, 72, 82, 84,
    137, 146, 147, 154
  earned income, 15, 84, 145, 147, 151
  effect on benefits, 11, 12, 90, 112
  employer-based, 23, 112, 146–147
  evolution, 40
  for home care, 72
  income splitting, 145
  legislative initiatives, 146, 147–148
  value to workers, 103
  wage levels and benefits of exemptions, 92
Technology
  and household responsibilities, 20
  and labor force composition, 24

Teenagers
  employment during pregnancy, 56
  unemployment rates, 39
Telephone
  contact arrangements for children, 133
  monitoring for elderly people, 69–70
Terms of employment
  effects on families, 3, 4, 42, 50, 52–53,
    184–195
  post World War II, 22
  and quality of dependent care, 42
  see also Leave; Location of work; Part-
    time work/workers; Schedules, work
Title XX, 70, 84
Transportation services, for elderly people,
  69–70
Travel, job-related, effects on families, 52
Travelers' Companies, 74

U

Unemployment, 38–39
  age and, 39
  education and, 39
  insurance, 8, 12, 23, 92, 112, 122, 138
  race/ethnicity and, 39, 49
  rates, 38–39, 40
  sex and, 38
Uninsured Americans, characteristics, 2,
  109–111, 112
Unions/unionization
  and benefit coverage, 101, 103, 112
  collective bargaining for benefits, 11–12,
    41, 89, 96, 131, 141–142
  and employment and earnings, 36
  and family-related benefits, 140
  industry differences in representation,
    36–37
  opposition to home-based work, 130–131
  public-sector, 11, 132, 140
  race/ethnicity and, 36
  sex and 36
  and wages, 36, 41
  and welfare capitalism, 22, 88
United Auto Workers, 141
United Food and Commercial Workers, 142
United Kingdom
  economic performance, 171, 173
  holiday and vacation leave, 160, 161
  home-based workers, 168
  income distribution, 175
  part-time work, 165, 166
  quality of life, 174, 176
  social welfare expenditures, 157, 159

United Mine Workers Association, 140, 141
United States
  economic performance, 171, 173
  income distribution, 175
  part-time work, 164–165, 166
  quality of life, 174, 176
  social welfare expenditures, 157, 158, 159
  social welfare programs, 156
United Steel Workers, 141
Universal benefits, 158
U.S. National Income and Product Accounts, 111

V

Vacation leave, 2, 11, 23, 101, 105, 112, 115
  employee participation, 97, 102, 107
  firm size and, 102
  occupation and, 119
  policies in United States, 88, 89, 96, 161
  policies in Western Europe, 160–161
Veterans' Benefits and Services Act of 1987, 71
Voluntary benefits and programs, 11
  alternative schedules, 166–167
  alternative work sites, 167–168
  availability, 112
  death benefits, 23
  disability insurance, 100
  employer costs, 96
  factors affecting, 11, 90
  growth, 144
  health insurance, 23, 98–99
  life insurance, 23, 100
  outlook for improvements, 113
  paid leave, 23, 100–101
  part-time work, 164–166
  pension plans, 23, 98
  regulation, 96, 117
  tax status, 13
  in Western Europe, 164–168
  see also Family-related benefits
Volunteerism, labor force participation by women and, 13

W

Wages
  and benefits coverage, 101
  economic conditions and, 24

and labor force composition, 24
  minimum, 20, 150–151
  unions membership and, 36
  see also Earnings; Income
Walsh-Healy Act, 130
Welfare capitalism, 21–22, 88
Western Europe
  child allowance programs, 147, 151
  government expenditures, 159
  leave arrangements, 150
Women employees
  earnings, 24, 34
  effects of work, 2–3
  and employer support programs, 139
  family pressures, 31
  scientists and engineers, 60–61
  in unions, 36
  see also Married women
Work
  characteristics, *see* Schedules, work; Terms of employment
  and children's well-being, 47–48
  effects of families, 3, 23, 54–62, 181–183, 241
  effects on family, 2–3, 44–54, 181, 240–241
  and identity, 44–45
  incentive programs, 150
  interruptions, 3, 62
  and health, 45–46
  and marital satisfaction, 46
  problems related to families, 3
  sharing, 127
  see also Employment; Labor force participation; Occupations
Workers
  productivity measures, 10
  supply, 23
Workers' compensation, 8, 85, 88, 91–92, 112, 131
Workplace
  changes in, 21–24
  culture and employer-supported programs, 140, 143
  modern era through World War II, 21–22
  post World War II, 22–23

Y

Yale Bush Center Advisory Committee on Infant Care Leave, 149